FORTUNE FAVORS THE BRAVE

Fortune Favors The Brave

❧ The Life and Times of
Horace Bell
Pioneer Californian

BY BENJAMIN S. HARRISON

THE WARD RITCHIE PRESS : LOS ANGELES

1953

Made in the United States of America by
ANDERSON & RITCHIE · LOS ANGELES

To

Virginia Herrick Bell Phillips

ACKNOWLEDGMENTS

MORE than a score of interested people contributed in some way to the production of this book. To all of them I am grateful.

Preëminent on the list is the name of Virginia H. B. Phillips of Pasadena. She gave her time to provide descriptions, incidents, and anecdotes—all facts which no biographer could obtain elsewhere. The many hours spent in interviewing this delightful daughter of the Bells have been the most pleasant part of the work. Besides lending her parents' album she granted free use of all her father's remaining papers. Wholehearted was her assistance, so is my appreciation. For the loan of letters forming much of the last chapter I am indebted to Daisy Bell Overton of San Francisco, the other surviving member of the family.

J. Gregg Layne, past president of the Historical Society of Southern California, not only bestowed his encouragement but designated certain informed persons to call on. George William Beattie and his wife Helen, historians of southern California, furnished information on various topics.

A rare advantage came from two journalists: John B. T. Campbell, managing editor of the Los Angeles *Herald & Express*; and Harry G. Miller, assistant to the president of the Los Angeles *Times*. Both accorded me the privilege of working in their offices and having free access to old files of their respective papers.

Among those who knew Horace Bell and were able to speak intimately of his life and personality were these citizens of Los Angeles: Frederick Baker, LeCompte Davis, William C. Anderson, Frank G. Finlayson, and Joseph F. Chambers, all lawyers; others include Joseph Mesmer, Mary Foy, Geraldine Cole and her brother Edward Fitzgerald, and Ana Begue de Packman. In Redlands, N. Lee Levering.

Either for their assistance in finding historical items, or for permission to use rare materials, or for both, I am obliged to the following librarians:

In California—Leslie Edgar Bliss and his staff in the Henry E. Huntington Library; Esther Hile and her staff at the University of Redlands; Lenore Greene, formerly of the Los Angeles County Museum of History, Science, and Art; in the Los Angeles Public Library, Althea Warren (recent city librarian), Mary Helen Peterson, and Laura Cooley; the staff of Mabel R. Gillis at the State Library; and Eleanor Bancroft of the Bancroft Library in Berkeley. In Indiana

—Marguerite H. Anderson, formerly of the State Library; and Elsa Strassweg of the New Albany Public Library.

My colleague, Dr. Lawrence E. Nelson, was helpful in reading the manuscript, and Dr. Robert G. Cleland of the Huntington Library enhanced the book by writing his Foreword.

Thanks are also due to President George H. Armacost and the Trustees of the University of Redlands for a leave of absence in which to finish my opus.

Finally, there is one whose contribution was unique and personal, one who has sustained me throughout the entire project with her unfailing faith and cheerfulness—she is my wife, Dorothy A.

BENJAMIN S. HARRISON

University of Redlands

Foreword

FOR NEARLY two decades after the beginning of the Gold Rush, southern California remained a rough, lawless, isolated cattle frontier. Its population was scant, its means of communication were almost primitive in their simplicity, it had no cities in any true sense of the term, and its few towns or pueblos—by whichever name they were called—were widely separated, still in the early frontier stage of cultural development, often exposed to the danger of Indian or bandit attack, and accustomed, almost to the point of indifference, to incidents of violence and bloodshed that ranged from individual homicide to multiple hangings by self-constituted Vigilance or Citizens committees.

Los Angeles was by far the largest and most important of these southern California settlements, but the population of the former provincial capital, according to the federal census of 1850, was only 1,610. It had "neither newspaper, hospital, college, academy, library, public school, nor Protestant church," and violence and crime were so prevalent in the mid-fifties that the lawless little settlement, according to one reliable historian, actually averaged a homicide a day for one entire year.

Small, culturally backward, and socially turbulent though it was, however, Los Angeles of the fifties and sixties had among its few hundred inhabitants far more than its share of forceful, independent, intensely interesting figures.

Among those long-ago makers of Los Angeles and contributors to the romantic tradition of its early days, none was more colorful or arresting than Major Horace Bell. Of Scotch-Irish ancestry, a product of the semi-frontier settlements of Indiana, and a nephew of Alexander Bell, one of the leading American citizens of California before the Mexican War, Bell came to Los Angeles in

[ix]

1852, when he was twenty-two years of age, and died in Livermore in 1918.

During his first three fast-moving, often adventurous decades in Los Angeles, Bell played many roles. He was lawyer, ranger, filibuster, soldier, editor, author, land-owner, and rancher. He participated in many of the stirring events of his stirring day and time and watched the drama of others with shrewdly appraising eyes. He was a highly controversial figure, the target for many enemies, a man of admirable if sometimes contradictory qualities. Though he was aggressive and self-willed, often violent in speech and temper, and sometimes reckless to the point of bravado, he was also the champion of the weak and oppressed, the bitter foe of injustice, the gadfly that none apparently could intimidate or suppress. According to his present biographer, he was grossly maligned by some of his bitter, irresponsible contemporaries, and is too little appreciated by our own forgetful generation.

It is difficult to understand why California historians have waited so long to write the story of such an extraordinary life. But in Dr. Benjamin S. Harrison, Professor of English at the University of Redlands, Bell's faithful biographer has at last appeared. The author has spent ten years in searching the country over for manuscript, newspaper, and other previously unknown or unused source material relating to Bell's activities and life, and in using that material as the basis for this present painstaking and comprehensive study. Dr. Harrison has thus made a valuable contribution to our understanding of one of the most interesting of all that vanished generation which set its stamp upon the rough cattle frontier town of Los Angeles a hundred years ago; he has also added to our knowledge of those formative and eventful years in the history of what is now one of the greatest of American cities and the even greater southern California of today.

Robert G. Cleland

That which I have myself seen and the fighting

A. MACLEISH—*Bernal Díaz' Preface to His Book*

CONTENTS

ILLUSTRATIONS

Introduction

DURING four decades Major Horace Bell stood out as a most picturesque personality in Los Angeles. His combative nature made many hate him. His generous spirit made as many love him. His life was one of public action and historic interest. For what he was and what he did numerous people in southern California long remembered him. Yet until now his biography has not been written.

It should be, for it is well worth knowing. Partly for the imprint of the man's life on his native Indiana, as well as Kentucky and Louisiana. Partly because he was active in the early history of Central America. And chiefly for the dramatic role he played during the boisterous youth of Los Angeles and for the influence he exerted toward the betterment of her society. In the words of Leslie E. Bliss, librarian of the Huntington Library, and a recognized authority on the historical literature of the state, "The history of California will remain incomplete until the full story is told of Major Horace Bell."

To a great extent the material in this book is new—in the sense that it has not been used by scholars, or that it has been unknown and inaccessible to the public, or that it has never been published. Much of it was gleaned from Los Angeles newspapers of the 1880s and from Bell's own weekly publication now little remembered and largely vanished. Some was obtained by interviewing early families in Los Angeles. One part preserves my conversations with his daughter Virginia. And then there are his private letters, biographical notes, and historical typescripts now brought to light for the first time. Many of the pictures were in Mrs. Bell's album. The explanatory notes are placed at the end of the book to prevent breaking the narrative.

The true story of Bell should correct the mistaken ideas which have grown up around his name. These have come largely from a defamatory pamphlet, proved in court to be libelous, which was published and circulated in his time by enemies. Except obituaries the few sketches of his life are based on this source. As Bliss said, "The Major has never had a fair hearing." But the biographer of Bell, or of any person, should do more than dispel error. He should avoid portraying the subject as an ideal hero and reveal both his faults and virtues. Using both light and shadows he should paint the man as he really was. This I have tried to do.

To know Horace Bell is to know many of his generation—those rugged pioneers who won the Far West and finished the foundations of our republic. His dominant traits and mental outlook were largely theirs, for like them he was stamped by the frontier.

Bell during his early years was a man of physical action. But he was more than that in his maturity, since he championed ideas. With his newspaper properly named the *Porcupine* he fought for reforms in California, political and economic. Moreover as an author recording his times in *Reminiscences of a Ranger* and *On the Old West Coast*, he gave to posterity a unique bequest.

Today there are still a few old-timers who can remember this colorful and controversial figure walking the streets of Los Angeles.

B. S. H.

FORTUNE FAVORS THE BRAVE

CHAPTER I

O Pioneers!

Come my tan-faced children,
Follow well in order, get your weapons ready,
Have you your pistols? have you your sharp-edged axes?
Pioneers! O pioneers!

WALT WHITMAN

The Birth Roll

EXCEPT for an Irish great-grandmother, all Horace Bell's known ancestors were of Scottish descent, the fourth generation back being natives of the Highlands or of Ulster.

His great-grandfather, David Bell, born in Scotland, came to America in 1773.[1] It was then that discontent sweeping over the Highlands caused many migrations to the New World. In the year of David's departure, James Boswell, who accompanied Dr. Samuel Johnson on a tour to the Hebrides, noted in his journal the signs of this exodus.[2] Quite naturally Bell gravitated toward a major center of Scottish colonization in America, which was in West Augusta county, Virginia, later to become a part of Pennsylvania. Here his son Alexander was born, who sired David Williamson, father of Horace Bell. These families, like many others in the region, had two traits in common: they were firm Presbyterians and fiery patriots.

On the distaff side the progenitors of Horace Bell were Scotch-Irish and bore the name of Wright. In the second decade of the eighteenth century the Scots in North Ireland were discouraged. High taxes and political discrimination against Presbyterians had made them bitter. Moreover after settling the country and increasing the value of the land by their own industry they were forced to pay higher rents.

About 1686 a young man named William Homes, a native of

[3]

Ulster, had come over to Martha's Vineyard, an island off Massachusetts, where he taught school at Chilmark. Desiring to preach he returned to North Ireland and became the pastor at Strabane. In 1714 he returned to Chilmark, this time settling down as a Presbyterian minister. He had a son Robert, husband of Benjamin Franklin's sister Mary, who as a sea captain made frequent voyages to Ireland. These journeys gave him the opportunity to inform his father's former parishioners of benefits offered by New England. Eventually father and son were conferring in Boston with Dr. Cotton Mather, a Puritan divine, concerning a possible migration of Scotch-Irish to Massachusetts. Having long desired to see the frontier, then only 40 miles to the west, defended by a hardy and God-fearing people, Mather gladly agreed to sponsor such a movement.

Most likely Captain Homes sent letters and plans to friends at Strabane and other towns in Ulster. Perhaps no one in Boston had so many relatives among the clergy of North Ireland and as a navigator he had a commercial interest in the new project. Messages from both Mather and Reverend Mr. Homes also had influence in stirring up a desire for migration. In the Bann river valley whole congregations became so interested that Rev. William Boyd, pastor of Mocosquin, sailed for New England as their agent to see what arrangements could be made for settling there in a body. Since he was well received he brought back favorable reports. Soon ships were chartered and their holds filled with the domestic goods of the Bann valley emigrants. Mr. Boyd was their leader. In August 1718 five ships reached Boston bearing a few hundred people, among them Horace Bell's maternal great-great-grandfather, whose surname was Wright. Possibly he came from Ballymoney, county of Antrim, since records in Ireland show that a John Wright was ruling elder of its church in that year.

Now Cotton Mather's dream of a great migration from Protestant Ireland was coming true. On the seventh of August he wrote in his diary:

[4]

What shall be done for the great Numbers of People, that are transporting themselves hither from the North of Ireland? Much may be done for the Kingdom of GOD in these Parts of the World by this Transportation.

Although the immigrants were viewed with distrust by most Massachusetts people, two leading citizens of Boston, Dr. Mather and Samuel Sewall, a jurist, showed their ministers marked kindness. On the ninth of August, so wrote the man of law in his famous diary, Sewall and his son dined with Mr. Boyd. But the civil authorities were anxious lest some of the new arrivals would become charges on the town, since they had brought only modest savings. The Bostonians feared also that "the confounded Irish" would reduce the supply of food — an apprehension which apparently came true, for in the following spring the prices of wheat and Indian corn nearly doubled because of an increased demand from a larger population.[3]

Then there was a worse difficulty. Mr. Boyd could not find desirable land for all his people to settle; consequently many in his colony, including the Wrights, passed on to what is now southwestern Pennsylvania. Hardened to privation and made self-reliant by their training in Ulster, the Scotch-Irish were not overcome by the frontier. Rather than that they throve. They opened the wilderness to civilization and formed a barrier between the hostile Indians and the settlements of the seaboard. They helped to lay the foundations of a new west in a greater America. Here not only the Bells and Wrights settled, but also the Williamsons, McKees, and Sullivans, families who through marriage were to contribute their qualities of brain and brawn to the inheritance of Horace.

The first of the Wrights to be born in America was Zadok. In 1755 as sergeant in a company of rangers he fought in the battle of Braddock's Defeat. In the retreat, which was conducted by young George Washington, Zadok held the crossing of the Monongahela river to cover the routed army. When almost all had passed over and Sergeant Wright was ready to follow, a

British officer rushed up begging to ride on his horse. But on mounting he was struck by a bullet. As he fell off lifeless a chain dangled from the pocket of his red coat. So Zadok with an eye to his own interest quickly possessed himself of a big bull's-eye watch. It remained in the family for generations as a souvenir of the French and Indian war.

After the English occupied Fort Duquesne, which they re-named Pitt, Zadok Wright with family and relatives moved to Peter's creek near the fort. Later during Washington's presidency, at the time of the Western Insurrection, commonly called the Whisky Rebellion because the western Pennsylvanians opposed a federal tax on liquor, Zadok saved the life of General John Neville, a regional inspector of the excise. On the seventeenth of July 1794, a mob of Scotch-Irish disguised as Indians and imitating the Boston Tea Party marched to Neville's house, burned it, and would have killed the officer but for great-grandfather Zadok, who being loyal to the government ran ahead of the rebels and warned Neville in time for him to escape. In an old historical novel called *The Latimers*, telling of the Whisky Rebellion, Zadok appears as a character, speaking with a Scotch brogue.[4]

To Zadok Wright and his wife Sarah Sullivan was born in 1762 a son whom they named Jeremiah. When only 14 the boy ran away from home to join the company of his uncle, Captain James Sullivan, in the Continental Army. At the end of a year he was honorably discharged, his parents having furnished a substitute. But later he re-enlisted and was commissioned as lieutenant in the same Virginia regiment. He served for a time as an Indian spy and continued his military career in the campaign of George Rogers Clark in the Illinois country, which ended with the capture of Vincennes. When the Revolutionary War was over, Jeremiah had served five years as a soldier and was only 21. On the twenty-fifth of December 1794, he became the father of Elizabeth Wright, who would some day be the mother of Horace Bell.

Sarah Sullivan, wife of Zadok Wright, had a brother Daniel, who was one of the most celebrated scouts and daring rangers of his day. In the year 1758 he was born on the present site of Pittsburgh. At the age of nine he and a boy named Cunningham were carried off by Indians in one of their raids on the white settlements. Following their capture they underwent an exhausting march through the wilderness, which lasted several days. Wornout from the hardships of the journey the boys finally reached their destination, an Indian town secluded in a region of lakes.

After a day's rest came the initiation into the fraternity of red men, when they were forced to run the gauntlet between two files of young savages near their own age, each of whom wielded a hickory switch. As the white striplings started down the double line of torture a chorus of frenzied yelling rang in their ears and blows began to fall upon their naked backs. The Cunningham boy when he reached the end of the row was barely alive, suffering excruciating pain from the beatings.

But Dan as soon as he felt the cut of a switch became so angry that he turned upon the first inflicter with a well-planted blow in the face and felled him to the ground. Like an enraged beast he sprang upon his aggressor and waged a tussle for supremacy. The bucks gathered around to revel in the sight. Some of the spectators wanted to give their racial brother an advantage, but the chief, who was present, demanded fair play. Some encouraged the young paleface, others the struggling redskin. The fight continued at length until Dan came out victorious. Delighted with his fighting spirit the chief adopted him and he quickly became a favorite with the tribe. Likewise the Cunningham boy was taken into another Indian family.

Quite naturally the white boys acquired the habits and manners of their foster people. Their sports and pastimes were those of the Indian youths in whose company they were thrown, such as hunting, fishing, and the rude games of the forest, in which the two became adepts, particularly Dan.

One day about six years after the kidnaping a number of the tribe appeared at Fort Pitt to trade and obtain ammunition, the two races being then at peace. With the party came the young Caucasians. Despite their Indian make-up they were recognized

[7]

and Dan's brother-in-law, Zadok Wright, who lived on the east side of the Ohio river about 10 miles below the fort, was sent for. At once he began negotiations to recover the captives.

There was little difficulty in obtaining the release of the Cunningham boy, who had grown tired of his mode of life and encouraged efforts to restore him. Not so with Sullivan, who was now 15. Dan had become completely adapted to savagery and was regarded by his Indian comrades with great esteem. Consequently the parley over the latter's ransom became tedious and prolonged, threatening to prove a failure. Not only were the demands of the chief exorbitant, but he retracted from several agreements just as they were about to be effected. Finally a horse, a packsaddle, a half-dozen hatchets, three red blankets, and a gallon of whisky closed the deal as far as the chief was concerned.

Throughout the dickering Dan remained a silent but not indifferent spectator. When told that he was to return to his relatives he emphatically shook his head, signifying a determination to remain with the Indians. Such a decision embarrassed the Wrights and required much tact to surmount. But after long persuasion the boy agreed to come home if his brother-in-law would buy him a beaver hat, which in that day was a great luxury. Believing that he was substantially complying with his promise Zadok purchased a wool hat, at the price of one dollar, and presented it to Dan. Giving it a contemptuous glance the boy handed it back with the curt phrase—"ram beaver!" Finally a genuine beaver hat was offered and joyfully accepted. But with great reluctance did Dan forsake his adopted people.

Young Cunningham cheerfully resumed the ways of civilization. Dan did not. He despised the customs of the palefaces. He refused to work and scorned the men who did, calling them squaws. All he wanted to do was to fish and hunt. His new life became a restraint which he could hardly endure.

One Sunday a year after his redemption, the people of the settlement were gathered in their log meeting house for public worship. Suddenly while they were absorbed in their devotions they were startled by an apparition in their midst, arrayed in Indian costume, adorned with feathers and paint and fully armed. Before the astonished congregation could quiet down, Dan let out a deafening war whoop and turning on his heel sped like lightning into the woods. Bored with culture he had gone back to his former friends to indulge in pursuits more congenial to his nature.

Years passed.

As his relatives received no tidings of him they became convinced that he was dead. But in September 1782, near the close of the Revolutionary War, when the British and Indians joined to attack Fort Henry (now Wheeling, West Virginia) he unexpectedly emerged from the forest to offer his services to the besieged. Because his instincts revolted at the thought of raising a hand against his own nationality he had left the Indians and gone over to the service of America. Even before the Revolution when he was one of the Indians, he always refused to take part in any expedition against his white people. He was now 24 and full-grown, having lived among savages for about 14 years. How did he happen to be in that area? He was on his way westward conducting a boatload of cannon balls down to the Falls of the Ohio river, opposite Louisville, where he would deliver them to the Continental Army. Passing by on the river he heard firing at Fort Henry and knowing that meant danger to his countrymen he made for the shore and hurried to their defense. In so doing he was discovered by the Indians, who gave him a close chase and severely wounded him in the foot. But a party of Virginians sallied to his rescue and helped him into the stockade. Soon his boat fell into the hands of the British, who shot forth the balls in a vain attempt to destroy the fort.

After the siege had ended, Sullivan was compelled to stay at Fort Henry because of his injury. Through the nursing of Mrs. Elizabeth Zane it was eventually healed and as soon as he could travel he visited the Zadok Wrights near Pittsburgh.

But his restless character would not let him remain inactive. The fight with England being over he renounced his unnatural allegiance and took the side of his people in their warfare against the savages, serving as scout and guide, penetrating the wilderness

with utmost confidence. His knowledge of Indians, their character, habits, and tactics, as well as their trails, made him invaluable
to the settlers. From the time that he ceased to live among them
he joined in almost every movement made against the red men.

About the year 1808 when William Henry Harrison assumed
command of the Northwest Territory, the Indians were com-
mitting many depredations in the region of the Wabash river.
This general, located at Post Vinscus (later called Vincennes,
Indiana), needed a company of woodsmen to act as scouts and
spies who could successfully cope with the aborigines in strategy.
So impressed was the general with Sullivan's reputation that he
commissioned Daniel to raise and captain the requisite number.
Accordingly this great-granduncle of Horace Bell selected 17
men all skilled in woodcraft and with them set out to the Falls of
the Ohio.

Having reconnoitered to this point they were returning. The
distance to be traversed from the falls back to the post was about
100 miles, extending through a dense and uninhabited wilderness.
Reaching a place about 30 miles from the post they stopped during the heat of the day to rest and refresh themselves. While they
were relaxing, Sullivan, who like an Indian believed in dreams,
related to them one that had appeared to him on the preceding
night. He informed his men of a supernatural warning that during
the day they would certainly be attacked. Consequently he cautioned them to be extremely vigilant. His story made but a slight
impression on his listeners, who treated the matter lightly, regarding it as an idle fear. Their unconcern led him to exact from each
of them a solemn promise that should an attack occur, regardless
of its magnitude, they would if need be stand by him to the death.
This pledge they all unhesitatingly gave.

Resuming their march they had progressed for two hours on
their way when they came to a spring in a beautiful grove. So
inviting was the spot that they halted for a brief rest. No sooner
had they sat down in the friendly shade of the trees than they
were startled by the wild whoop of savages. As they sprang to
their feet a heavy volley flashed toward them from an ambush.

[10]

Notwithstanding their promise of the morning nine of the 17 men fled at the first round of shots. Two of those who remained were killed outright. The rest took to trees according to custom in the wilderness.

Meanwhile the savages circled the group, firing upon it from all sides. Only seven men were left to defend themselves against a large and bloodthirsty pack of Indians, who called on Sullivan by name to surrender. He yelled back that he would die first. Whereupon they charged and attempted to take him alive. His companions rallied around him. Standing firm in cool fortitude they fought their foes hand to hand until all were slain except one man and the captain.

During the combat Daniel's rifle broke at the small of the stock, but using the barrel as a war club he dealt swift destruction to any who ventured within reach of his blows. The Indians closed around, intent on securing him alive, but his desperate courage prevented them from doing so. One of the scouts who had been stunned by a blow on the head and who was supposed to be dead recovered consciousness and lifted himself up on his elbow. He saw an Indian deliberately raise his rifle and shoot Sullivan, who fell dead. Now fully restored to his senses the last survivor tried to run away, but he was caught and bound. For an unknown reason they let him live.

The men whose prostrate bodies were scattered on the place of conflict were each scalped and mutilated. But Sullivan's remains the Indians respected. They cut out his heart and made of it a soup. This they partook of with the view, as they said, of making them brave. As a further token of admiration for his courage they covered his body with leaves on the spot where it fell. Then joining in a dismal death chant the whole party moved away on a dogtrot through the forest leading their single captive.

But he was not long at their mercy, for he soon managed to escape and reach his people. To him we owe this story of the fatal expedition.

The place of the massacre has ever since been known as Sullivan's Spring. The county of Sullivan, Indiana, washed on its western edge by the Wabash river, and also its capital town were named in Daniel's honor, forever preserving the memory of a dauntless, early-American scout whose supreme motive was patriotism.[5]

Such was the ancestral tree of Horace Bell. From a double line of forebears naturally endowed to survive the hardships and hazards of the wilderness he inherited a passion for adventure and an athletic body, tall and always spare. His rosy-white face turning to purple-red in moments of rage, his blond hair and blue eyes betokened a Scottish and Irish past. Ruggedness and self-reliance were gifts from both strains of his pioneer people. The fighting spirit, a dominant trait in his nature—note the name of Sullivan—came mostly from the line of his mother.

How Dear to this Heart!

David Williamson Bell and his wife Elizabeth Wright were born and reared in Washington county, which during their youth lay in Virginia. But when state lines were finally fixed they found themselves in the southwest corner of Pennsylvania. As the northern state forbad slavery the Negroes belonging to Mrs. Bell as an inheritance from her father were consequently freed. In their early married life David and Elizabeth moved due west across the panhandle of western Virginia wedged in between Pennsylvania and Ohio to Wheeling, where they lived for a brief period. Then in 1829 they floated down the beautiful river, passing the full width of Ohio and half of Indiana, to make a home at New Albany, a settlement on the Indiana bank, a few miles below Louisville. With them came Julia Wright, a maiden sister.

There were now five children—all girls except four-year-old John. A year after the Bells reached Indiana Horace made his advent into this western world on December 11, 1830. Like many pioneer mothers Mrs. Bell clothed her babe in a red flannel dress and gave him a strip of bacon tied to a string for an all-day sucker. Then in due time came two more sisters, followed by the last

[12]

baby named Charles, who increased to nine the number of young-sters seated around the table devouring hog and hominy. Later Charles would spend much of his adolescence with Aunt Julia and be moulded in mind by her.

Dissatisfied with prospects after nine years in New Albany David Bell conveyed his family farther down the river to a place in Harrison county, Indiana, directly across the water from Brandenburg, Kentucky, 40 miles below Louisville. With money saved in New Albany he bought an abandoned town-site formerly owned by the Boones and turned it into a farm. It was rich bottom land. Below rolled the majestic river, behind stood cedar-clad hills.

He bought also the ferryboat plying back and forth to Bran-denburg, as well as the right to operate it. Since early days there had been a ferry at this point, for it was a well-known crossing for emigrants moving from east Tennessee, North Carolina, and western Virginia into the Illinois country. Here the first settler, Solomon Brandenburg, installed a ferry where the river was less than a mile wide. In those days steamboats on the Ohio were owned entirely by individuals—truly an age of private enterprise. Bell's boat connected with a highway on the Indiana side running from the village of Mauckport, two miles west of the landing, to Corydon, the county seat. The ferry was thus a necessity to the Kentuckians of Meade county who wished to go on horseback or in wagons to towns in Indiana. Likewise people in the southern part of Harrison county used the boat, since most of them traded in Brandenburg. In this zone Bell had a monopoly of the boating business, for the state not only licensed but also protected the owners by fining those who rowed others across for pay within two miles of the ferry.

Not far from the boat landing Bell built a house on his farm. It stood facing the river southward at a place just above the high-water mark, beyond which the waters never rose. There were no other homes within a mile. Only nine persons were in the family now, two children having died. Attached to the Bell household were two Negroes. One named Oswald had belonged to Jeremiah Wright. In spite of his emancipation by Pennsylvania he had

[13]

fondly followed "Miss Julie" when she came west with her sister. In New Albany he had been one of the few freed slaves. Now he was working for David Bell on the river farm. Some years later came Ike, a light mulatto from Kentucky. This boy had been indentured to Mr. Bell with the understanding that at 18 he should be released.

When Horace was three years old, grandfather Jeremiah Wright, the Revolutionary veteran, visited the family just before he died. It was in the spring when they were making maple sugar. The child amused himself by sitting on his lap and dropping sugar lumps into grandpa's mouth—Horace's earliest recollection.

Living so near the river the Bells like others in that country were frequently sick with malaria. This condition provided Horace, years later, with a bit of drollery. He repeatedly told the story that in the late summer when the illness came and the youngsters were shaking violently with chills, their father would make them climb up in the boughs of the chestnut trees growing by the house and stay there until they stopped shivering. Then on the next day when fever followed he made them pick up the nuts which their quaking had caused to fall. So the nut crop was harvested with the least labor. Whenever Horace cracked this joke his father would laugh uproariously.

Here on the banks of the Ohio river Horace Bell grew to young manhood. He did what every frontier boy might do. He plowed the fields and planted, chopped down trees, broke colts, and raced horses. He swam in the creeks and river. He learned to hit his mark with a rifle or pistol. He fought with his fists, for as he later recalled, "A boy who could not fight was forced to take a back seat."

Beyond the farm flourished "the deep tangled wildwood," forests of tall oaks, walnut and poplar trees. He knew where to find the old trunks still bearing in their bark the inscription carved by Squire Boone, a brother of Daniel:

HERE I KILLED A BEAR

Inviting caves hidden among the wooded hills beckoned him. All these the lad explored. He liked best the one by Buck creek near the home place, which had saved the life of Squire when he was fleeing from Indians. Inside he gazed in wonder at the drawings of bird and beast and Biblical quotations cut in the walls by the old pioneer. He read Boone's lines engraved upon a large rock:

HERE I SIT AND SING OF MY SALVATION
AND PRAISE THE GOD OF MY CREATION

What a fillip this country gave a growing boy, especially during spring when the dogwood bloomed and fish began to bite! Like a pocket 20 miles wide beautiful Harrison county lay, outlined by the bending river.

The young Bells were better educated than most children in their locality. Horace, as well as his brothers and sisters, went for his Latin to Brandenburg, since Kentucky being the older state gave better training than Indiana. The school was taught by a man, for no woman could control a roomful of wild young frontiersmen and give them the whippings they deserved. In spite of his natural devilment Horace like many Hoosiers loved books and he read every one he could get in that backwoods community. His gift for narrative, which later turned him to writing, developed early. His favorite volume was the life of General Francis Marion, a Revolutionary hero of South Carolina. It was written by "Parson" Weems, the biographer of Washington, who fabricated the myth of the ax and cherry tree. Characteristic of the times the story glows with patriotism and abounds in heroic deeds and moral platitudes. Throughout his boyhood Horace read it over and over again.

Then came the momentous year of 1849. Up and down the Ohio river men went wild over the news of gold discovered in central California. John Bell now 24 set out at once to get his share. A year later Horace, completing his teens, could not resist the call. His father, willing for him to go, sold the boy Ike (whose indenture had not expired) to a relative in Kentucky. The price of $500 he gave to Horace for the trip, who prepared to travel with three other men from southern Indiana. The four obtained a covered wagon and six horses to pull it. Father Bell also gave his son an extra horse to ride when he chose.

There were many supplies to pack in the wagon for the long haul across the continent. Besides a tent and many blankets there must be plenty of warm clothes and boots. John's letter from California, which took over three months to reach Indiana by way of Panama, had not only given advice about the route but had listed other things to take: carpenter tools with nails, ropes and chains, also an ax and hatchet. They would need tin cups and plates and by all means a coffee pot. John warned them to carry sufficient flour and bacon, coffee and sugar, lard, crackers, and cheese. As for weapons each man should have a good rifle, a pair of pistols, at least five pounds of powder and 10 pounds of lead, as well as a bowie knife. All these things and many others John advised buying near home where they were cheaper.

At last the outfit was ready to move and the steamboat stopped at Bell's Landing. All the family walked down to the dock to see Horace off to California. When the wagon was placed on the lower deck and the horses stood in their stalls, the time had come to break home ties. Fondly hugging his mother he kissed her under her black sunbonnet. He embraced his sisters, first Anne and Elizabeth, then Caroline and Virginia. He gripped the hard hand of his father and slapped Charley, too young to go, soundly on the back. When the farewell whistle blew, the first period of Horace's life closed. Wearing a worried look David Bell thought of the chances his reckless boy would take. Mother stood longest, gazing at the boat as it paddled down the bright river—her face expressionless. She had too much grit to betray emotion. If ever a woman was a Spartan it was Elizabeth Bell, daughter of the Wrights—so everybody said who knew her.[6]

To Hangtown or Bust!

The four friends floated down to Cairo, Illinois. Here they transferred to a boat going up the darker waters of the great stream, passed St. Louis, and turned into the Missouri river. Ten miles east of the Kansas border they got their wagon and horses off and drove a short distance south to Independence. This was the "jumping off" place for many emigrants en route to the Far West, the one John Bell had recommended.

The little town of less than 2,000 residents hummed with business. Its 30 stores and 20 wagon and blacksmith shops were crowded with customers buying their last supplies and equipment needed for the long journey. The four Hoosiers observing that they were not dressed like most gold seekers bought red shirts with collar attached, and rough woolen coats reaching nearly to the knees. Their trousers they thrust into high topboots. But their slouch hats were in style. Feeling that his blond hair made him less impressive as a man of action, Horace dyed his long locks deep black—a practice he would continue until his marriage, when his wife would put a stop to it. His group also noticed that many of the wagons bore slogans. So after much thought they painted in black on their white wagon cover the words: Hangtown or Bust.

The time for beginning the journey was all-important. Trains of lumbering prairie schooners should not start out until the swollen rivers of early spring had subsided. They must also wait until the grass on the plains was tall enough to feed the animals. Once under way the emigrants moved as fast as possible to miss the snows falling in October, blocking the trail through the High Sierras. Now it was just right for "jumping off."

Having made friends of a number of gold seekers the four Indianians joined their caravan for mutual protection. So at dawn on the twenty-second day of May in 1850 they set forth on their perilous journey across the continent—a distance of 24 hundred miles. Leaving Independence they traveled over the old Santa Fe trail now worn into ruts by recent traffic, ruts so deep that the drivers had to take a parallel course. On the second day when they were 40 miles out, the party saw a crude sign reading

ROAD TO OREGON

and pointing to the right. They could not continue westward through Kansas, for in case of a drouth they would find no water and probably no grass for the stock. Then farther on they would

[17]

meet the unopened Rocky mountains. Therefore they followed the sign and bore toward the northwest.

It was not an unpleasant journey going northward and parallel with the Missouri river—not until the sameness of things palled on everyone and dampened enthusiasm. On the prairies the grass was high, sometimes half covering the caravan. The valleys sloped gently and were not hot. Occasionally near the river bank they could see a few lazy savages staring at the wagons lumbering past. Each noon the party halted to rest and feed man and beast. At sundown the day's journey ended. On the spot chosen for the night's camp the wagons were rolled into a circle making both a bulwark against enemies and a corral wherein the animals grazed.

Tents were put up, fires started, pots and pans appeared. While cooks prepared the evening meal, others tinkered with the wagons or tended the horses and oxen. Supper over, there came a lull. The camp fires leaped higher revealing a circle of contented faces. Someone told a tall tale. Then the musician of the party pumping on his accordion sang, among other pieces, *Oh, Susannah*. On the chorus all joined in with the revised version:

> I'm off to Sacramento
> With my wash bowl on my knee

the wash bowl being the tool used for separating the gold nuggets.

When the fire subsided a hush fell over the camp. Dark figures stole away under tents and into wagons, all but two—the sentinels who stalked about guarding the spot against surprise and watching the animals until relieved at midnight. When the first streaks of dawn appeared everybody began the new day. At six the caravan was again moving.

When Horace's band had been out of Independence two weeks they reached the Platte river in southeast Nebraska and followed it west. Near its banks were pleasant meadows to delight the cattle. Game was plentiful and Horace when his turn at driving the wagon had ended made short side-trips on his extra horse to shoot antelopes and prairie chickens. Farther on, the train struggled through marshes until it reached the southern branch of the Platte, where the drivers finding the stream shallow enough to ford turned up to the north fork. From there the route ran along the river to Fort Laramie, a government outpost in Wyoming.

This was the first important stop on the long expedition and a good place to pause, for just beyond waited the mountains. June had now come and Horace's group lingered for a week beside the Laramie river. What a beautiful and romantic scene it was! Here they cut up their wagons and made them into packsaddles to which they balanced their diminished loads. Here they met Kit Carson, the famous scout, and traded to him their fine American horses for Mexican mules. Thus prepared they entered the great barrier.

The road led them across rugged country farther up the North Platte river. They followed the stream until they came to its Sweetwater tributary, which brought them up to South Pass on the Continental Divide. This was a low natural gap in the Rocky mountains, its elevation being little more than 7,000 feet. The ascent was so gradual that the emigants hardly knew they had crossed a continental watershed. Nearby at Green river stood a monumental butte looking like a ruined stone edifice with majestic pillars and dome. It seemed as though the Creator had set it there to mark the origin of the Pacific water system.

Not long out of the pass Bell's companions choosing a right-hand branch of the trail, called Sublette's Cut-off, followed it over to Soda Springs on Bear river in Idaho. Here Horace stopped for a day and became acquainted with Peg-leg Smith, a notorious horse thief. A native of Missouri he had turned Indian, acquired numerous squaws, and become a Blackfoot chief. Smith made a business of stealing horses from the Los Angeles country and selling them at the junction of the California and Oregon trails to passing emigrants. Early in his career, while escaping with a herd of horses through Cajon Pass northeast of Los Angeles, his leg was shattered by the bullet of a pursuing *ranchero*. When out of danger he had an Indian amputate his leg with a hunting knife. A special stirrup made to fit his wooden stump enabled him to ride. When young Bell saw Smith at Soda Springs he had 15 hundred horses.

[19]

Farther on, the government had located Fort Hall on the Snake river. This was the second main stop, 12 hundred miles from Independence, half the distance to the gold fields. But the worst was yet to come! There were still the desert to be crossed and steeper mountain passes. After another rest the party started out to meet their double ordeal. Onward they traveled now southwestward, following the bank of the Snake river in Idaho, then passed the Goose Creek mountains, and reached the headwaters of the Humboldt in Nevada. They rode beside the river throughout its crooked length until it ended in a sink. On entering this waste land the first emigrants were frequently driven to despair. Often many who had endured the hardships of Nebraska and were undaunted by the Rockies now turned back. There was no avoiding the Humboldt desert, this most dangerous part of the whole route. The soil was alkaline and the dust fine as flour floated in the air, choking men and mules. It blotched the face and blistered the lips like poison ivy. But the Bell party survived this greatest hazard.

From the sink the trail led them straight west up over the exhausting Truckee Pass in the Sierra Nevadas close by the northern shore of Lake Tahoe. Thence it turned southward and following more rivers stopped at Hangtown, California, now called Placerville. It was on the nineteenth day of August 1850 that Horace finished the terrible journey, 90 days after leaving Independence—and he was still under 20.[7]

Among the Diggings

A few miles north of Hangtown lay the placers. These were the sandy beds of streams which during the rainy season were covered with rushing torrents, but now the upper sides were exposed. Some in Bell's company dug among bushes nearby, others with pick and shovel delved in the banks and under tree roots. Placing their rockers beside a stream they filled them with soil, then threw in water, and separated the gold, if any, by washing. Sometimes they stood waist-deep in icy water while the sun beat down on their heads. At the end of a week Bell and his friends grew sick of their job, for in spite of back-breaking work they had each sifted out less than 50 dollars' worth of gold. Being discouraged they would go to Sacramento and see what it was like.

That city was bursting with a population of 60,000 and suffering from a housing shortage. For only one person in 10 had either a house or tent. The rest camped under big trees standing in town or beside the river. Horace and his mates lived on the levee just below the foot of J street near the boat landing, having nothing over their heads but the leaves of a wide-spreading oak. A beautiful stream it was, so clear he could watch the salmon playing 15 feet below and so deep that when the *New World* and the *Senator* came steaming up from San Francisco they ran in close to the bank.

Sacramento was boiling with excitement. On the day before the Hoosiers arrived there was a riot. The site of the city with land surrounding was owned by Captain John A. Sutter, who got it as a gift from the Mexican governor Micheltorena for help given in a war against the rebel Alvarado. But squatters had moved in, refusing to pay rent or vacate. What were Mexican grants worth? they argued—California was American. When Sutter served writs of ejection a battle followed. Barricading themselves behind wagons, the squatters threw rocks and broke windows. In the melee the sheriff was killed.

During the year before, when rains were heavy, the Sacramento river had overflowed its banks. Now the young city proposed building a better levee to prevent a recurrence. Engineers were trying to obtain laborers at four dollars a day, but men would not accept the offer. They held nightly meetings and vowed they would not work for less than eight dollars and board. Their price was finally accepted. Coming from Indiana where men toiled for eight dollars a month with board, these wages looked like affluence to Horace and so he gladly accepted a job.

In the middle of October 1850, while he was camping under the oak tree a steamboat brought the news that California had been admitted into the Union. At once several patriots started out beating gongs, calling for volunteers to go to Sutter's Fort, a few miles away, to bring in a cannon for celebrating the great event. Dust and sand lay deep on the road, but men were ready to go, Bell being one. They pulled in the big gun, placing it at the foot of J street. At dawn the firing began. It continued throughout the day and the fun with it. Fifty years later Bell told the Pioneer Society of San Bernardino honoring the event at a picnic, "There was no parade, but no end of speeches. The river front was lined with lumber piles and on every pile stood a speaker surrounded by listeners. The cannon kept on firing and the orators kept on orating."

December came and Horace found new excitement by joining in a brief war against the local Indians, the Mocosumnes, who had been molesting miners. His company set out on the immigrant road toward Carson valley. On the way they met a savage who killed their captain, but in three weeks the campaign was over and Horace returned to his quarters under the great oak tree.

Fortunately the winter was one of prolonged sunshine. Spring drew on. It was time to be moving. Having lost heart for mining near Hangtown he expected better luck by trying a new location, and there were other men near the river who thought as he did. But a stronger motive demanded a change. Bad sanitation caused by the housing shortage had produced an epidemic of cholera; consequently all who could leave were ready to flee to the mountains. So Horace joined a party of 25 to explore the country northward. In February they broke camp on the river bank and turned their bearded faces toward Mount Shasta, 200 miles away. They hoped to pry open with pick and shovel the lockers of fortune on the Klamath, the Salmon, or Scott rivers, which in 1851 were as little known to the government as the tributaries of the Amazon.

Pugh Price, being 52, was the oldest one in the party and Horace the youngest. Because of his seniority Price was made captain of the band. He was a superb sample of Missouri manhood, standing six feet, two, and weighing 240 pounds. His nephew, W. B. Royal, was also in the company. The men were well armed and provisioned, but took no tents. Nor was there a wagon among them (pack mules being the only means of transportation in the Sacramento valley). The winter sunshine had deceived them into believing that tents would be only a burden. For this mistake they would pay heavily. But they carried plenty of ammunition, having heard tales of the warlike Indians on the Trinity and Pitt rivers.

On the first day's advance Price killed a raccoon which Sam, his Negro servant, cooked in Southern style. Fat coon stewed with sweet potatoes! Sam served that popular frontier mess on tin plates. A blanket spread on the ground sufficed for a breakfast table. On the second day out, an owl, a crow, and a hawk were the captain's trophies, for he was the only man with a shotgun. Kentucky rifles, Mississippi yagers, and Hall's carbines made up the rest of the armament, except for various patterns of revolvers.

The only big game obtained in the march up the valley was a California lion killed by one of the rifles. He was a tremendous fellow with muscles like those of a mule. Juanito Ramirez, a native boy, dragged him into camp with his *lazo*. The captain put Sam to work skinning and preparing him for the spit and pot. Then followed a lecture by Price on the edibleness of all carnivorous animals, including the lion and catamount.

"Better than veal! better than kid or mutton!" insisted the captain, and to prove his assertion he invited the whole company to breakfast. Some of the men modestly suggested while admiring the muscular monster that "he might be tough." "Tough!" snorted Price indignantly. "Tough? Why, gentlemen, it's all in the cooking. So would a sirloin of beef be tough if not cooked properly. When Sam dishes him up for breakfast tomorrow, if there is just one of this company who says he's tough, then I will agree never to sit down again to feast on lion or wildcat."

It was a beautiful frosty moonlit night. They were camping in a lovely grove somewhere near Red Bluff. Everyone sat up until midnight telling stories of adventure, interspersed with song and jest, meanwhile chaffing Sam about the lion. The poor fellow had pressed into service every kettle and had each marshaled in line on an improvised furnace made of two large green oak logs, where he kept up such a firing as grandmothers were wont to do at old-fashioned sugar camps.

At gray dawn Sam came to the man on guard and inquired the

time. Shaking his head gravely he muttered, "Dat beats all! Dis chile hab trabeled from de Potomac to de Sacramento an' damned if eber I seed de like. Won't de cap'n swar!" At a late hour in the morning when the cook announced breakfast Pugh Price was in ecstasy. He attacked a piece of sirloin and pronounced it capital. The lion had been chopped up and stewed with salt pork and potatoes. Some hardtack was also thrown in. Except for the lion meat the kettles contained a beautiful lobscouse. The pork, potatoes, and hardtack had resolved into a general amalgam, but the lion refused to mix.

Everyone behaved soberly while all eyes watched the captain. Quickly the lobscouse disappeared but without the lion. Happening to get a piece of hind leg Juanito gnawed energetically at it. Then slyly he slipped it under the blanket, muttering, "*Carajo!*" A titter now passed around the festive board—or blanket. Looking sharply at Juanito, the captain asked, "What's the matter, boy?" The young Mexican to add emphasis to his faltering English words got up, walked to his saddle, and returned with his riata. Holding it up, he said, "Cap', you eatee lion, we eatee rope." Roars of laughter followed which Price himself joined in. And that ended the feast on California lion.

About midnight it began to rain. It kept on raining from day to day, sometimes snowing. They were completely without shelter. Rock creek was in front and Cottonwood creek behind—both unfordable during the storm. Using their blankets they tried to improvise tents, but could not. Sometimes the rain became a deluge. The discouraged campers would lie down on wet blankets and cover up with blankets and be rained on all night. They waited for short cessations during the day to cook their meals. Finally after two weeks the storm abated and, strange to say, not a man suffered from that unparalleled exposure.

Two days of sunshine followed and a subsidence of the creeks, permitting the company to resume its march. They camped the next night at Redding's Springs (now called Shasta), then headed their mules westward toward the Trinity river, and on the second night bivouacked on a steep but grassy mountain side. After graz-

[24]

ing until dusk the mules were caught up and secured. Guards were posted with warnings to be vigilant, for they had passed beyond the peaceful valley and were penetrating the mountain fastnesses of the fierce Trinity Indians. Except for the occasional snorting of a fearful mule it was a quiet night. But at dawn the adventurers picked up in and around camp a few dozen barbed arrows. These, like triangular notes, forewarned them that if they wanted to stay alive they had better be watchful.

On the morrow they reached Weaverville, a little mining camp of log houses on a mountain bench overlooking the Trinity river. It was now March 1851. Up to this time little mining had been done here. But several Cornishmen were working some rich deep bank diggings opposite the mouth of the north fork. On the same stream Price's party found fair prospects of coarse gold. So they settled down to swing their picks, willing to abandon earlier hopes of shaking nuggets out of the grass roots beside Scott river and picking up gold by the bushel on the Salmon. The company divided into small groups. Each staked out its claim and began to dam and divert the stream and dig in its former bed.

Bell passes over his mining experience on the Trinity river, merely calling it "satisfactory." By this we may infer that success was only moderate. At any rate he gave up digging for gold and turned to something less monotonous and perhaps more profitable.

The mules belonging to the company were divided into two pack trains. Price's nephew, Will Royal, took the management of one and Bell, near his age, the other. Horace set out with his beasts to Uniontown (today called Arcata) 80 miles distant on Humboldt bay to be followed in a few days by Royal. Bell had 21 mules, one man to help him, and Rose, a dog, to stand guard. These sturdy little Mexican mules were indispensable. Each one could carry for a long distance across mountains a load of 300 pounds—sacks of flour, kegs of whisky, bags of beans, and other supplies needed in the gold fields.

Uniontown, so Horace saw, was a live place with one street, a square, and a gambling house where monte was dealt to packers coming in from the Trinity and Klamath rivers. It was the rival of

San Francisco and the leading settlement on its newly discovered bay.

He made the return trip without meeting Royal, who in error had taken the trail to the town of Humboldt. Unloading his cargo at camp Bell started again for the bay determined on following the trail to Humboldt and joining Royal for mutual protection, since all packers feared the Indians, who were known to be bold and dangerous. No place in the world, thought Horace, could be as lovely as this region of the Trinity river and the great forest of redwoods enclosing Humboldt bay. It was truly an arcadia swarming with all kinds of game. He saw thousands of elk and deer in herds and they seemed as tame as domestic sheep.

Where the trail divided, one branch going toward Uniontown, the other to Humboldt, Horace camped for the night. In the morning he set out for the latter. Descending the slope toward the south fork of Trinity he wound his way through thickets of hazel brush at the head of his mules, little Mack, his helper, bringing up the rear. Suddenly as he was riding along carelessly at a sharp turn of the road, Horace was confronted by a wild-looking, heavy-bearded man, bareheaded, and holding a Mississippi rifle in the position of "ready." At the same moment he lowered his weapon, gasping, "My God, young man, you were never nearer your end!"

Then looking behind, the man cried out, "Hurrah, boys! it's all right, we're safe!" By this time the mules had crowded up, halted, and commenced browsing on the hazel brush, and little Mack called out impatiently from the rear, unable to see on account of the thicket the cause of the halt. The stranger shouted, "Look out for yourself and mules. The road's alive with Injuns!" Will Royal now appeared, pale and haggard, and armed with rifle and revolver, a red handkerchief tied around his head, his clothes tattered. Horace grasped the situation. They had been attacked by redskins!

His first move was to lead his mules to Will's camp on a small bench down the trail. Then he put Rose on guard. He convinced his friends that the faithful dog was ample assurance against un-expected assault. Their minds at ease explanations followed. But there was no need for words; the dead mules and the barricade of saddles and flour bags told the story. The six men in the other party had left Humboldt three days before with 50 mules now decreased to less than 20. Royal introduced the stranger who had almost shot Horace as Captain Dixon of Humboldt, formerly a Texas frontiersman. On the day before, the two parties of packers after uniting had been desperately harassed while descending the mountain to South Fork. At four in the afternoon on gaining their present camp they were forced to unload and form a defense. Here Horace had found them.

The next thing to do was to pack up and substitute Bell's mules for those that were killed. Soon Rose commenced barking and encircling the camp. So Dixon and Royal took to the brush as scouts while the six other men loaded the beasts. After burning the pack-saddles of the dead animals the combined party set out for a lake four miles off which Horace had left in the morning. Along the way they were shot at by Indians until the trail emerged into more open country where they were comparatively free from attack.

Unpacking at the lake when the sun was still two hours above the western peaks, they picketed their frightened mules to graze on the luxuriant grass, Rose being the only guard. Dixon killed a fat buck for supper. After eating it they opened a five-gallon keg of cherry brandy and were as happy a lot as ever camped in the wilds of the Trinity region. During the night Rose gave a few alarms which Mack and Bell attended to, letting the others have their much needed sleep.

A man named McLaughlin kept the Mountain House on the road from Shasta to Weaverville. From his place at the foot of Trinity mountain to its summit the distance was a half-mile as the crow flies, but by the zigzag trail four times that far. With his pack train Horace stopped there one night. Besides Bell's helper the only other guest was Mr. Anderson, a butcher from Weaverville who was driving over some fat cattle. The three visitors ate their supper and went to bed in the tavern. During the night Rose became uneasy and in the morning while the stock was feeding she ran barking up to the summit and returned in great excitement. Feeling sure that Indians were on the road Horace proposed reconnoitering.

But Anderson would not agree. As soon as breakfast was over, without waiting for the others to pack up and go with him, the butcher turned his cows out of the corral and started up the mountain. Rose whimpered her fears. The rest were an hour getting ready and more than an hour in reaching the top. Before gaining that point Bell and his comrade, Fred Stacer, heard a dismal wail from the dog and spurred their mules forward. Just over the summit they found the dead body of Anderson with a half-dozen arrows sticking in it.

On the next day Horace passed through Weaverville and camped at Oregon gulch. Another day and his mules reached their destination, a trading post on the north fork of Trinity river.

Several months more passed and Bell wearied of this kind of life. He had experienced about all he cared to know in central and northern California. Then an idea came. He recalled that he had an uncle living in Los Angeles. He would go down there on a visit and explore the south country. So strapping on his gun he picked up his carpetbag and went to the wharf in San Francisco. He handed over a fifty-dollar octagonal slug of gold for his single-cabin fare and boarded a little steamer named *Sea Bird*. She was a side-wheeler and churned her frothy course down to San Pedro in about four days. Now in October 1852, Horace Bell was on his way for the first time to Los Angeles.[8]

And while we wait for the *Sea Bird* to finish her watery flight, let us turn our eyes away from the young man to view the life of the uncle he had never met and with whom he would stay.

Adobe Days

Back in Pennsylvania when the nineteenth century had just begun Alexander Bell was born. Named for his father he was a few years younger than his brother David. In his twenty-third year the spirit of adventure carried him off to the unknown City of Mexico. Here and in various parts of that country he lived as a merchant. What he sold, there is no telling, since he has left no memoirs. But we do know that after spending nearly a score of years in Mexico making money he gave up his business and moved. Crossing to the west coast he embarked at Guaymas, and passing Mazatlán sailed up the Pacific to the port of San Pedro. It was in 1842 when he arrived and California was still a Mexican province.

Alexander settled down in the pueblo of Los Angeles 20 miles inland, selling hides, tallow, and general merchandise. Two years after his coming he married Señorita Maria de las Nievas Guirado, a Spanish lady of the upper class. To provide the proper setting for his bride he built a *palacio* on land held in his wife's name. Made of adobe it stood on the southeast corner of Los Angeles and Aliso streets and had the distinction of being one of the few structures in town boasting a second story. A long roofed balcony ran along its north side and looked down on Aliso street. From here you could see the Plaza not many steps northward and to the west a stretch of elevated ground later called Fort Hill. The rooms were large and adorned with furniture of teak carved in China. Outside the house in boxes on the second-story porch red geraniums bloomed the year round.

Near the middle of the house and cutting through its thick walls on Aliso street there was an imposing entrance surmounted by an ornate arch. When its wide door by the sidewalk swung open you could pass through to a cozy patio at the rear of the building. Here grew a garden of flowers and blossoming shrubs within a circle of orange trees. The *zanja* flowing nearby provided precious water for irrigation and for the spraying fountain at the center. It was a pleasant place, where Spanish doñas could enjoy a secluded airing.

At the west end of the mansion an ell extended down Los Angeles street about 300 feet, which contained Alexander's general store and a number of shops rented to other merchants. For many years it was a trading center and known as Bell's Row.[9]

Though he had spent many years in a foreign country, Alexander Bell remained a loyal American. Most of the early pioneers who married *Californio* women became naturalized Mexicans, for only by doing so could they possess land. But Bell refused to give up his national birthright and never owned a foot of Mexican soil. As his nephew later expressed it, "His patriotism was always at the boiling point." During a dinner party given by John Temple, a local merchant, in 1844 at which all the *Americanos* of Los Angeles were guests, the conversation turned upon visiting the United States. Abel Stearns had just returned; others proposed to make the trip soon. As Bell remained silent he was asked when he would be going.

"Never," he answered bluntly. "I have been away so long that I will wait a year or two longer and then the United States will come to me. Yes, gentlemen," he shouted, rising to his feet, "California will soon be an American possession."

Bell's guess was not wrong, for a year later Commander Sloat's squadron appeared off the coast. He had been instructed by the Secretary of the Navy to communicate with Abel Stearns, who it was thought would inform Sloat as to the military defenses of southern California. Dropping anchor in San Pedro bay the commanding officer dispatched Pancho Johnson[10] to find Stearns and give him a letter. Stearns answered that being a Mexican citizen he could not help the commodore, but he would hand the letter over to Alexander Bell, who was not a naturalized Mexican.

After reading Sloat's message Bell, risking his life, abandoned his store, his house, his wife, and hurried through the night to San Pedro. Boarding the ship he placed himself at his country's service. On the next day the Mexicans confiscated his merchandise and under the pretense of searching for enemy papers ransacked his house from garret to base for money and valuables. Other Americans, more than 50, followed Bell to the fleet where they organized a company and elected him captain.

Bell's soldiers did good service as riflemen. They covered Mervine's disastrous retreat from the bloody battle on the Dominguez ranch. They garrisoned Los Angeles until driven out by an uprising led by Cerbol Vareles, who forced them back to San Pedro. His company then boarded Sloat's fleet and sailed down to San

Diego. Here they joined General Kearny, whose troops had crossed the plains, and with them fought the battle of San Pasqual. Returning to San Diego Captain Bell's company joined with Commodore Stockton's men and marched northward on Los Angeles. The united force met the enemy at the San Gabriel river near Ranchito where a battle was fought. Bell's riflemen waded through the water and held the crossing while the artillery was getting over. On the following day another engagement took place at Evergreen cemetery, called the battle of La Mesa, and the little army camped for the night at Lugo's ranch. Then on the next day, the eighth of January 1847, with band playing and flags flying the Americans marched into town by way of Alameda street and took final possession of Los Angeles. The patriot's dream of his country's coming to him was now realized.

When on the fourteenth day of the same month Colonel John Charles Frémont and his men rode in from Cahuenga valley where the articles of capitulation were signed, Bell contributed the use of his home as headquarters for the new governor of California, who lodged his troops on the first floor and in the area back of the patio. To celebrate his self-appointment to office, Frémont gave an inaugural ball in the upper story of Bell's place. It was too public an affair to suit the aristocratic Spanish families, yet they accepted the courtesy in the spirit with which it was offered and danced the hours away with the bluecoated *gringos*. Here Frémont remained until the following June when he went east with Kearny.

Alexander Bell neither asked for nor received from his government one cent for his services. He never claimed the 160 acres of land which he was legally entitled to as a soldier. He paid off Frémont's battalion with his own money and gave the first governor $4,000 in cash for the proper maintenance of his dignity. For this he neither requested nor received reimbursement.

The soil of California being no longer foreign he was ready to buy land in his own name. He purchased Rancho Providencia, occupying in part the present site of Burbank. For his expanding business he needed a warehouse at San Pedro. In the first book of

[31]

records kept by Los Angeles county one may still see the copy of a petition which he sent to the military governor stationed at Monterey in 1849. He informs the chief that "the Port of San Pedro is insufficiently provided with a Warehouse to accommodate the rapidly increasing trade of this section of California of which it is the Entrepôt." Bell explains that "for this cause much inconvenience and serious losses result to shippers from the exposure of their goods to the water while awaiting transportation." He humbly requests his Excellency for the "grant of a lot 200 yards front by 50 yards deep North of the Landing for the erection thereon of a Warehouse." In this old book we can also read General Riley's reply. With certain restrictions he grants the pioneer merchant's request.

In that year, 1849, so the same records show, Bell was elected to the city council, having received 451 votes.[11]

Aunt Nievas, the wife of Alexander Bell, must have been an admirable lady—to judge from her family and host of friends. She had two sisters who lived in Los Angeles: Anita, wife of Don Santiago Johnson, an Englishman who had come up from Chile, and Gertrudes, who married Don Manuel Requena. By the marriage of a niece, daughter of their brother Rafael, the sisters were related to John G. Downey, a native of Ireland who became a governor of California. Through these connections, as well as by her own name of Guirado, not to mention her husband's worldly goods, Señora de Bell belonged to the élite of Los Angeles.

A devout Catholic she furnished a room at her home as a private chapel for herself and friends. On the wall she hung the picture of a saint dear to Spanish hearts and before it candles burned. To this shrine supplicants came to kneel and beseech the favorite saint for a special blessing. When the prayers were for healing, these Latin folk left at the sacred place an image made of precious metal resembling the ailing member, say, a hand or heart, which remained while prayers continued throughout nine successive days. So good a woman she was and so consecrated to religion that many called her Santa Nievas.[12]

[32]

The Bells had no children, for she was 51 at the time of her marriage. But because of their wealth and good nature they were *padrino* and *madrina* to more youngsters than any other couple in town. Henry Dwight Barrows, an early historian, records that the Bells were godparents of his oldest child.[13]

Boom! boom! belched the cannon on the deck of the *Sea Bird*. Thus Captain Haley on nearing Timm's Point announced the arrival of the little craft to his 20 passengers and those waiting on shore. To do so was necessary because of the heavy fog hanging as usual over San Pedro bay and the low sun ready to drop into distant waters. Now Captain Phineas Banning and his men began to bustle, for they made a business of transporting sea passengers to town. His two lighters, the *Cricket* and the *Los Angeles*, pushed by tugs moved toward the steamer while deck hands cast anchor. Among the arrivals to be ferried across was Don Benito Wilson, a prominent Angeleno, whose name would some day be given to a mountain near future Pasadena.[14] And with him there came a tall, erect stranger answering to the name of Bell, who was now stretching his long legs for the first time on the soil of southern California. Little did these people at the landing know that this young newcomer would record their period and describe their region in prose as lasting perhaps as Wilson's fame.

On shore they found two stages waiting. To each one several Indians quickly hitched up six broncho mules. As soon as everyone was seated the passengers offered bets on which carriage would reach town first. Young Horace like others gambled a fifty-dollar slug that his own would win. When all the stakes were made, Banning called, "Now lads, let her drive!" Then the chief of the Mexican mule-skinners yelled out, "*Suelto, carajo!*"[15] and away plunged the coaches, bumping and bouncing the travelers mercilessly in a race to the City of Angels 20 miles away.

The course ran through the great Dominguez estate. Horace saw in the twilight vast open spaces without a tree or building. But near and far ranged thousands of cattle, which were kept from wandering into the road by outriders stationed along the way.

After two hours of furious driving the bruised passengers neared their goal by a narrow road called San Pedro street. Bell could now descry in the starlight a wide stretch of grape vines bordering the town. At Second street the road turned diagonally left. So the mules raced for two blocks more to the northwest pursued by a growing band of frantic dogs. Entering Main street the coaches sped two blocks farther to the north, then stopped in front of a one-story flat-roofed adobe. (Horace lost his bet.) It stood on the east side of Main street in the second block south of the Plaza. This was the Bella Union, the town's only hotel. From there, so Horace learned, it was only a few steps east to Uncle Aleck's.

In the morning young Bell wanted to see what the town was like. His uncle's place he observed was in the commercial center, most of the stores being on Los Angeles street. In front of Bell's Row the road widened making a larger space for turning wagons. Here were the city scales where farmers weighed their produce—hay and grain, hides, tallow, and wool. Standing on the upper veranda he surveyed the length of the street. To the left appeared a small two-story adobe. Over its door hung the sign *Imprenta*; so he guessed that this was the place where the *Star* was printed. It stirred his fancy, for he had an ambition to write for newspapers. On his right he noticed that the street narrowed to about 40 feet. The scant passage he later learned was *Calle de los Negros*—capital of the underworld—or as the Americans called it in blunt English, Nigger alley.

Horace now turned his eyes straight ahead and looking up saw on a wide-topped hill the walls of Fort Moore where American troops were garrisoned during the late war. It thrilled him to think that the Stars and Stripes had been fluttering there for the last five years. Leaving the gallery he walked north through the notorious alley and found himself on the Plaza. It was a large open irregular square, the cartographic center of the town from which the longer streets emanated. Bare of trees and grass it was cut across by crooked paths. On its south side squatted the gambling dens close to the alley. On the east lived the Lugos and Del Valles; on the north the Olveras, close to a gambling house. Back of its northwest corner clustered the hovels of the poorest Mexicans, their section being called Sonoratown. On the west side of the Plaza the Catholic church lifted its cross overhead.

Passing its door Horace strolled up Main. Many people were moving through the street, horsemen in Mexican costume, natives riding in creaking *carretas* crawling along on solid wooden wheels, and *Americanos* driving covered wagons. Most of the houses were built of adobe and whitewashed. A few stood on Main street south of Third and some west of Main on Spring. But the better homes lay closer to the public square. How small he observed was the settled area!

Evening came and Horace with a new friend set out to see the town's night-life. First they strolled to El Dorado, a saloon and billiard room on Main street, thence to Gibson's gambling house on the Plaza. His place was jammed. Many men drank at the bar, while others played monte at the tables stacked with gold slugs. Horace watched but did not play. He never gambled with professionals, but of course racing was different. From here the boys cut across the Plaza and entered Nigger alley. It was slow work elbowing their way through the passage and entering the gambling dens where noisy crowds shoved in and out. At each place the pair saw more gold slugs laid hopefully on the tables to be left behind for the house. Unbroken confusion almost drowned out the savage music of Indian bands. Fiendish howlings made the night hideous. Every half-hour or so the uproar grew louder when someone was knifed or shot. Only a few yards away slept Mr. and Mrs. Bell undisturbed no doubt by all this bedlam, thanks to thick walls which made adobe houses practically soundproof. Then too they must have closed their doors and grated front windows, ventilating their bedroom from the patio.

One Sunday afternoon Horace standing on his uncle's gallery witnessed a bloody fight, an ordinary occurrence in Los Angeles. Ricardo Urives, a local desperado, was attacked by enemies in Nigger alley. Though shot, stabbed, and stoned, he fought his

[35]

way, revolver in hand, bowie knife in the other, to his horse hitched in front of the Bell place. Bareheaded and bleeding he mounted, while his enemies returned to succor his victims. What was young Bell's surprise when he saw Ricardo ride back to the alley! He had fired the last shot from his Colt's revolver, but using it as a club he drove away his foes like sheep. Ricardo then rode past the Plaza to Sonoratown where he had his wounds dressed. Though he had been shot three times and stabbed, he spent an hour riding up and down Main street in front of the Bella Union, defying arrest. No one making an attempt, he loped out of town to his sister's rancho.

In such an environment was Bell to spend his middle twenties.

Shortly after his arrival Horace attended a ball given by Don José Antonio Carrillo, whose house graced the south side of the Plaza. It was a grand affair, for Carrillo was rich and his family ranked at the top of Californian society. The genial don had been both a congressman to Mexico and at home a military leader. The ball opened the social season of the winter of '52. All the patrician families from San Diego to Monterey were represented. The music Horace thought was exquisite, being furnished by a skillful performer playing an immense harp. He heard no primitive Indian music and saw no crushing of hollow egg shells over the heads of favorite señoritas. Instead the young Yankee was impressed by everyone's serene formality. All the natives dressed as Spaniards, gorgeously, expensively. He marveled at the beautiful dancing of both the gentlemen and ladies. Until two o'clock in the morning the party continued with unbroken dignity.

In the following February Abel Stearns, an American merchant who had married a native Californian, celebrated the birthday of the father of his disowned country. His ball was meant to be as genteel as that of the Carrillos, but it turned out otherwise. For the Stearnses committed the *faux pas* of inviting a couple of gamblers and ignoring others of their profession. This angered the rest of the American gamesters, who felt that for patriotic occasions one American was as good as another. So they decided to break up the party. More than a hundred of them in the darkness brought out an old rusty cannon and pointed it at the Stearnses' front door. They also found a large beam to use as a battering ram. At midnight when the dance was at its climax they shot off the cannon, which being poorly trained missed its aim. But with the battering ram the gamblers broke through the entrance. A gentleman dancing past the door when it fell stepped to the opening and fired off his gun at the first assailant trying to enter. More shots were fired and several gamblers dropped. Strangely enough only one guest was perforated.

Bell also went to see the fandangos. Unlike the *bailes*, such as the Carrillos gave, these lower-class dancing parties were rowdy and open to all who wished to attend. At such democratic entertainments it was wise to have your revolver ready for quick firing. Then too you must wear a red vicuña hat with a broad brim and sugar-loaf crown, a gold cord being wound twice around it with heavy tassels. Otherwise you would be taken for an *Americano* and be socially ignored.

Horace was a frequent guest at the *casa* (house) of Don Manuel Dominguez, who owned the lordly Rancho San Pedro. From Wilmington bay its broad lands reached about 10 miles out on the road to Los Angeles. The good old don was rich and distinguished. He counted his cattle by tens of thousands. When California was a Mexican province he refused the governorship; when it became an American state he took an important part in the constitutional convention. From the first he liked Bell. Then acquaintance warmed into friendship. Besides riches and influence Don Manuel was blessed with six good-looking daughters. But Horace favored Maria Dolores. No wonder! for her soft brown eyes and black lashes would catch any young fellow's attention. She was eight years younger than he and she enjoyed his dancing.

One day Uncle Aleck approached his nephew, saying, "See here, Horace, you are now past 22. It's time for you to find a wife and settle down. Why don't you court Maria Dolores? She's a nice girl and seems to like you and some day she will have her share of the Dominguez fortune. You get busy with Maria and I'll say a word for you to Manuel. That ought to help along the match."

Horace looked interested, while his uncle concluded: "I'll tell you what we will do, my boy. Your aunt Nievas and I want to give you a present for your birthday. You can have a fine horse, and besides, a bridle and saddle of carved leather both silver-mounted, the best riding gear that $5,000 can buy. But if you will marry into a good California family and settle down, you can have the San Pasqual Rancho. It has 20,000 acres, but I can buy it cheap from Don Garfias. Which shall it be?" Alexander summarized, smiling, "a horse or a sweet señorita?"

Horace debated inwardly and then replied, "Oh, I'll take the horse, uncle."[16]

So equipped like a gay *caballero* Bell rode forth to explore the southern country. He attended a big rodeo on the San Joaquin Ranch, 40 miles east of Los Angeles. Arriving late in the afternoon he was surprised by the large number present. A score of *rancheros* or their agents had come from as far off as San Fernando and San Diego. As ranchos were unfenced, cattle wandered great distances from their owners. The men were there to separate, brand, and drive back to their proper places the cattle which had strayed to this ranch. When Bell unsaddled he saw groups of *vaqueros* (cowboys) seated on the ground beside a blanket playing monte. Inside the house Don José Sepulveda received the visitors. Fully a hundred men sat down to eat at his tables.

Before daylight the camp was astir and nearly everyone went to the field for work. By nine o'clock 30,000 head of horned cattle were brought into one herd and surrounded by *vaqueros* swinging their riatas. After the cattle were separated according to their owners, the calves were marked in the ear and branded. The round-up being over, the great herd was broken into many small groups and driven homeward.

About this time Bell visited Los Cuerbos, the country place of Don Antonio Maria Lugo, located on the present site of Compton. He admired the old man's generosity and uprightness. Horace also won the friendship of Isaac Williams, who owned the great Rancho del Chino near the present city of Riverside, and spent many weeks with him as his guest. From here he roamed as far east as San Bernardino, where he acquired an admiration for the Mormons.

Early in '53 Joaquin Murietta, a Mexican desperado formerly of Los Angeles, began robbing and killing in Calaveras county. His success drew to him thieves and cutthroats all the way from San Diego to Stockton. Soon the whole southern country was in arms, for the bandits seemed to be everywhere. In June two companies of volunteer rangers formed, one in Calaveras, the other in Los Angeles, the latter being headed by Alexander Hope. About a hundred men joined in the southern town, including Bell. They received no pay for risking their lives, but the legislature voted a small sum for forage and equipment. Their barracks stood on Requena street (now called Market) where it met Los Angeles street three blocks south of the Plaza.

Horace for a time was stationed at San Gabriel Mission as a solitary guard. But his duties did not interfere with social life, for he appeared at all the fandangos, wearing the dress uniform of a Ranger. This included a blue jacket with gold embroidery, a red sash, sky-blue pants with gold fringes down the legs, and a red vicuña hat of broad brim and sugar-loaf crown, wrapped twice around with gold cord bearing heavy tassels.

When Isaac Williams sent word that some of Murietta's men were camping in Temescal valley, Captain Hope laid plans to bag them. He and his rangers set out late in the afternoon so that during the latter part of their course darkness would hide them from view. At 10 they reached Fort Jurupa, near the future site of the city of Riverside, Bell riding in with his comrades. At midnight they moved on the robbers, whose rendezvous lay just above the hot springs. Entering the valley the mounted police charged up the road and came in sight of the camp fires. The bandits had fled, but their horses' hoofs were heard clattering through Coldwater canyon. In the darkness it was impossible to chase them over mountains and through gorges. But in the morning they took up the trail. It led them south all day. Late at night they reached San Juan Capistrano and slept in the courtyard of the dilapidated mission. In the morning knowing that further pursuit was useless the disconsolate rangers saddled their horses and headed homeward.

September came. Small bands of Joaquin's men drifted south toward Los Angeles marking their way with blood and pillage. A party of seven including one woman had murdered some people near San Luis Obispo. News came to Captain Hope that this detachment was camping behind a willow hedge in the rear of Billy Rowland's vineyard, south of town on Alameda street above First.

Hope divided his company into three parts. One he sent south up San Pedro street to block the bandits in case they fled in that direction. Another he dispatched to Boyle Heights across the river to prevent an eastward retreat. The third including the captain and Bell left the barracks and moved quietly up Alameda past Rowland's house, where they heard the clatter of horsemen breaking through an adjacent cornfield. A long bugle blast warned those in waiting to look out for the gangsters. Hope's group now separated and each picked a man. By sunset all were taken, including the queen of the pack, a little brunette, who escaped for a time, by using her gun, until she was caught by the rangers at Boyle Heights. Many citizens in the morning insisted on lynching the prisoners, but the district attorney convinced them that San Luis Obispo deserved this pleasure.

In the same year, Murietta was killed in Monterey county with his accomplice, Three-Fingered Jack. As their bodies were too heavy to carry over the mountains, Joaquin's head and Jack's hand were cut off and placed in a bag. These were sufficient evidence for claiming the reward of a thousand dollars. Times now threatened to be dull for men of action.

In the Los Angeles *Star*, the town's single newspaper, appears the only account of an early unsavory episode in Bell's life. The young adventurer (if the reporter's story is correct) had repeatedly threatened to whip three men of Los Angeles. Riding into town on New Year's day of 1854 Horace met one of them, Mr. H. Z. Wheeler, in front of the Bella Union. He announced to Wheeler, "One of us must die!" and dismounting advanced to strike him. (There is no mention of his having a weapon.) But Wheeler was too quick. He shot the twenty-three-year-old man and then flogged him.

The justice of the peace told the editor that if Bell had died from Wheeler's gun, he would have cleared him on the ground of justifiable homicide. And then the writer concluded, "It would have been better to have thrown oneself upon the protection of the law, which is much pleasanter and ought to be more powerful than knives and pistols."

Bell never told of his defeats—but who does?[17]

After two years Bell had seen all that Los Angeles county offered for interest. Restless for new sights he made a solitary journey northward through the San Fernando pass to the Tehachapi mountains. He was the first white man ever to visit that country, or rather he thought he was. He found no people closer than San Fernando a hundred miles south. The valley and pass delighted him with their beauty. Over wide grassy plains ranged deer and antelopes. Forests of pine and oak, springs and meadows, lay before him like a romantic painting. But terrific winds howled through the pass causing the trees at Tehachapi to lean eastward. He found three Indian families living in a sheltered nook by the great gap, overlooking the Mojave desert. His gifts of powder won their good will.

Early in '55 with three companions he explored the Kern river country. Near the water's head they dug for gold. But what they found was of low grade and in small amounts. The trail going over the mountains beyond the San Fernando Mission was a rocky climb and the descent horrifying to wagon drivers. At one point a precipice on the edge dropped hundreds of feet straight down. To cross over this pass was an experience pioneers never forgot. Inspired by the hope of trading with the north the merchants of Los Angeles raised a large sum and improved the way. But still it was difficult. In February of this year Bell and a ranger friend each drove a ten-mule team over the San Fernando road. This was the first wagon train ever to leave Los Angeles for the north.[18]

It was late in 1855 when Horace bade *adiós* to southern California. December found him back in San Francisco.[19]

CHAPTER II

Soldier of Fortune

What strange strong bearded man were these
He led toward the tropic seas!
Men mighty-thew'd as Samson was,
That had been kings in any cause,
Who dared the West when giants were,
Who erred, yet bravely dared to err;
With blendings of the worst and best
Of faults and virtues that have blest
Or cursed or thrilled the human breast.

JOAQUIN MILLER,[1] *With Walker in Nicaragua*

I N October 1855 James King of Wm.—so he signed his name
—had founded the San Francisco *Bulletin*.[2] This was a crusading journal designed to fight corruption in city government. Its fearless editor exposed dishonest politicians,
assailed gamblers, and named every person or practice harmful to
civic virtue. As a consequence it was not long before King was
assassinated. Soon after the paper began, Horace Bell joined its
staff. Though he served for only a few months, this experience
gave him a vision and training which later affected his life.

Meanwhile trouble was brewing elsewhere—in the far-off country of Nicaragua. Migrations to California had brought a lucrative business to Cornelius Vanderbilt's transit company which
conveyed easterners across Nicaragua to the Pacific coast. For
the privilege of operating, the corporation paid to the Nicaraguan
government a large revenue. There were two political parties in
that country: the Legitimists, who were the aristocrats and in
power, easily recognized as those wearing shoes, and the barefooted Democrats. A few years before, Castellón had led the un-
shod in a revolt against the government, their main motive being
to possess the income. The revolution was almost put down when
Byron Cole, an adventurous New Englander living in Nicaragua,

suggested to the Democratic leader that he enlist Americans in his cause and told him of William Walker lately returned to San Francisco from an unsuccessful filibustering expedition in Lower California. Castellón jumped at the chance.

Soon 55 armed men came with Walker and turned the scale for the Democrats, who seized the government. Hailed now as liberator Walker became commander in chief of the Nicaraguan army and a new president was named—Patricio Rivas. Americans kept on coming, some from New York and New Orleans, but mostly from California. With the approval of President Franklin Pierce the United States recognized the changed regime. Alarmed by the new control over Nicaragua and the influx of foreigners the neighboring country of Costa Rica declared war on the Walker-Rivas government.

When the Democrats came into power Vanderbilt's company owed the government $40,000. Now it refused to pay, causing Walker to make the fatal blunder of his career. He confiscated the company's steamers on the San Juan river and Lake Nicaragua, as well as all other property in the country.

To meet the emergency of war with Costa Rica, President Rivas called for more Americans to come down and fight for Nicaragua. During the rule of the second Vigilance Committee in San Francisco, Horace Bell became the recruiting officer for the Nicaraguan army.

In and Out of Granada

In March 1856, with 40 other daredevils, he sailed through the Golden Gate on his way down to Nicaragua. It is hardly fair to call him a filibuster, since he went on the invitation of a recognized government. Being young he gave little thought to the war's implications. His sole motive was adventure. Unable to land on the western shore because of the Costa Ricans, the company debarked at Panama. After a week's delay they crossed the Isthmus by rail. On the Atlantic side they coasted by schooner up to the town of San Juan del Norte. Here they boarded a steamer, and passing up San Juan river entered Lake Nicaragua, gliding over its broad waters to their journey's end, Granada. Trumpets brayed and drums clattered to greet the Californians. Escorted first to the grand plaza they were later marched into their quarters.

On the morrow Bell appeared at the national palace to meet General William Walker. To his great surprise Horace learned that his commander was now himself the president of Nicaragua. For recently when a plot was hatched against the general and he had put it down by shooting the chief conspirator, President Rivas had fled fearful of his life and Walker had seized the highest office.

There were many sentries on duty and many officers lounging in the place and also a guard of honor composed of 100 Cubans, all gentleman refugees from New York or New Orleans. They had come to Nicaragua with General De Goicouria, a Cuban patriot, now commissioned by Walker. He hoped to form a nucleus of soldiers for waging a future revolution in Cuba. The honor guard, observed Bell, was less useful than ornamental. They wore Panama hats with red ribbons and their officers were liberally adorned with gold lace. Well supplied with native cigars the Cubans whiled away the hours in smoking and showing off their finery. At last Walker appeared dressed in a rich uniform having two golden suns on the shoulder straps, the insignia of general in chief. Receiving the young captain with formality he assigned him to De Goicouria's command. Bell long honored the Cuban as one of the few men of character in Walker's regime.

By this time the signal for dress parade sounded and Horace took leave of his Adventurous Excellency to walk to the plaza and see the review. He was not impressed by the soldiers as they fell into line. Most of them looked sick. Many officers seemed unsteady on their legs both in marching and standing at "parade rest." On dismissal there was a rush of officers (who had been an hour without a drink) to the liquor dispensary. Meanwhile the men were marched to their quarters to await the coming ration of whisky. Bell inferred that in prosecuting the war liquor was second in importance only to gunpowder—that if "blue ruin" were cut off, the army's courage would vanish.

Granada was the most forlorn place he had ever seen. The upper class of citizens had departed. About 25 hundred filibusters were quartered there and also 800 native soldiers. The daily mortality was fearful. Though recruits kept coming the army did not increase. It was only a matter of time until the whole establishment would disappear. Surrounded by a dense forest lay Granada, a half-mile from the great lake, and every breath one drew in that wretched country reeked with miasmic germs. Everybody in the town it seemed had but two objects: one to leave, the other to get drunk. A soldier's rations even in time of plenty were low-grade beef, green plantains, chocolate, rice, and a half-pint of whisky. Bread and flour were unknown. The army subsisted by foraging on the small farms near the town and on the islands.

When Bell arrived Walker controlled the greater part of Nicaragua. He had small garrisons along the transit route from coast to coast and as far north as Managua. His enemies, composed of natives who had rebelled against his dictatorial rule, and their Central American allies, were centered at Leon on the northwest coast. They were now collecting a force in the Chontales country to the north of Lake Nicaragua. A recent expedition into this section had resulted in Walker's defeat. So Captain Bell was ordered to march his men to Tipitapa, the river joining the two lakes of Nicaragua and Managua, lying close to the enemy's line. Judging from what men had done in the mining country he thought his company could easily complete the journey before sunset. But he soon discovered that climate and good beef had much to do with marching. Night fell and a deluge of rain. They were still trudging on the road through a tropical forest. His men waded and floundered until midnight when a light gleamed in the black and a shrill voice cried, "Who comes there?"

"Friends!" answered Bell, "reinforcements from Granada."

Then the first voice asked, "Did you bring any whisky?"

"Yes, lots of it."

"Then the countersign's correct! Friends, advance!"

They did, the rain still falling in torrents.

Next morning Bell led his men in the sunshine to a plaza not far from the river, thence to their quarters, where he set them to work cleaning and drying their guns and clothing. The village of Tipitapa was a squalid place in a somber forest, the people mostly Negroes. But for the magnificent church on the central square a stranger might believe himself to be in an African jungle. Bell noticed the absence of men and when he inquired the cause the women would roll the whites of their eyes, shrug their shoulders, and say nothing. So he assumed that they were a part of the hostile garrison at San Jacinto.

After visiting the wounded in the church he walked to the bridge a quarter-mile distant to inspect the picket. What a beautiful landscape! he thought. Here the connecting river was about 200 yards wide. Upstream it looked perfectly straight and far off in the distance he could see Lake Managua, its silver surface shimmering beneath verdant hills. While Bell was gazing at the panorama Charley McIntosh, one of Frémont's old guides, stepped out on the bridge with the warning: "Cap', don't stay here too long. Them saucy greasers on the other side come down two or three times a day and exchange shots with us." No sooner was this said than a party of enemy cavalry galloped out of the timber and fired at the pair. The picket responded with a few bullets. But shooting at that distance was ineffective.

Bell remained in command of Tipitapa about a week, sending in a few wounded, galloping down to the bridge at the sound of firing, and foraging for his men. The situation was dangerous, for his force was small and the only defense they could make would be from the church, which like most Nicaraguan sanctuaries, had loopholes in the walls to shoot through. So he felt greatly relieved when orders came to mount the wounded on horses and fall back to Masaya, where Walker was now located.

On leaving, the problem arose as to what to do with the church's precious metal. When Bell assumed command of the place the colonel whom he relieved turned over to him all the sacred gold and silver plate stored in a big box. There were 250 pounds of it —highly valuable! One surgeon stationed in the church wanted to take it along, the other doctor wished to bury it for future recovery. But Bell being in command overruled them both. In the morn-

[47]

ing when the wounded were ready to be moved and he had formed a rear guard in front of the church while waiting for the picket to come in from the bridge, Horace took one of the medical officers and went to the altar. After raising some of the loose planks of the floor, they shoved the box of plate under, then quickly left. Though he might be a filibuster now that his chief had turned usurper, this young man of Presbyterian upbringing would not loot. For this act he felt a great sense of inward peace.

As soon as they reached Masaya everyone, including the garrison, was put to work fortifying the plaza against the approaching enemy. When the last barricade was built three new companies arrived from New York making the army feel they could hold Masaya against any force.

On the same day, Bell's company was sent three miles out on the Managua road to a place called Nindiri to take a position and hold the enemy when they came. The next morning Bell paid his respects to the governor of Nindiri, which was a large well-built Indian town without a Spaniard or *mestizo* (half-breed) in it. The chief ruled like an absolute king, as his ancestors had done for centuries. The American captain dined with him and thought he had never eaten from a better table nor from a whiter cloth. He found the Indian to be an intelligent, dignified gentleman—a direct descendant of King Nicarao, who controlled the land when the Spaniards discovered it and gave his name to the lake on which he dwelt. Moreover the whole country got its name from him, the word Nicaragua being a Spanish corruption of Nicarao (pronounced *Nic-ar-rów-o*).

The enemy were not long in attacking. They forced Bell's men into the plaza of Nindiri, but at dark ceased firing and camped on the edge of the town. Orders came that night to retreat. On reaching Masaya Bell's company was astonished to find the rest of the army ready to leave. Walker had ordered them to abandon their fortifications and return to Granada.

All night long they floundered through mud over the eighteen-mile road leading back. In the morning at 10 they marched into Granada feeling as though they had been sold out. Such seemed to be Walker's policy: always on the approach of the enemy to abandon his position, to await the perfection of his foe's defenses, then to sacrifice his men in vain efforts to drive them out.

Within a week after the retreat from Masaya Walker started back to retake his own fortifications. His organization of about 2,500 men consisted of two battalions of rifles, two of infantry, one of cavalry, a battery of twelve-pounder howitzers, a battery of twelve-pounder mortars—also a company of sappers and miners, and the quartermaster and commissary departments. It was a splendid little army, well equipped, every man eager for the fray.

With drums beating and flags flying they marched out of Granada loudly cheered by the invalid garrison left behind. Driving the hostile pickets back they bivouacked in front of the enemy's barricades in Masaya. At daybreak the army formed and stood ready to fight. A moment later the buglers and drummers sounded the charge. Forward rushed the filibusters, capturing the enemy's loopholes, scrambling and boosting each other over obstructions, making a devil's din. In two minutes Walker's men held all the barricades, and the smaller plaza swarmed with combatants, each side thrusting the bayonet with deadly effect. Soon this plaza was carried by storm as well as the enemy's breakfast, still hot.

Refreshed by the meal the invaders advanced toward the main plaza, their course swept by both cannon and rifle fire. Though flanked by the foe they worked their way from garden to garden, from house to house, into and out of kitchens, dining rooms, bedrooms, parlors. The enemy met them in almost every building, contesting every foot of ground, giving blow for blow. Night found Walker's army within a few yards of the big plaza ready to make a rush at daylight to retake their old fortifications. Feeling certain of victory on the morrow they set out guards and slept until 11 when suddenly the camp was aroused and told of a terrible mishap. During the day the Central Americans had flanked them and captured Granada, the filibuster capital! The news was stunning!

Bell now received orders to withdraw his company, for the whole army would at once march back to Granada. When he halted his command for a short period, his men sank down and went to sleep, while their captain stretched out on the stone steps of the church to think. Soon Captain Watkins approached him and asked what he thought of the situation. Bell answered, "We'll have to go down and whip the enemy out of Granada." To this Watkins retorted:

"Why didn't we whip them at Masaya today? We never have whipped them and we never will with such a damn fool for general. Walker I tell you is a military fraud.

"And look here, my friend, do you know that we are in the wrong? We are trying to rob these people of their property and country. They are fighting for all they hold dear—and right always prevails over wrong.

"Let me tell you something, Captain. Tomorrow we fight for our lives and the chances are 10 to one not a man of us will ever get out of this country. But right here under the shadow of this old church, if God spares me and permits me to get out of this infernal scrape, I solemnly swear never to fire a gun or draw a sword unless it be in defense of the Star-Spangled Banner."

A killing forced march now began through the mud and rain. Bell managed to get all his wounded and worn-out men mounted, sometimes three on a horse, a fourth holding on to the tail to be dragged through the mire. The strong carried the muskets for the weak. The night was dark as only a night can be in a tropical forest. There was only one road and that was bad and narrow. Behind, a fortified city cut them off. The only way of escape led them through Granada now held by the enemy. Ammunition was low. Every bit of food had vanished. The whole army was hungry and exhausted after two days of marching and fighting, having had only two short intervals for sleep. What a terrible night it was!

But at sunrise they began to hear the clatter of musketry, rousing the hope that their invalid comrades were yet holding out. "Close up, close up!" came the sharp command. The poor fellows revived as though 40 demijohns of whisky had been passed along the line. Wounded men jumped off their horses, seized their guns, and took their places in the ranks. The music began. The line

[50]

closed. "Forward! Quick time! March!" shouted the officers. A great cheer went up joined in by the weakest. And so the trapped army pushed hopefully on to Granada.

The roar of cannon and the rattle of muskets in the city now became fearful. Every man's face wore the question, "Will we get there in time to save our comrades?" And to many a man came the distressing thought, "What may happen to my wife and children?" For not a few Americans had brought their families down from the States.

The sun was now two hours high as the haggard army neared the Jalteva church, a half-mile from the plaza. Suddenly the line stopped at the sound of terrific firing ahead. Within 200 yards of the building the filibusters saw on their left an immense chasm, caused by an earthquake, coming up to the edge of the road. On their right side appeared a jungle. Within it crouched the enemy behind a battery of three guns belching grape and canister, their infantry support concealed farther inward.

Bell's company was ordered to the front. The column broke into platoons in time for the first one to deliver a volley as the hostile battery wheeled into position for another round. Bell yelled, "Charge 'em!" and both platoons rushed upon the artillerymen. The battery blazed away again and Bell felt his heels fly up and his head and shoulders strike the ground. When he regained an upright position the first thing he saw was Colonel John Markham—brave fellow—standing on a gun carriage waving his bloody saber and hurrahing while the foot soldiers bayoneted the artillerists, who stood by their guns until the last man was killed. The enemy infantry now retreated a short space within the jungle.

Thus with a fearful loss of life Walker's soldiers captured the battery and thought that the way was now open to their beleaguered comrades in Granada. But they soon learned of more warm work to be done. Another battery awaited them at the Jalteva church. Another charge, another slaughter, and Walker gained this second position. During a temporary halt Bell found that he had been struck on the ankle with a canister shot at the ambush, but his blood being at boiling heat he scarcely felt it.

[51]

No time could be lost. Leaving a guard at the church to help the surgeons in caring for the wounded and to hold the place, the little army reformed its depleted ranks and with flying flags, beating drums, and buoyant hearts it began to advance. Coming within three blocks of the plaza the attacking force split into three columns, pressing down the three streets leading to the plaza. Within this space of less than 20 acres the two foes fought in deadly conflict—neither one giving quarter. At every barricade you could hear the command of the officers: "Give them the bayonet, boys! Save your cartridges!"

"Here goes for the rifles!" came the shout as some party made a rush.

"*Vive la Louisiane!*" the Creoles would yell as a New Orleans company hailed a California command.

Less than one block from the plaza on the street where Horace Bell was fighting there remained but one uncaptured barricade. Colonel Jack Allen with his riflemen proposed to keep the enemy's heads down. He called to Bell, "You wade in with your bayonets!" Bell and his men waded in. But in so doing he was wounded again. Consequently when the plaza was finally taken he made his entry recumbent on a stretcher.

So closed the campaign after 60 hours of continuous marching and fighting in a tropical climate with only a few hours of sleep, nearly half the time the rain falling. It was a grand exhibition of pluck and endurance, but it cost the lives of more than half of the brave little army, and many who escaped the bullets sickened within a few days and died of fever.

Bell was carried to a church in Granada where his wounds were examined and dressed. Nolan, his servant, made him as comfortable as possible. The building was crowded with the dead, the dying, and wounded. All the time more were brought in. Good old Father Vijil, the priest, did noble service. About dark he passed through the church with a tureen of soup and vessels of tea. When Bell addressed him in Spanish he sat down on the rawhide bedstead and while pouring out the beverage informed the wounded captain of the siege. The holy father had stood musket in hand

and defended his church against the natives through 24 hours of assault, for he was a friend of the filibusters. His example, it was said, helped to save the church from capture.

In another half-hour Bell was in dreamland from which he awoke at midnight with a violent chill. Although Father Vijil had thrown a heavy green priest's gown over him, he wanted more covering and called Nolan, but he was unable to wake him. The church lamps threw a dismal light over the scene. The great room was quiet but for the weak groans of the dying and the heavy breathing of sleepers. Bell could not reach his servant with the saber that hung at the head of the bed. Seeing a man sitting with his back against a pillar of the church quietly smoking a cigar, he politely requested him to step over and wake Nolan.

The man looked up at Bell with contempt, saying, "Step! did you say? Damnation! don't you see I've got both my legs shot off!"

Horace could find no words for reply. Although the convulsive chill racked and tore his wounds, he kept silent, and when fever came he dropped off into a stupor. When he woke in the morning the sun was shining through the window. Nolan still slept and the man who sat beside the pillar was dead.

Soon the good padre came. He felt of Bell's feverish brow, gave him tea and kind words. Looking around mournfully he sighed, *"Los de más son muertos, hijo!"* [Most of them are dead, son!] Few of the injured in that terrific butchery recovered. More died from exhaustion than from wounds.

So on the thirteenth day of October in 1856 when Granada was retaken, the first year of Walker's rule ended.

Retreat to Rivas

Bell was soon moved from the church hospital to a fine house on the plaza. One day a couple of paroled officers were brought to his quarters and introduced by a Cuban. While the group was pleasantly chatting about the war and smoking some first-class Havanas, a staff member of Walker's came in and showed the visitors an order for their execution. They received the news coolly, even good-naturedly, and having 15 minutes in which to prepare for death, they presented the officer bearing the order a cigar, sent over to the church for a priest, shook hands with Bell and his wounded roommate, and left. In a few minutes a volley of musketry sounded and it was all over with the brave fellows. Before dying they acknowledged the justice of their sentence, since they had shot two of Walker's officers in Masaya. To Bell the incident was shocking, but such things he learned were a mild feature of Central American warfare.

Father Francisco de Paula Vijil came daily to see Bell in his new quarters. One morning the two were talking over the probable fate of the filibusters. "I have told General Walker," the good priest remarked, "that it is certain destruction to stay here. I want him to go to Rivas. It's a healthy place and close to the transit line. By staying there and acting on the defensive, in two years he can wear out all Central America. But," he shook his head sadly, "Walker is *muy cabezudo* [very obstinate]. He is determined to drive the enemy out of Masaya—absolutely impossible with his small army."

Delicately Bell inquired of the priest why he favored the foreigners, seeing that they had been deserted by both parties of Nicaraguans. "Well," explained Father Vijil, "for this reason: I am a native here and have seen all the disgraceful butcheries that have gone on for 20 years. I have wept and prayed over the sins of my countrymen in their struggle for power. Our people have forgotten their country and their God. It is all self. For 20 years our ears have been greeted with *Viva Carrera, Viva Morazán, Viva Chamorro, Viva Castellón*, and now *Viva Walker*, but never *Viva la patria*. This country must have relief. Revolution has become chronic and I hope Walker and his Americans will bring us peace. *Quién sabe?*" [Who knows?]

Soon after, Bell witnessed an interesting ceremony—that of discarding the volcanic flag of Nicaragua and adopting a plain blue one with a single star in the center. The old flag was blue, white, and blue, with a volcano in the center of each stripe—

[54]

certainly emblematic, he thought, of the combustible nature of the country. This was pulled down without a word and the new one run up, while artillery thundered, bands played, drums rolled, and filibusters hurrahed.

The day after the ceremony Walker marched under the new flag with 15 hundred men to try again to capture Masaya. To Bell's great joy his company remained to garrison Granada. Though convalescing he did not want to be away from his men. The generalissimo utterly failed to dislodge the enemy and on the fifth day out returned with the most horribly used-up body of men Bell had yet seen.

On the morrow began the evacuation of Granada. The first maneuver was to send Bell's battalion southward to Virgin bay on Lake Nicaragua; then all the sick and wounded were put on board the steamers and moved to the island of Ometepe in the great lake. Walker would soon follow leaving Henningsen, one of his generals, behind with orders to sack and burn Granada, and afterwards join him at the bay.

Bell was then hardly able to hobble on crutches, but he lost no time in having his baggage packed up, and taking his cook and orderly prepared to go with the last shipment of invalids to the island. On the boat he met a superior officer of his battalion, Leonides McIntosh, sickened by fever. "Bell," confided the colonel to his captain, "don't you wish you was at home, sitting alongside your gal?"

"No, I don't," replied Horace. "I am well satisfied to stay here and stick it out."

"Then you have less sense than I thought you had," remarked McIntosh, "if you are content to fall a victim of such mismanagement as we have seen for the last month. Why, my dear sir, with the force we had at Masaya behind our fortifications, we could have whipped all Central America. But what did we do? We marched out like cowards—never fired a shot. I'm sick of it all. I wish I was out of it."

"But there's no way to get out but by fighting," ventured Horace.

[55]

"Then," concluded the colonel, "we are sure in for it. Our commander mistook his calling."

When the steamer reached the island Bell decided it would be more independent to share the dangers of his comrades than to stay in a miserable hospital, and so without consulting anyone he remained aboard the steamer and returned to Virgin bay where he was received with joy by his company—but not as they were when he first marched out of Granada leading a column of 47 as brave fellows as ever fired a gun. Of the original company there were now only a sick lieutenant and five miserable wretches that on marching staggered under the weight of their muskets. The whole battalion to which Bell's group belonged—the only force Walker now had outside of Granada—mustered for duty but 35 men. The Costa Ricans situated at Rivas, 18 miles southward, numbered a thousand.

Soon the unit of 35 headed by Walker himself plus the convalescents set out for Rivas to attend to the Costa Ricans. The general sent Bell a good horse which so pleased him that he pitched his crutches into the lake, mounted with assistance, and volunteered to command the advance guard of 10 other convalescents. Walker riding up told Bell that he wished to take over the village of San Jorge, three miles from Rivas, on the lake shore. If they failed to capture the plaza they would take possession of some houses near the lake and be ready to receive the remaining army when it came down from Granada.

The little detachment reached the edge of San Jorge by midafternoon and passed noiselessly to a spot 100 yards from the plaza. Then Bell's advance guard raised a shout and dashed for the public square. As the village market had just opened, the plaza was crowded with women. The small force of the enemy being distracted by their interest in the market ran out on the other side leaving their horses and arms behind, permitting a bloodless capture. The invaders next set their pickets and went into quarters.

Captain Bell sought out the home of the village priest as the most likely place to find plenty of food. Arriving at the house he dismounted and started toward the high stone steps. To his amazement he found he could not walk. So he called a couple of his soldiers, who helped him up to the door. Then in the name of the "Lone Star Flag" of Nicaragua he took possession of the place, ordering his men to quarter themselves in the back yard. Good-naturedly the fat padre accepted the intrusion. That evening he sat down at his own table as a guest of the foreign captain, the pair lingering long over a five-gallon demijohn of port wine, old and mellow. The large house was clean and comfortable.

But this earthly paradise was soon abandoned. The Costa Ricans having left Rivas, Walker decided to move into that city, only three miles away, and reorganize his force. Since Bell entered the service in Granada only a few months ago, the number of deaths had been staggering, more than 3,000. The generalissimo filled up the two rifle battalions, and consolidated the two battalions of infantry into one. His army now consisted of 720 rifles, 360 infantrymen, 360 rangers, 100 artillerists, and 100 in the quarter-master's corps. Of this total, however, only 1,000 could report for duty, the rest being in the hospital.

He now appointed Captain Horace Bell as commander of the consolidated infantry of 360 men and advanced him to the rank of major, a title which he never relinquished. Such a promotion over the heads of other officers naturally aroused resentment. But Walker quickly silenced objectors by placing them on half-pay. Flattered by such recognition of his ability Bell's unfavorable opinion of his chief vanished—for a time.

Rivas lay on high rolling country rising like a ridge between the Pacific ocean and Lake Nicaragua and in the center of a culti-vated area 40 miles long and eight miles wide. As this region was now entirely free from the enemy, the foreign army could go anywhere without danger. So Major Bell's infantry took long marches for exercise and pleasure, enjoying the sight of brooks rippling over pebbly bottoms, shady lanes, and broad orange groves decked with golden fruit. This tropical country, thought Bell, must be as beautiful as any place in the world. Then too it seemed as healthful as California, for those who were weak grew strong and the slightly injured reported for duty. But alas, there

[57]

was no liquor, except occasionally when some fortunate officer obtained a limited supply. Then among his friends there followed jubilation.

Vanderbilt's Revenge

While Walker and his men were relaxing in Rivas during January of 1857 disaster fell. Two years before when Cornelius Vanderbilt heard that Walker had seized his steamers and properties on the transit route and had revoked his franchise, his rage knew no bounds. According to Bell the baffled millionaire of New York raved and roared like a captive sea monster. He swore that he would spend his last dollar to be avenged on the audacious fellows who presumed to cross his path. So he sent agents to all the Central American governments, loaned them money, gave them arms, and outfitted an expedition to recapture his company's steamers on the San Juan river and Lake Nicaragua.

This project was led by a renegade filibuster named Spencer. With only 50 Costa Rican soldiers he succeeded in regaining all of Vanderbilt's steamers and the forts at Serapaqui, Costillo, and San Carlos—the three strongholds on the transit route lately held by Walker. All this Spencer did by surprise and strategy without losing a man, killed or wounded. It was the only brilliant achievement of the whole war. The wresting of the transit line from the filibusters broke the backbone of their army and assured the speedy end of their stay in Nicaragua.

When the news of the captured steamers reached Rivas it seemed like a clap of thunder in a clear sky, so little was it expected. At first the men did not believe it, but when the time came for the semi-monthly crossing of passengers and the Californian ship arrived, landed her recruits, and steamed on down to Panama with her through-passengers, then the painful truth was confirmed. Walker became morose and irascible. He began to levy fines and force loans from the natives. He squeezed all the money he could out of the priests. Those who would not contribute he imprisoned or forced to work on the new fortifications. Father

[58]

Lugo, who refused, followed for months in the wake of a wheel-barrow.

Word now came that the enemy was advancing on Rivas; so the filibusters marched to San Jorge to meet them. The two rifle battalions detoured to attack the two flanks. The infantry was to remain inactive until the rifles had tried their strength; then Bell's men would go in. When the firing on the flanks ceased, the rifle battalions came dragging back, cut to pieces and horribly used up. The enemy now threw themselves upon the Walkerites with terrific violence. Startled, Bell's infantry fell back, while the Costa Ricans made a rush to capture the howitzers. This gave the infantry time to recover. When the foe came pushing forward a second time they were again driven back behind their barricades on the San Jorge plaza. Walker's men were outnumbered two to one, but they whipped their enemy decisively, picking up 130 muskets after the fight. This was called the battle of the Plantain Patch and was regarded by the filibusters as the best fight they had had so far.

By the time the smoke cleared away, the afternoon was well advanced. General Henningsen then took the victorious infantry and marched them close to the plaza. After placing a battery he called for volunteers to storm the public square. Sixty-three men stepped to the front, among them Major Bell. It was now near sundown and all was quiet. They were ready to move. Suddenly the army's mascot, a shaggy old dog named Filibuster, came capering along in front of the detachment, wagging his tail and smiling in the men's faces. The army believed that good fortune would follow the company that carried the dog on its rolls. He had an uncanny way of deserting a company just before disaster came. When he joined the present unit the men felt sure of victory. So they advanced carefully, the dog frisking before them, until they reached a street corner within 40 yards of the plaza.

On passing this point the dog gave a growl, the party raised a yell and rushed up to the barricade. It was 20 feet high and pierced with three tiers of loopholes. Bell saw one man's head exposed and deliberately fired his revolver at it. This was the only enemy seen. The attackers tried to get possession of the lower tier of loopholes,

[59]

but 39 of them were shot down and nearly everyone was wounded. In a minute more not a man of the 63 would have been left alive; accordingly they fell back. They left their dead on the ground and most lamented of all, the dog Filibuster. His death cast a gloom over the army, for a superstitious veneration attached to him. His loss was believed to be ominous of defeat.

So ended the first fight at San Jorge. All night the survivors lay on the ground in front of the enemy to cover the removal of the wounded. At sunrise they marched back to Rivas utterly dispirited. More than 300 filibusters died in this fight. Their failure blasted the men's hope of an offensive plan. It seemed to them that Walker's policy was to have them whipped in detail. Their whole force thrown against one point, many believed, would have taken the town. Seven hundred and twenty men failed to carry the plaza in the morning and 63 were expected to do it in the evening.

Immediately after the defeat at San Jorge General José Maria Cañas commanding the Costa Rican division issued a proclamation to the filibusters asking them what they were fighting for, what was their pay, and what were their expectations. He pledged the faith of Costa Rica and his own sacred honor to give free passage to New York or San Francisco to all *Americanos* who would abandon Walker and present themselves at San Jorge or any place in Costa Rica.

During Cañas' first occupation of the transit route while Walker was fighting at Masaya and Granada, several filibusters fell into his hands, whom he treated with greatest kindness, leaving them free and unmolested. When the Americans recaptured the transit route, shortly before its final seizure by Spencer, these men refused to give the Costa Ricans a bad name and were loud in their praise of General Cañas; whereupon Walker sent them all to the guard house and threatened to have them shot, calling it treason to speak well of the enemy.

Such a proclamation coming from Cañas at the time it did was gravely considered—so much so that in less than three days after its issuance two companies of rangers saddled up and cleared out for Costa Rica. The next day a party of artillerists followed on foot. The latter group was pursued and overtaken near San Juan del Sur on the Costa Rican road and by Walker's orders they were all killed on the spot.

Shortly after these desertions Walker had all his army mustered in a hollow square on the Rivas plaza. In the center he stood and made a speech. He referred to the brilliant record of his soldiers, their many victories, their great and manifest destiny,[3] the perfidy and cowardice of the enemy, the noble profession of arms, the ignobility of labor, and promised them that in a few years they would not only be masters of Central America, but would muster their legions on the grand plaza of the city of the Montezumas. He grew vehement, shouting that the cowardly enemy had insulted them. "We have sent them the olive branch. They returned us the knife. We will throw away the scabbard and the knife let it be!"

A major who lost an arm at Tipitapa threw up his cap in the air and screeched, "The knife let it be!" He was the only one who responded. Not a cheer. No applause. Silently the troops filed off, going to their quarters in disgust.

On the following day the whole army under the top general's command marched back to San Jorge. This time they moved up close to the plaza, established their batteries, and bombarded for six hours, but the enemy fired not a single shot in reply. In the afternoon the filibusters returned to Rivas without any bloodstains on their garments, but they were covered with ticks that had crawled on them while they lay on the beautiful greensward. The foe always waited to be attacked. They knew the advantage of fighting behind adobe walls—something which Walker never learned until it was too late.

A week afterward he marched again to San Jorge to make a night attack and surprise the enemy. His men silently flanked the barricade and at a given signal went to work bayoneting the startled soldiers. The order was not to shoot unless they were fired upon. One officer not having a musket and bayonet used his bowie knife, but becoming excited discharged his revolver, thereby giving an alarm. Then commenced an infernal din of drums, bugles, and tom-toms, the shouts and *carajos* of the enemy officers, and the cheers of the attackers.

The assault was fierce, the defense brave and determined. Walker would have succeeded but for the officer's firing of his gun. This defeat so near a victory did more damage to the morale of the filibuster army now reduced to 700.

Two weeks later another steamer came down from California. With 300 men one of Walker's generals went down to receive and escort the newcomers to Rivas. But the enemy also sent a force from San Jorge. Taking a position in a wood bordering a prairie called the Jacote Ranch, directly on the transit route, they waited for the Walkerites. About noon the head of the filibuster column appeared, reinforced by 100 recruits, making the whole force about 400 men. Equal in numbers the enemy advanced to meet them in the open field. Here occurred a most humiliating thing. The Central Americans whipped Walker's men like dogs, scattered and drove them into the woods. So remarkable was their defeat and such good time did the filibusters make in reaching Rivas that the fight was called the "Jacote Races."

Within an hour, a rider having brought the news, Major Bell's command was ordered forth to rescue the defeated general. On the way out of Rivas Bell called on Mrs. Sanders, wife of the unfortunate officer, to see if she had a message for her husband.

"Oh, laws a massy, yes!" she gasped. "Here's a bottle of whisky. Take it to him quick. I expect he's out of liquor. Oh, dear, how he must need it!"

Before Bell could take hold of the bottle the heroic general came charging up, his horse covered with foam and dust. Without a word to his wife or a look at Bell he grabbed the flask and drained it at one draft—then looking around wildly panted, "Surrounded by 5,000 men! and me the only survivor!"

Bell at once rode off to catch up with his command. Two hours later they returned accompanied by 300 survivors, about 100 being missing. It turned out that 25 were killed. The remaining 75 had taken the road to Costa Rica and claimed the benefit of General Cañas' proclamation.

The filibusters were now put to work preparing defenses. They labored hard, although dispirited, some murmuring that they would be forced to abandon Rivas as they had deserted Masaya—so what was the use of killing themselves in building fortifications?

In the middle of March the California steamer again arrived bringing 150 recruits—all mountaineers, as fine a body of men as ever came to Nicaragua, and commanded by an old United States army officer. After being supplied with arms at San Juan del Sur they were marched into Rivas and given a three-days' drill in the manual of arms and in firing. When this training was completed Walker marched his whole army to San Jorge to try the enemy again, who now outnumbered his men three to one.

The Nicaraguan rebels and their allies did not wait to be stormed but came out and attacked their foe on all sides. Bell's command faced about to protect the rear. After three hours of desperate fighting in the gardens and orchards of the village, the rear attack was driven off and Bell's men got a breathing spell and time to clean their guns. They followed the natives a quarter-mile down the road, who instead of retreating to San Jorge went on toward Rivas.

Bell now surmised that his adversaries would try the same strategy played at Masaya—they would slip behind the filibusters and capture Rivas. He lost no time in reporting his suspicions to Walker, who was still sorely pressed in front. The general dispatched a handful of rangers to reconnoiter. Returning they reported that the road to Rivas was occupied by the enemy. Meanwhile the foreign army picked up its wounded and prepared to retreat. Walker ordered Bell to take the lead and open the way. Bushwhacking and gaining in numbers as they went, the natives led their pursuers on to the suburbs of Rivas.

At the intersection of four roads called Cuatro Esquinas stood a large adobe strongly barricaded. Here the Nicaraguans waited to block the entrance to Rivas. Riding along with his advance guard Bell passed through a deep cut in the road and emerging saw the improvised castle 40 yards ahead. Taking in the situation at a glance he reined his horse back into the gorge just in time to miss

[63]

a volley fired at him. He halted his battalion as it came up panting, covered with dust and blood.

Bell now posted a man as sentinel (whose head barely showed above the bank), dismounted, and reconnoitered. To his right he saw a point where artillery could be run into position to cannonade the house. In a moment General Walker and his staff came trudging along in the dust like private soldiers. Being bushwhacked as they were it was less dangerous to go on foot than on horseback. Angrily Walker inquired the reason for the halt. Bell answered that the *hacienda* [main dwelling] was strongly fortified and manned—that he thought it prudent to wait for the artillery to come up and help in dislodging the enemy.

"There is no enemy here!" stormed Walker, stepping up on the side of the bank. Three soldiers out of curiosity did likewise. Just then the Central Americans fired and hit two. "General, is the enemy there?" asked Bell.

Then Walker, who by this time had completely lost his senses, turned to the commander of the rangers and said, "Colonel Waters, I want you to lead these men to Rivas." But the colonel neither stirred nor spoke. Feeling himself reprimanded Bell inquired of his superior officer, "General, will you be kind enough to follow me?"

At the same instant the Major spurred his horse forward and rode the gauntlet of 200 feet of loopholes in a hurricane of bullets. His beautiful horse was riddled but carried Bell beyond range of fire, then dropped dead. The filibuster general did not follow, neither did the rangers' commander. Only one of the whole advance force did. That was Bell's orderly, a sixteen-year-old Irish boy who gloried in the name of Charles O'Malley. Mounted on a jackass he dashed past unharmed, being protected by the smoke of the volley fired at Bell. "Well," panted the Major to his companion when they reached the plaza of Rivas in safety, "fortune favors fools as well as the brave."

With 10 men they returned to Cuatro Esquinas and found the highway full of dead bodies. The whole force including the artillery had taken to the plantation on the side of the road opposite

[64]

the fortification, intending to flank it. While the sun was setting, the straggling filibusters with Walker at their head emerged from the plantation about a hundred yards from the adobe, having successfully skirted it. Bell's auxiliary squad now fell into the rear of the column, which dragged into Rivas without order, completely broken up. On this day the filibusters lost about one-fourth of all engaged. Their only achievement was to march to San Jorge and succeed in getting back, leaving the road strewn with their dead.

On the morrow when Bell called on the president general he failed to treat the Major with common courtesy. He was angered no doubt by the superior courage of his subordinate officer.

Trapped!

On this day of their return, the twenty-third of March 1857, the siege of Rivas began. General Walker on re-entering the town went to his quarters and although during its investment the battle raged within a block of him he never left his room. He feared being shot by his own men.

Notwithstanding the president's coolness toward Bell for having led where he declined to follow, the great *Pomposo Furioso* seemed to feel a sense of obligation to the infantry and its commander. Soon after the engagements at San Jorge and Cuatro Esquinas he issued a general order complimenting and thanking the infantry for its gallantry on that day. The order declared that the battalion of foot soldiers should be known in the future as the St. George Fusileers and its commander should be entitled to wear as a decoration a golden Maltese cross, properly inscribed and called the "Cross of St. George." Within the order appeared a sketch of the badge showing its shape and size. Ah, thought Horace Bell at the time, who would not march through fire and blood, month in and month out for nearly two years, willingly breathe the deadly miasma of Granada, starve at Virgin bay, charge bayonets on a barricade 20 feet high, run the gauntlet of 600 men and be fired at by all of them at 25 yards range—all for the reward of a cross of distinction! For the moment Bell believed that surely Walker was the perfection of noble generosity.

[65]

On the day following the reading of the order the St. George Fusileers were commanded to report for duty on the plaza. Here they found a force assembled to make a sortie and drive the allies from a position called the Bull Pen. This was an elevation from which the enemy could cannonade the plaza; so they must be dislodged. The sortie was to be led by Walker's favorite officer, the hero(?) of the "Jacote Races."

The filibusters got within 100 yards of the Bull Pen before they were shot at. At the first fire the "whisky general" made a sudden personal flank movement to the right and taking position behind a big tree shouted at the top of his voice, "Go on, you damned sons o' bitches!" The men made a weak charge, then fell back, carrying off their dead and wounded comrades.

At the evening parade the sergeants informed Major Bell on the part of the men that they were willing to meet the Central Americans at any time in the field, but they had charged the last barricade. They also told Bell that of his original battalion that had marched out of Masaya less than eight months before 360 strong, only 18 remained—that all had fallen victims to the murderous policy of charging barricades.

The next day Bell waited on Walker and informed him of the determination of his men. He also suggested that because of their limited supply of provisions, the weakness of their force, and the increasing strength of the enemy, it would be good policy to retreat to San Juan del Sur where at the worst they could not be starved out, having their boats to forage for them up and down the coast.

Walker was furious, first at the failure to drive the enemy from the Bull Pen and then at the soldiers for presuming to think for themselves and worst of all that anyone should dare to suggest a retreat. After the order complimenting the infantry he thought they would go anywhere. No, he was mistaken. They were unfit to be soldiers, he chided. Walker had lost his senses.

On the following day the men began to eat their horses and the enemy's lines advanced to encircle the city.

About this time General Cañas sent in another proclamation and a document printed in English signed by all the deserters present in Costa Rica. The paper certified to the honorable manner in which they had been treated. Some of those who had deserted at Jacote attested that many of the officers in that debacle had been guilty of brutality toward their soldiers and had been shot down by their own men. This tended to demoralize the more cruel officers. It helped to explain the unequal ratio of mortality in battle, there being at least three officers killed to every private.

This announcement had something to do with Walker's seclusion. The republic of which he was president was getting so shaky that he seemed to lose confidence not only in the army but in himself. Fifty men came from California a day after the Bull Pen defeat and a company of rangers went down to escort them up. They were not molested on their march and reached Rivas safely. Yet Walker made no effort to extricate himself when he could. He had lost the power of action.

By the seventh of April the Central Americans had completely surrounded Rivas and were so close that many soldiers on both sides could converse with their foes by shouting from the barricades, the nearest being about 300 feet apart. The besiegers now yelled out this message:

Since it was Holy Week they proposed not to desecrate it with fighting; the tenth of April, which was Good Friday, would be followed by the Saturday of Glory, celebrated in Nicaragua by crucifying Judas Iscariot in effigy; they would spare Walker and his troops until that day; they had 4,000 men and knew he had only 500; they could break in any time and finish them up; they promised to give them until Saturday, the eleventh, to repent and get ready to leave; but if the little army did not, they would commemorate the great day by coming in at four in the morning to slaughter them and make a Judas of Walker. To emphasize this threat they raised a black flag.

The filibusters well knew their prospects were desperate. During the three-days' respite, though it was Holy Week, the Walkerites did no praying but a vast amount of swearing, and when the noble Latins would send over a shower of *carajos*,[4] their oppo-

nents always sent back a volley of fluent American profanity. So
Holy Week wore on. Walker had about 500 men and fully 3,000
rifles and muskets—all nicely cleaned, loaded, and ready at hand.
This supply gave each man at least a half-dozen guns. Every prep-
aration was made by strengthening the barricades and clearing
away obstacles. Good Friday came and passed away in gloomy
silence, for the allies did not fire a shot. They truly observed the
holiness of the day.

The besieged army retired early feeling certain that the foes
would do their best to annihilate them on the morrow. Asleep on
their muskets at three in the morning the garrison was silently
aroused to prepare for the coming storm. Every man stood at his
post, calm, determined, every nerve set. They were ready to show
the insolent adversaries that 500 Americans would not quietly
submit to being butchered, and if they failed they would make the
victory costly. At exactly four o'clock an enemy gun boomed
forth its thundering command. In a moment the Latins were upon
the Walker army.

The Costa Ricans rushed toward the western side of the plaza,
while the Guatemalans assaulted the east side. Hondurans poured
in from the south. The Nicaraguans and Salvadorans under the
intrepid Chamorro charged on an isolated position, a half-mile
from the plaza, held by Bell's battalion. A three-gun battery of
howitzers had been placed by the defenders to sweep the ground
when the enemy passed over it to reach the west line of the plaza.
Riflemen were also stationed to enfilade this space. But the Costa
Ricans passed over the ground so rapidly in the dark that they suffered little and quickly occupied the whole west side.

On the eastern boundary the besieged had stationed their artillery. In a minute the whole force of big guns opened on the Costa
Ricans. Half of their number was killed. The others surrendered
and were marched to the guard house. In the meantime the Guatemalans and Hondurans pushed up to the barricades, and Chamorro's men succeeded in firing one of the houses occupied by
Bell's Fusileers, who put out the fire and drove them away. Time
after time in regular column the attacking troops came up only to

[68]

be shot down. For four hours the battle raged; then the foe slowly retired leaving 800 dead in front of the barricades and 300 prisoners. Walker lost only two men, killed. The foreigners now saw the advantage of fighting behind barricades. But it was too late to profit by the lesson. They could have done the same at Masaya.

Having achieved a glorious victory the filibusters assumed that Walker would take advantage of it by leading them out of their beleaguered camp. They felt that they could break out and go to San Juan del Sur with little loss. But no move was made. On the day following he held a cabinet meeting and stopped issuing sugar. He set men to work breaking up the church bells to be cast into cannon balls. His soldiers now assumed that he intended to let the enemy starve them into submission. They were compelled to gormandize on horse meat without sugar and to gloomily await the end. By the next morning 50 of his heroes, including several officers, deserted.

"Why withdraw our sugar?" the disgruntled men asked of each other. If they had to starve, why could they not have sugar to sweeten the horse meat? A week later they learned the reason. The cabinet had found a small still in the country used for the illicit production of liquor. So the sugar was being made into *aguardiente* to sustain the courage of the general and his staff. Bell's impression formed at Granada of the importance of alcohol in fighting a war was verified.

The men continued to eat their disgusting food and tighten up their belts. Soldiers stood at the barricades night and day, but the enemy remained quiet, letting famine do its work. So time wore on until the first of May when daily rations of horse and mule meat were reduced to half a pound. Then the men began to butcher the dogs and cats. Bell went to Walker urging him to take action, but got nothing out of him.

Ten days later Lieutenant Stockton from the American sloop-of-war *St. Mary's* came in with permission from the enemy to take the women out of the besieged quarters and a truce was observed while he was in either camp. The Latins affirmed that they did not wish to cause the American ladies any privation—that they would

[69]

be glad to escort them to San Juan del Sur, where they would be under the protection of the warship lying offshore. Here they would be lodged in the American hotel which was owned by the United States consul. In Walker's camp there were fully a hundred women. As they would encumber any attempt to break out, the men rejoiced at their departure. Some were wives, but many more widows. Most of them were amiable and virtuous women who had followed to Nicaragua the fortunes of their adventurous husbands. Arriving at the enemy's camp they were politely and hospitably treated. In a spirit of true chivalry the Latin generals not only feasted the half-starved ladies but gave them delicacies to send back to their husbands. During the truce the enemy sent Walker's army a large supply of cigars.

General Victor Zavala, head of the Guatemalan army, who had been educated in the United States and spoke fluent English, entertained several ladies, one of them being the wife of the "hero" of the "Jacote Races," another Mrs. Max Strobel of Anaheim, California. Dinner being over, the general told the ladies that he hoped they would deem it no offense if he offered to supply them with whatever provisions or delicacies they might wish to send to their besieged husbands. The wife of the adjutant general asked for a box of cigars. Another guest requested sardines for her husband. When he came to the wife of the Jacote leader he urged, "Madam, be kind enough to say what you would like to send General Sanders, and please, madam, do not be sparing of my stores. Your husband is a true soldier and it gives me great pleasure to contribute to his comfort." Without a moment's reflection Mrs. Sanders replied, "Please send him a half-dozen bottles of whisky."

When the twenty-four-hour truce ended in the afternoon, the allied armies began a vigorous cannonade. Darkness set in and morning came, bringing no prospect of a move. The only hope for the filibusters was to accept the enemy's terms and lay down their arms. There were men who objected either to surrendering or being sacrificed, the conviction being that Walker intended the latter. Horace Bell like others who had come to Nicaragua in the early stage of the war believed he had a right to be there, for he had been invited to come by proclamation of President Rivas and had received his commission as captain from the lawful head of the government. Though he had blindly followed Walker in his usurpation and so had outlawed himself in the eyes of the natives, still he felt he had a right to be in the country. He was unwilling either to surrender or be sacrificed. The situation now reached a climax. The men had only a few horses and mules left. These were kept alive on plantain and banana leaves—poor forage but the best available.

Among the desperate soldiers admiration for General Cañas increased. Drifting back from the Costa Rican camp came stories of his generosity. His kindness did more to break up the filibuster force than shot and shell. So vexed did Walker become at his noble enemy's popularity that he sent a man to assassinate him. The one selected for the purpose had come from California on the mid-March steamer. He was a sergeant, a muscular, brave, and determined fellow, eager for any enterprise however desperate. In the character of a deserter he slipped over to the Costa Rican camp with a revolver concealed in each boot. As all runaways on being caught were sent to General Cañas, the sergeant was to seize an opportunity to kill the Costa Rican general, escape, and make his way back to camp. On going over he was taken to Cañas who treated him with such kindness that the sergeant's heart softened. Making a full confession he threw himself upon the mercy of the man he had intended to murder. Instantly Cañas forgave him and treated him with undiminished graciousness.

This magnanimous general was a small, slightly built, light-complexioned Spaniard with blue eyes. He looked more like a store clerk than a military leader. In manner he was as gentle as a woman, but in battle as brave as a California cougar—so agreed his foes. About the time the ladies left, one of Walker's cabinet, the attorney general of the republic, deliberately walked out and claimed the protection of General Cañas.

The garrison now numbered 300, fully one-third being in Bell's command. The position held by his men was a half-mile from the

[71]

plaza on a hill. All the intervening houses had been burnt down, except one used for a hospital. This was garrisoned by the surgeons and convalescents. If it were captured the enemy could cut off communication with the plaza and quickly annihilate St. George's Fusileers. During the entire siege in addition to having his barricades well-manned Bell had 20 picked men who slept at his quarters. These he used for reinforcement whenever needed. The Major let everyone know, including Walker, that this force was his own independent unit.

On the second morning after the women departed, about daylight the Fusileers were startled by rapid firing at the hospital. It was a large structure built around an inner court. The front and two sides contained the rooms; the back was closed in with a thick wall. From the front you entered by a wide passage into the courtyard; an exit could be made at the rear through an immense wooden door. The wall was loopholed, the door firmly shut.

Approaching from the rear the Hondurans rushed up, captured the loopholes, and battered a hole through the door large enough to admit one man. Bell and his 20 soldiers ran to the hospital thinking of their destruction if the enemy got possession of the place. Reaching the front entrance they saw a sheet of flame coming in through the apertures in the wall. The situation was desperate. They must recover the loopholes. Bell ordered his men to trail arms and run low. In they rushed through the courtyard. Crouching down until the Hondurans withdrew their muskets for reloading they ran their own through the vacated gaps.

As he entered the courtyard Bell saw a solitary man standing close to the wall, covering the broken passage in the door, a high pile of enemy dead lying before him. In his left hand he held a carbine, in his right a navy revolver. The Major rushed to his side just in time to see him blow a man's brains out as the victim plunged through the breach. "My God! old fellow!" he gasped recognizing Bell, "you're just in time. I've fired my last shot!"

Recovering the loopholes the picked men drove the Hondurans off, but only after 15 minutes of desperate fighting. At every shot the grim doorkeeper had killed a man. Seven lay before him—one for his carbine, six for his revolver.

[72]

"Well, Doc," inquired Bell, "if we had not come, what would you have done?" "Oh," answered Dr. John Brinkerhoff of Los Angeles coolly, "I'd have knocked their brains out with the butt of my carbine."[5]

By now the situation at Rivas had become horrible. The constant watching for two months had begun to tell. Sometimes Bell would meet a man he had not seen for a week or two and it would be difficult to recognize him because of his emaciation. He found that only 250 fighting men were left with 20 horses and mules. Every day officers and privates would go over to General Cañas and surrender. One day it was announced that another of the president's staff, a colonel, had laid his sword at the feet of the Costa Rican. Such news created no wonder whatever. Thus the garrison, or what was left of it, awaited the end, which could not be far off, as almost the last horse had been slaughtered.

Meanwhile the president general had been secretly negotiating through Commander Charles Henry Davis of *St. Mary's* for terms of surrender. Three days after the assault on the hospital the announcement that "tomorrow we march out," fell on the camp like a bursting bomb. The terms of surrender provided that at sunrise Walker and his staff should leave Central America for the United States—that at nine on the same morning his men should park the artillery, stack their arms on the plaza, and march out. Then the allied army was to march in. The vanquished soldiers were to be fed by the victors; one half of them to be sent out of the country by way of the San Juan river; the other half through Puntarenas in Costa Rica. All expenses for rations on the way and transportation would be paid by the Costa Ricans.

It was now late in May 1857, the Walker rule having lasted for nearly two years. At the dawn of the final day, with its band playing, its burnished arms reflecting the sunlight, the Stars and Stripes waving gently overhead, the United States marine guard in full uniform marched into Rivas and formed in platoons before the quarters of the retiring president. Then for the first time in 42 days William Walker put his head outside his bombproof castle and he with his well-fed and well-liquored staff filled the space between the platoons. This curious cortege marched through the

[73]

enemy's lines, not halting until it stood safely on board the American warship at San Juan del Sur.[6]

Nine o'clock came. Men and officers walked to the plaza, some with arms, some with none. Then a great row started. Walker, the enemy declared, had violated the treaty. He had caused the trunnions to be knocked off the cannons, had thrown the ammunition into wells, and broken hundreds of rifles by striking them over anvils. Walker was safe, but he had left behind his unarmed followers to brave the wrath of an outraged foe. A spark would have fired the fumes of their disappointment and every American in or near Rivas would have been murdered before noon on that day, but for the prompt action of the generous Cañas. He marched his Costa Rican column into Rivas and served as a safeguard to the unarmed foreigners.

Bell believed that this last act of deviltry was Walker's stratagem. Had these veterans been murdered after laying down their arms it would have made great capital for the exiled president in the slave states of America. A hundred men would have come to avenge the death of every man killed. But the scheme did not work, thanks to the benevolence of General Cañas.

Costa Rica carried out faithfully her part of the treaty. The filibusters were shipped out of Nicaragua to the United States except a few who wished to remain, some of whom became wealthy.

So sounded taps for the fight in Nicaragua.[7] In Horace Bell's opinion it was born of the spirit of adventure engendered by the Mexican War and the wild rush for gold to California. For the most part—he thought—Walker drew forth as his soldiers the flower of American knights-errant, men who went to war chiefly for the love of action.[8]

CHAPTER III

Champion of Freedom

All ages shall speak with amaze and applause,
Of the courage we'll show in support of our laws;
To die we can bear—but to serve we disdain,
For shame is to freemen more dreadful than pain.

JOHN DICKINSON, *A Song for American Freedom*

I N the year 1857 there lived in Brandenburg, Kentucky, a
Negro blacksmith named Charles, who was owned by
Dr. C. H. Ditto. Charles had a wife, Mary Ann, belonging
to A. J. Alexander, a Brandenburg merchant. The pair lived
in a small house beside the Ohio river. Being a skilled workman
Charles was more valuable than most slaves. His trustful master
gave him a skiff in which he was allowed to cross the water for
fishing and to shoe horses for people living in Indiana.

On the afternoon of September, the twenty-sixth, Charles Bell,
the seventeen-year-old brother of Horace, was seen with the
Negro mechanic in Brandenburg at the blacksmith shop. Late in
the evening young Bell left the wharf in a skiff headed for the Indiana shore. Early the next morning the Negro passed the word
along that he was going across the river to fish, the day being
Sunday.

When Monday morning came and the slave did not return, the
cry arose that he had run away to freedom, which was true. Never
again was he seen in Brandenburg.

Suspicion at once pointed to the Bell boy as an accomplice in
the escape, for he was known on both sides of the Ohio as a fiery
abolitionist. He had lived much of his youth with his aunt, Julia
Wright Jones, a militant opposer of slavery. Through her influence the lad had accepted the arguments for abolition and she had
filled his mind with stories of the daring deeds done by his older

brothers. Though the boy's father did not openly object to human bondage, he was believed to be unsympathetic since he had once refused to join a party of Kentuckians pursuing a runaway slave. And he had made matters worse. On the day when the Negro escaped, the elder Bell rode on horseback from Corydon to New Albany and thence by ferry to Louisville to cash a draft from Horace. On the next Monday when he was nearing home late in the day he was stopped by a group of Kentuckians searching for the fugitive. They demanded to know where he had gone and what he had been doing. He returned the curt answer, "That's none of your business."

As soon as it was clear that Charles Ditto had run away, his master dispatched handbills and runners in the direction of Brownstown in Jackson county, Indiana, hoping to head him off. He believed that Charles would take this route since it was at Brownstown that the Underground Railroad connected with trains going north. Early in October the handbills and newspaper notices began to bear fruit. C. B. Johnston and a Mrs. Withers, both of Brownstown, wrote to Dr. Ditto that they could supply him with the names of persons who had effected the escape of his man.

Mrs. Withers asserted that a free Negro named Oswald Wright, who lived in Corydon, had come to her house begging breakfast for himself and a fleeing slave named Charles. After she had provided food Wright took the fugitive to the train and saw him off on his way to Canada. While eating his breakfast Oswald, she wrote, had told her that a family named Bell who lived on the Indiana shore opposite Brandenburg had aided in the flight of the Negro and that they were planning the abscondence of his wife Mary Ann.

The other correspondent, Mr. Johnston, had read of the reward offered in the papers and desired to obtain it, since it was unusually large. So he came to southern Indiana to search for more evidence, plying this business under the guise of horse trading. He visited Corydon and won the confidence of Oswald, who confided to him that he had taken Charles Ditto from the Bell farm to Brownstown on a horse. Wright declared further that young Bell had enticed the slave away from his master and harbored him until the colored man could be sent north.

Assuming that the escape of Mary Ann was being planned Johnston endeavored to find out more about the Bells as agents of the underground. He and a group of associates from Jackson county went to their neighborhood under the pretense of horse trading. They put up their mounts at the Bell farm and went over to Brandenburg, where with the aid of some slave owners they hatched a scheme for catching the Bells.

As their first move the Jackson county men became friendly with Charles Bell and with him plotted the running away of Mary Ann. They chose a night when they would bring her to the river at a place agreed upon. On the signal of striking a match, which could be seen clear across the Ohio, young Bell would pass over in a skiff and ferry her to the Indiana shore. Oswald Wright was to receive and escort her to Brownstown. At eight on the appointed night the matches were struck and in less than an hour Charles Bell reached the place of the signal on the Kentucky side. It was so dark that he was not seen until he whispered, "Where is she?" The detectives replied that she was hiding in an old mill near the water-line. At once Charles got out of his skiff and started to the place to get the colored woman. But on his way he walked into a hollow square of men who seized and put him in the Brandenburg jail.

With oars wrapped in rags to prevent noise in rowing, some Kentuckians now crossed the river to apprehend Oswald, the free colored man, and David, young Bell's father. The Bell house stood back from the river a short space above high-water mark. Quickly they surrounded it to prevent an escape. Two men stalked to the door and knocked. They were told to come in. They saw the Negro Wright propped back in a chair, his sock-covered feet warming near the stove, the elder Bell reading a newspaper. On entering, the strangers ordered Wright to put on his shoes and go with them. This he refused to do until they compelled him by force. Oswald accompanied them to a ferryboat now waiting at the landing. The Kentuckians also led off the two horses that he had planned to use in taking away the colored woman.

So far nothing was done to Bell. But a little later the men returned and told him that since they were taking the Negro's horses he had better come with them to see if they had any of his property. This Mr. Bell did. But instead of going to the barn they led him down to the ferryboat. Here a man held his arms while a Kentucky constable read a warrant accusing Bell of complicity in stealing a Negro named Charles, belonging to Dr. Ditto, and ordered that he be brought before the magistrate in Brandenburg. The constable's action was assumed by the Kentuckians to be legal since their state claimed jurisdiction over the Ohio river to low-water mark on the Indiana side and as the river was then low the boat lay well within the line. It was not long before Wright and David Bell also found themselves inside the Brandenburg jail.

On the next day a preliminary trial was held, the chief witnesses for the prosecution being Johnston and Mrs. Withers. Wright denied he had given them information. Likewise Bell and his son denied complicity in the Negro's escape. But Charles and his father were each placed under a $5,000 bond, Wright under $3,000. As bail was not forthcoming the three were remanded to jail. This happened on the twenty-fifth of November 1857. Here they would remain until court met in the following May.

Meanwhile frenzy raged up and down the river. People in Harrison and Floyd counties were furious because of the high-handed and illegal way in which citizens of Indiana had been arrested and taken out of the state. Old Colonel William C. Marsh of Corydon, a friend of David Bell, raised a band of armed neighbors bent on freeing the prisoners, but plans miscarried because the boats failed to reach Leavenport, the rendezvous, in time. Residents of New Albany were also ready to help. On the Kentucky side people armed to defend Brandenburg. On guard were the Meade County Rangers, the militia, and companies of the Kentucky Legion ordered by the governor to prevent the prisoners' release. All were under command of Captain Jack Armstrong, who had served with Horace Bell in Nicaragua. It looked as though there would be war between the two states if only a spark were set to the powder.

[78]

Fortunately no violence was done by the Hoosiers and soon the guard grew too strong for a rescue. A committee then called on Governor Willard of Indiana to demand of Kentucky the return of the abducted men, but he refused to interfere.

Within a few months news of their father and brother reached California causing Horace and John to start hotfoot for home. They came back by way of Panama, the Mississippi, and Ohio rivers. John got off the boat at Tobacco Landing, the first one above Brandenburg on the Indiana shore, and went to his mother on the family farm. It was now May 1858. Horace rode on to New Albany, thence to Corydon, where he walked into the law office of his friend, Walter Q. Gresham, and secured his legal service. While visiting their mother the boys were approached by friends who offered to help in a rescue, but they politely declined, saying they would try legal means. They crossed over to Brandenburg to secure bail for the prisoners and finally found two slaveholders who agreed to go on their bonds, but on learning of the excessive amounts demanded, the Southerners later refused. So the three men remained in jail.

While the trial was in progress many friends of the defendants ferried over to Kentucky to hear it. One noon during an intermission Colonel Marsh, who had attempted a rescue, was standing near the Brandenburg hotel discussing the case when he was shot and killed by a young man secluded in the balcony. But this was another affair—merely a family feud, and the killer was not apprehended. Though it had no connection with the Bell suit, it shows the spirit of the times.

Feeling ran high. The Hoosiers were angry because of the manner of the arrest and the Bell brothers were jeered in the streets by the Brandenburgers. One day after the court's adjournment a crowd followed them to their hotel, whereupon Horace made a short speech. He declared that he and his brother did not want border warfare—that they had declined the aid of armed friends and neighbors—all they wanted was justice. But if they did not get it, then he and his brother would come alone, break the jail and free the prisoners in broad daylight. This the Kentuckians took as a joke, many remarking that "a man who talked that big would attempt nothing."

Delay seemed to be the state's strategy. When preliminaries were finally over and the trial was about to begin, the prosecution announced that it was not ready and called for a six-months' postponement. This request the court granted. As the Bell party had already been confined several months, this was more than Horace could stand. Bolder steps must be taken.

The brothers now disappeared, giving out the word that they had returned to California. At length the Kentucky governor withdrew the armed guards, but to prevent surprise the Brandenburgers swore in 200 minutemen and placed a stand of arms in all the county offices in the town. Excitement having subsided, the two brothers conspired to raid the jail. They discussed the plan with their Spartan mother, who approved. At a late moment John hesitated, fearing failure. But Mrs. Bell spoke from her sickbed:

"Johnny, you go with Horace. Ye won't fail. I would ruther see ye baith laying here at my feet dead than have ye do nothing fur to help your poor Pa and Charley. And may God go with ye!"

So on the twenty-ninth day of July in 1858 near to noon the two brothers strapped on their pistols, filled a carpetbag with six-shooters and ammunition, and stepped into a skiff. A young mulatto boy indentured to their father rowed them over to the Brandenburg shore. He was threatened with horrors if they did not find him in the boat on their return. This day had been chosen because a barbecue was in progress at Garnettsville, Kentucky, a few miles up the river and they knew that many of the people of Brandenburg would be there. Moreover at the noon hour those persons remaining in town would likely be at home eating dinner.

To avoid attracting attention the boys took different streets leading southward to the jail, which stood on the south side of the public square about a quarter-mile below the river. On the north side of the square and facing south was the Meade county courthouse. Here were stored the arms and munitions to be used by the minutemen in defending the town. They were mostly the county officeholders, the lawyers, and merchants of Brandenburg. The lawyers' offices lined the west side of the public square; on the east were the stores. As the brothers expected, the streets were empty.

Horace reached the jail first. The jailer and his wife with two guards sat at the dinner table. Pointing his revolvers at their heads he drove them into a corner of the room, but not soon enough to prevent one man from jumping out a rear window and giving an alarm, which created a frightful din. Now John arrived. He took the jail keys from a bureau drawer, the boys having previously learned from a spying friend where they were kept. Then he sprang upstairs, unlocked the jail doors, armed his father and Charles, and locked the other prisoners in. (Oswald having been removed temporarily could not be rescued.) As the three ran downstairs Horace dashed to the courthouse before the minute-men who were in town could assemble. When they arrived to grab their guns he held them off until his party was near the river, then ran for the water himself. Faithfully the mulatto had waited in the skiff. As the Bells were descending to the levee their pursuers opened fire. But being discharged from an elevation the bullets passed overhead. Father and sons returned a volley, purposely shooting high, but close enough to make the town guard retreat. Then they jumped into their boat and without more annoyance, except for a few straggling shots, crossed safely back to Indiana. Nobody was hurt on either side.[1]

Horace Bell found himself the hero of the hour and on his own admission celebrated victory by drinking too much of "John Barleycorn." The exploit of the two brothers was heralded by the local newspapers. While many Brandenburgers writhed in mortification, people on the Indiana side of the river exulted. The New Albany *Ledger* declared Horace Bell to be "as brave as Julius Caesar." The *Tribune* of the same city observed that the heroes were not only "Bell-igerent but Bell-impudent," and on the tenth of August published a ballad celebrating the rescue. Composed by Forceythe Wilson, a local poet, it was called

[81]

A Chime of Bells

We have heard how Leander swam over from Sestos,
 To the warm heart of Hero,
 To the white arms of Hero,
Through the storm of the Straits when the flood was at Zero.
And the heart thrills to think how a much sterner hero,
 The old Roman hero who sitteth in story,
 At the head of his host in the red fields of story,
 On his war horse in story,
Rode over the river to Rome and to glory.

We have read of ten thousand old knights and grim monarchs,
 In myth and tradition,
 In stirring tradition,
Who dared for devotion and died for ambition;

But we never have read in the annals or legends,
 Of swordsmen or bowmen,
 Of spearmen or bowmen,
Of the feuds and the combats of deadliest foemen,
Of gods or of giants, of high men or low men—
We have read of the deeds or the daring of no men,
Whose hearts were as strong as the hearts of the yeomen,
Whose hearts were as *true* as the hearts of the yeomen,

Our brave Yankee yeomen—the Bells of the river—
Who crossed the deep river, the bright tranquil river,
Unmasked and at noon, in the name of their Mother,
 To demand and deliver
 Their father and brother!
Whose skiff skimmed the river when the day was arisen;
Who thundered and walked through the doors of the prison—
 Of the Brandenburg prison!
 In the name of their Mother,
 Of God and *Affection*;
And took out their father, and took out their brother,
And brought them both over without dereliction.[2]

One would think that since the Bells were all safe at home the affair would be ended. But such was not to be. The hotheads on the south bank, wounded in pride, must vent their wrath on

Horace. They bided their time until the next scene of the drama opened, offering a reward of $500 for his capture and transportation back to Kentucky. Before long this yielded fruitage.

In 1858 the Floyd County Fair began on October nineteenth in New Albany. The event was attended by many people from southern Indiana and northern Kentucky. On the last day of the exhibit, October 23, Mrs. Bell and a daughter were present and on leaving crossed over to Louisville for a visit. Horace accompanied them as far as the Duckwall ferry. Returning from the wharf he waited at the Depauw House, chatting with friends. As it was early in the afternoon most of the townspeople had gone to the fairgrounds, leaving the streets almost deserted. At the last minute he left the hotel to hop on the stage for home.

When Horace reached the corner of Main and Bank streets he was suddenly surrounded by five Kentuckians girded with guns. They quickly disarmed and hustled him down to the wharf, telling those whom they met on the street that their captive had committed a murder on the other side of the river. The seizure attracted little attention, for the New Albany magistrates commonly allowed the police of Louisville to pick up suspected Kentuckians escaping to the Indiana town, without the formality of a warrant. As soon as Horace was placed on board, the ferry by previous arrangement at once put off to the opposite shore. For a few hours he was held in the Louisville jail and later that night driven under heavy guard to Brandenburg and locked up.

Again New Albany and the surrounding country were infuriated by the kidnaping of an Indiana citizen. At once men armed for his rescue. A party of 25 went to the Floyd county courthouse where they outfitted themselves with muskets, pistols, a swivel gun, and munitions. They procured the ferryboat *Adelaide* and by the time it left its mooring there were 75 men on board. At Tobacco Landing in Harrison county, four miles above Brandenburg, 40 more joined the expedition. When they came within two miles of their destination about 60 of the crusaders debarked. They were to go overland by a roundabout course and reach the rear of the town at the same time that the steamer should touch

[83]

the opposite side. Of those who marched inland all lost their way but 18, being unable to find their route over strange roads at night. In the morning when the 18 descended on the jail they discovered that Horace was gone.

Having heard of the approaching posse the jailers had removed Bell to Big Spring, 20 miles south of the river. The boat now arrived with its cannon and anchored in front of Brandenburg, whereupon the prisoner was transferred farther away to Elizabethtown. Impressed by the display of force the propertied citizens of Brandenburg, particularly the merchants, became conciliatory. They feared that a mob of invaders might set fire to their town. Moreover some of the slaveholders deprecated the aggressiveness of hotheads on their side. So influential citizens called a town meeting and appointed five Brandenburgers and three Indianians to settle the affair peacefully. The committee agreed upon three points: First, that the armed party should leave; second, that Bell should be given an immediate examination and, if not discharged, a moderate sum would be assessed as bail, the bond to be subscribed by citizens of Brandenburg; and third, that Governor Morehead of Kentucky should be asked to pardon all the Bells.

Accepting these proposals the Hoosier brigade returned home and Horace was tried before two justices. Charged with jail-breaking he pled guilty, was admitted to bail of $750, and ordered to appear before the Meade county circuit court in November. Two slaveholders went on his bond. On being released—it was now the twenty-ninth of October—he took the first boat for New Albany with friends, reaching there at nine in the evening.

When he arrived a large crowd greeted him and insisted on his going to the theater in Woodward Hall. Here a three-act play composed by a Louisville editor was in progress, dramatizing the Brandenburg adventures. It was called *Horace Bell: Champion of Freedom*. The room overflowed with spectators who responded, wrote a local newsman, with "rapturous applause." Of all incongruities—the hero's part was played by a woman, Miss Susan Denin! At the end of the last act the manager announced that

[84]

Horace Bell himself would soon appear. The audience was moved but seemed unbelieving. Ten minutes elapsed. Then the curtain rose again and Susan came forward dressed as the Goddess of Liberty and leading by the hand Horace Bell. Round upon round of shouting and stamping burst through doors and windows. The crowd demanded a speech, but poor Horace was too embarrassed to say more than a few words. Cheers then followed for the committee who had negotiated his release and also for the state of Indiana. The stirring scene closed with the goddess singing the French *Marseillaise*.

Instead of appearing in November before the Meade county circuit court, as he was supposed to do, Horace left Indiana. His bail was declared forfeited at the May term of 1859 and acquittance demanded of his sureties. According to the agreement that his bondsmen should never pay, the governor of Kentucky set aside the judgment. "But," remarked Captain J. M. Phillips, a merchant of Brandenburg, "we could not get the prosecuting attorney to remit his fees, so we had to pay him."

It was believed by his neighbors near Corydon that David Bell was innocent of the plan to free the slave and his wife Mary Ann. But a different story was told of his son Charles. Since he was widely known as an ardent abolitionist no one doubted that he had plotted the escape. Charles, historians agree, was surely an underground agent operating on the border. Aunt Julia, daughter of the Wrights, had played her hand well.[3]

The indictments against David and Charles Bell were stricken off the Kentucky dockets. Oswald Wright was convicted of stealing Charles Ditto and sentenced to the penitentiary for five years. But he was soon pardoned and returned to Corydon.

Among the anti-slavery people of Indiana there was great rejoicing. Moreover a considerable number of Kentuckians approved the action of Horace and John. For example Dr. Ditto's brother, himself a slaveholder by inheritance, publicly commended Horace for his gallantry, and Captain Phillips, another such owner, remarked, "I admired Horace Bell's nerve and was glad to go on his bond."[4]

[85]

CHAPTER IV

Wanderlust

Thou Italy of the Occident!
Land of flowers and summer climes,
Of holy priests and horrid crimes;
Land of the cactus and sweet cocoa;
Richer than all the Orient
In gold and glory, in want and woe,
In truth and treason, in good and guilt,
In ivied ruins and altars low,
In battered walls and blood misspilt;
Glorious, gory Mexico!

JOAQUIN MILLER, *The Tale of the Tall Alcalde*

INSTEAD of returning immediately to California, Bell drifted down to Mexico and joined the army of Benito Juárez.[1] In 1859 under the command of this revolutionary patriot he fought against the reactionary president, Miguel Miramón for Mexico's freedom. His martial experience he recorded in a manuscript long ago destroyed by fire. Thus was lost to the world what must have been a unique tale of historic adventure.

Though this is missing we do have his story of what he did shortly after leaving the service of the rebel who became president. Since his filibustering days Bell had longed to explore southeastern Mexico from its Pacific side to the shores of the Yucatan peninsula facing the Caribbean sea. He had heard of its network of rivers and lakes, its primeval forests of cedar and mahogany, its cabinet and dye woods, and also its wild Indian tribes, descendants of a prehistoric race that had left behind them ruined cities and mouldering temples. This vast region was as little known to the outside world in 1859 as it was when Cortés, guided by the captive Aztec emperor Guatemozin, cut his way through forest and marsh from Chinameca, a town on the southern shore of the Gulf of Mexico, to the infant Spanish colony in Honduras. In this broad realm, so Bell had been told, there were populous Indian towns unvisited by Catholic padres, where the inhabitants practiced the rites of their heathen religion as they had done before the coming of the mailed *caballero* and his companion, the missionary priest. Indeed one might travel a lifetime in this part of Central America and still not know all its secrets.

Such a wild and singular country appealed to Bell's imagination and so with the urge for more adventures he wandered still farther southward in Mexico until he reached Tehuantepec, situated on the isthmus of the same name which keeps the gulf from joining the Pacific ocean. This city lies close to the sea and within the western edge of the territory he wished to explore.

On reaching his starting point he found himself, as he says, "flat broke," and accordingly became a schoolmaster to replenish his purse. It was a pleasant occupation, he tells us, to teach in a place of 25,000 inhabitants where possibly less than one in a hundred could read or write. Because of his work he was regarded as one of the *sabios* or learned men and next in social prestige to the priest, *El Fraile* Romero.

"This rollicking soldier of the Cross," declares the Major, "dealt out religion in one of the Tehuantepec churches when not engaged in dealing monte to the light-hearted female portion of his not overpious charge. And it is no libel on the padre to tell of his dealing monte and betting on that game so dearly loved by Mexicans. *Fraile* [friar] Romero would play monte, quaff his wine, comb the girls' hair with his delicate fingers, and pat them on the cheek with his soft palm. He would pull and haul them around, push them under the arm with his thumb, tickle them in the ribs, and all that sort of innocent fun. And he was a more popular person than I imagined myself to be with the bright belles of Tehuantepec."

Soon Bell became the friend and companion of the jolly sky-pilot, loving him dearly, and after the lapse of many years he considered it no detriment to his dignity to confess that he also loved more than one of the feminine favorites of the roistering Romero. "No one of flesh and blood can help it," was the way the priest

[87]

would absolve them both and to this doctrine Horace was ever ready to agree with a hearty "Amen!"

As a learned man the Yankee schoolmaster frequently engaged in theological discussions with the friar and since he was the reverse of reverent in his arguments the good father gave him the nickname of *El Bárbaro*. But the ladies to tease the young padre added the word *Hermoso*. So by many he was called *El Bárbaro Hermoso*, or the Handsome Heathen. A half-year passed in this happy circle presided over by the jovial *fraile* with whom—to use military parlance—Bell messed.

One day Romero came to him looking sorrowful. "What is the matter, *amigo*?" asked Horace. "Are any of the girls to be married?"

"*Válgame Dios!*" [May heaven help me!] he answered. "I wish it were nothing worse."

"Have you been promoted?"

"Promoted?" said he. "That is just what it is. But Santa Maria! what a promotion! I am ordered by the bishop to shoulder my cross and go forth to convert the *bárbaros* of the Coatzacoalcos country. And worse than all to that hotbed of heathendom, Chinameca!"

"And where is that place?" Horace anxiously inquired, "and why do you dread it so?"

In reply the disheartened priest sat down and told him of its location and something about its past. Bell learned from him that Chinameca was a large Indian town near the Coatzacoalcos river, about 20 miles from the Bay of Campeche, the southern bulge of the Gulf of Mexico. It was noted for having been the birthplace and early home of an important woman in Mexican history.

Her father had been a rich and powerful *cacique* or chief over the region of Coatzacoalcos, who died when she was an infant. His widow then married another chief and by him bore a son, who they decided should rule as their successor. Accordingly she feigned that her daughter was dead and secretly gave her to wandering Indian traders, who in turn sold the child as a slave to the *cacique* of the neighboring province of Tabasco.

[88]

In 1519 Hernando Cortés appeared with his Spanish fleet near its shore and overcame the Tabascans. Wishing to placate his victors the *cacique* sent gifts, including 20 female slaves. They were soon baptized as Catholic converts, thus becoming the first Christian women in New Spain. Conspicuous among them was the unwanted princess of Chinameca. Besides a handsome figure and personal charm she possessed a generous nature, as shown by expressive features, and also a fearless spirit. At her christening in the town of Tabasco the priests gave her the Spanish name of Doña Marina. But the Aztecs being unable to place their tongues so as to pronounce the word aright called it instead Malinche.

In his attempts to converse with the natives Cortés was baffled. After leaving Cuba he had picked up a Spaniard at the island of Cozumel off the coast of Yucatan to serve as his translator. This man, who had been stranded there by shipwreck several years before, could use the Mayan language of Yucatan, but he was ignorant of Aztec. Fortunately Doña Marina could speak both. Thus was she able to converse with the interpreter, who in turn changed her words into Spanish. In her the conqueror found a means of communication necessary in warfare. It was not long before Doña Marina being a natural linguist gained such a command of Castilian that Cortés made the Indian slave girl his sole interpreter, then his secretary. Finally because of her charm she became his mistress and the mother of his son. Her knowledge of tongues and native customs, besides the revealing of plots against them, more than once saved her adopted countrymen from disaster. She went with her lord on his marches and did more for his happiness than either of his colorless wives in Cuba and Old Spain.[2]

The Chinamecans, according to Father Romero, still preserved a tradition that when Cortés came to their town on his way to Honduras the native priests reproached Malinche. They accused her of causing the bloodshed and ruin that her people had suffered from the rule of the Spaniards. Although she was then a Catholic — so tradition insisted — she entered the same heathen temple which was still standing and vowed that she would return some day to Chinameca and restore their freedom and religion. More than 300 years had been registered on the cycle of time since then, while day and night, year in and year out, an Indian had stood on top of the ancient tower as a sentinel to apprise the Aztecs of her approach that she might be properly received. Each dawn a watcher proclaimed in a loud voice the coming of day and the nonappearance of Malinche. He was then relieved by another sentry beginning a twelve-hour look. Thus throughout centuries had these peculiar people remained true to their hope of a promised liberator.[3]

In manners, dress, and religion the Indians of Chinameca and the surrounding villages had changed but little since the year when Cortés fought at their capital. They were still averse to the Christian religion, even hostile to priests sent to convert them. So stubborn were they in adhering to the faith of their fathers that the Catholic missionaries were always glad to hurry away.

Such was the place where Bell's comrade was ordered to go.

Romero begged Horace to accompany him to Chinameca. "After I am settled down you can return," he promised. Then recovering his usual mood of gaiety he added, "We will have a goodly supply of coin, for I will confess the whole town at half-price before I leave and make hard times for the fellows who remain here." *El Fraile* now filled his goblet and pushed the bottle toward his friend, who followed suit. After great persuasion Horace consented to go.

Ten days later they were ready to set out. So provident was the priest in collecting the comforts of good living that it required 15 mules to carry his baggage. Their journey would take them through the mountains to Suchiltepec, a point of embarkment at the head of the Coatzacoalcos river, a two-day journey from Tehuantepec. "And," sighed Father Romero dolefully, "I am doomed by my bishop to stop a week at San Juan Guichicova and minister to those infernal mule worshipers, and then stay another week with the Africans. *Mal rayo les pegue!*" [May the wrath of heaven fall upon them!]

At the first place lived a tribe of Indians who kept great herds of mules fat and fine, which they petted and pampered, regarding

[90]

them with religious veneration, such as the Hindus had for the sacred cow. At the second halt they would find a colony of vigorous Negroes who were descended from a cargo of slaves. Years ago their ancestors had mutinied and killed the crew of a slaver. Then having ascended the Coatzacoalcos river they settled in the mountains of Tehuantepec. Their offspring still spoke their language and retained the customs of Africa.

When Bell visited the Indians they were suffering from emotional shock because agents of the Louisiana-Tehuantepec company had offered to buy some of their sacred mules for service on the overland route across the isthmus. "We did not do much business at San Juan Guichicova in the way of confessing," writes the Major, "and absolutely none among the Africans, but we took in quite a quantity of small coin at monte in which I became very proficient. The father in the meantime instructed me in the mysteries of the mass and the confessional—and could I chant *Dominus vobiscum et cum spiritu tuo* with great unction! But the heathenish Guichicovans refused to take any stock in me in the religious role. So I corralled in their *reals* and *medios* at monte and did about as good a cash business as did *Fraile* Romero at confessing." They did not find the mule-worshiping Indians to be a bad people after all; so it was with something like a feeling of regret that the pair left them.

Resuming their journey they rode on to the river, where their muleteers turned back to Tehuantepec. Father Romero and Bell engaged a large *bongo* [boat] to carry them with their freight down the stream. They hurried to get away and by midafternoon were gently gliding past its somber banks. At sunset the *bongo* landed in an open space near the foot of a mountain. Said the captain to his two passengers, "I and my peons will stop here for the night. But your worships can ascend the mountain and stay at Doña Margarita's." In answer to their questions the head boatman merely said, "*Doña Margarita es muy rica y de muy buen corazón.*" [Lady Margaret is very rich and hospitable.]

Accordingly the two men climbed the mountain, which was steep and a half-mile high, and found on its level summit a large,

[91]

well-built plantation of oranges and bananas, plantains and pine-apples. But who might this Doña Margarita be? They discovered she was Mrs. Margaret Brewer from the state of Maine. The lady and her three grown full-blooded American daughters lived in this isolated place—not one white person near—surrounded by 20 Mexican peons and their families, their only security being their brave hearts and strong wills. Bell's astonishment knew no bounds. Had these Americans dropped down from heaven his surprise could not have been greater.

Doña Margarita was rich and a power in the land. The girls would manage the plantation while their mother in a fruit-loaded *bongo* would float with her crew of peons down to Minatitlán. Here she would sell her cargo, purchase supplies, and then steer her boat back to the plantation. She had a magnificent place. But why was she there?

Her husband had been a sea captain from Maine, trading in mahogany. He died at Minatitlán, leaving a cargo and other properties in the country. When his widow came down to settle the estate she was forced to stay so long that she grew fond of Mexico and decided to remain. Seemingly all the Brewers were happy, but on closer observation Bell sensed an air of discontent among the young ladies. This feeling was confirmed when he inquired of their mother where she would find eligible husbands for her daughters.

Early the next morning the two guests said good-bye to their hostesses of the wilderness and drifted down to Minatitlán where they stopped for a day and then went onward to their destination several leagues farther. On the way they passed over a beautiful prairie where Cortés fought one of his early battles on Mexican soil. Chinameca they found to be a large town. Its houses were built in the common style of the country. That is, posts were set in the ground to which canes were tied horizontally and then plastered with mud, the better dwellings being whitewashed. All had thatched roofs.

The old Aztec temple was quite prominent, though small, and rudely constructed of a kind of concrete in the form of a tower.

It was 30 feet square at the base and rose 50 feet to a flat summit of 10 square feet, mounted by a palm-thatched sentry box wherein stood the perpetual watcher for Malinche. On the ground floor was a large room, opening into small compartments on one side, while from the opposite side a stairway ascended to a room above and then with a zigzag turn it led to a higher room, thence in the same way through two more chambers empty and rude to the summit over the fifth floor. Under the stairs on the ground floor was a closet-like place with a small opening. But both Bell and his friend failed to notice this when they visited the temple shortly after their arrival. In the middle of the large room on the first floor stood a pyramidal pile of rough masonry or concrete about four feet high. Its base was six feet square, its top about four square feet. The building was without light or ventilation. Guided by the governor of the town the newcomers inspected it with a burning candle. They gave little attention to *el edificio anciano* except to climb to its top where they saw the Indian looking for Malinche and had a fine view of the surrounding country.

As there were few even nominal Christians in Chinameca, Horace greatly deplored the misfortune of *Fraile* Romero, who was doomed to live here until recalled by his bishop. The governor, or alcalde, with whom the two friends were lodging, was an elderly Indian, soft and benevolent. He declared himself to be a Christian, but he said his people were *muy cabezudo* [very stubborn] about changing their religion.

There had been trouble, he reported, between Chinameca and a neighboring town called Cosaleacaca. Although the two communities were of the same people, an ancient feud had made them mortal foes. On each side blood had long been freely spilt. A short time ago the Chinamecans had invaded the town of Cosaleacaca and committed some great outrage, which the alcalde feared would soon be followed by a gory retribution. As the nearest Mexican authority in that part of the country was only a customhouse officer at Minatitlán, the neighboring Indians would feel no restraint in seeking their revenge. Being unfamiliar with the situation Bell and Romero did not realize the danger until one morning 10 days after they arrival, when the storm burst in demoniac fury and Chinameca was invaded by about 200 raving Cosaleacacans.

Not a firearm was used. Machetes (heavy knives) and clubs were the only weapons. The surprised Chinamecans were mercilessly slaughtered and their homes set afire. Men and boys were sliced into pieces; even women and children suffered mutilation. From the alcalde's house the padre and Horace witnessed many of these frightful crimes, expecting every minute that their place of refuge would be carried by storm and they would be served in the same manner as the Chinamecans. Along toward noon, however, the defenders by dint of desperate fighting drove the enemy out of town. But at four o'clock they came back reinforced and the conflict became more frenzied than before and continued until a night of pitchy blackness threw its mantle over the scenes of devilish cruelty and victory again favored the Chinamecans. How many were killed outright the Major never knew, but he thought there was enough fighting to have butchered half the Indians in Mexico had the combatants fought like the Indians of North America. It seemed to him that he had witnessed more cowardice and cruelty on that day than he thought could possibly belong to the human family.

He and his partner supposed the danger to be over, but they were mistaken. For about nine o'clock that night the Indian mayor came in and informed them that their lives were in peril, since his house and authority could no longer protect them. The cause for the coming wrath was an incident that occurred late in the afternoon. One of the invaders becoming separated from his comrades was chased by some Chinamecans and ran toward the mayor's house. Seeing his plight Father Romero opened the door and beckoned to him. The poor fellow rushed in and was saved. His pursuers would have knocked the door down had not Horace threatened them with his revolver. For this deed of mercy they were both to be murdered. No time should be lost, warned the alcalde, but where were they to go?

The night being dark, as only tropical nights can be, made it impossible to follow the trail that would lead them through the forest and over the prairie to Minatitlán. As the moon would not be up until three in the morning the good alcalde declared their only safety would be for him to conceal them in the temple until the planet appeared. Then he would take them to Minatitlán. So emerging from the back door, preceded by their guide, they reached the old tower after much difficulty and by his direction hid themselves under the stairway in the closet-like place on the first floor. Their departing host promised them that as soon as the moon arose he would return. To be in such a situation was far from pleasant, but they were bound to endure it.

Facetiously Horace suggested to his fellow prisoner that he should have brought some "holy water" to sanctify the infernal place. Whereupon Romero replied that he had and passed him an earthen vessel from beneath his priestly gown. Being thirsty the Major took an exhilarating draft and then restored the flask to the friar, who advised him by a gurgling sound that he likewise knew how to use "holy water."

Soon they heard a great clamor. It grew louder and seemed to be approaching their secret place. As the opening through which they had entered the cubbyhole was small, they were able to close it quickly with rubbish while the noise drew nearer. When it sounded as though it came from the entrance to the temple, they blew out their candle and found themselves in Stygian darkness, but only for a minute, since a throng of Indians now appeared with flaming torches, dragging along two naked brown captives.

Forming into two parallel lines the party, about 20 in number, ceremonially faced the pyramid in the center of the room. The pair of prisoners bound together by neck and heels were dropped helpless on the floor, while two Indians placed on the flat top of the pyramid a dark concave block apparently of mahogany. Two others with an instrument called a *macana* began to remove some adobes from the wall right in front of the terrified white men, who breathlessly watched through the crannies of their improvised barrier and wondered what would happen next.

In a few minutes a niche was exposed and on each side torches were planted revealing an image, the most hideous that the very devils in hell could conceive. Now a team of six more Aztecs stepped out from the lines. One arrayed himself in a scarlet robe and walking up to the image took from its hand a knife, saying something in a sepulchral voice. Instantly the other five seized a prisoner and spread him out on the block, face upward, and held him fast, one at his head, one at each arm, and one at each leg. Then the demon in the red robe deliberately cut out the victim's heart and with a guttural chant dropped it into a steaming cauldron which had been placed before the idol. The body was dropped on the floor and the second prisoner served in the same way. At this a stifled moan escaped the lips of Father Romero and a dizzy, sickening feeling overcame Horace, who must have fainted, for when consciousness returned, the temple was silent as the grave. A cold sweat oozed from every pore in his skin. He thought he had just awakened from a frightful nightmare. But where could he be?

Then he heard footsteps and a voice. The gleam of a candle appeared from the outer room and the alcalde began to pull away the rubbish of their barricade, expressing surprise that they had walled themselves up so suffocatingly. On turning to *Fraile* Romero the Major found him senseless and put the liquor to his lips. Slowly he revived. Then they silently emerged into the large room, which had the same appearance as when they first entered.

"Come on! Hurry!" ordered their guide. So quietly and limply they followed. What with the fresh bracing air and their *aguardiente* they recovered both speech and strength enough to whisper with each other. They realized now that what they had been through was no dream, for each had seen the same sight, detail for detail. But they said not a word about it to the alcalde, who seemed ignorant of what had happened.

A short time later the three men were mounted on gentle ponies provided by the government official and went cantering over the plains to Minatitlán which they reached at breakfast time. On leaving the pair the governor promised the *fraile* to send in his baggage as soon as possible. He appeared glad to get them safely off his hands. In three days their nerves returned to normal. Meanwhile Reverend Romero's luggage came in and they arranged for transportation by *bongo* back up the river. The good father declared that he was returning to Tehuantepec even at the risk of excommunication and back they went. Both agreed to keep in secret the horrible sights they had witnessed in the Aztec temple of Chinameca. "For," said the friar, "it would be a great scandal not only on the government of Mexico but also on the church."

How Padre Romero came out with his bishop Horace never learned, because soon after their return to Tehuantepec he took passage by steamer to San Francisco and never again saw the genial companion of his visit to the birthplace of Doña Marina. He had given up his dream of unveiling the mysteries of southeastern Mexico, for he realized the folly of endeavoring to penetrate its wilds without a large company of fellow explorers and adequate guides.[4]

CHAPTER V

Confined to Quarters

They were the first hot wave of youth too-ready to die,
And they went to war with an air, as if they went to a ball.
... They were much like the men you know,
Under the beards and the strangeness of clothes with a different fit.

s. v. benét, *John Brown's Body*

WHEN the war between the states began and President Lincoln called for volunteers, Horace Bell left Los Angeles for Indiana. On April 27, 1861, he appeared in Indianapolis and began service with the first regiment of infantry organized in his native state. The term of enlistment was for only three months! This unit was named, however, "the Sixth Indiana," since the state having furnished five regiments for the Mexican War did not propose to start a new set of numbers. Recruits arriving from the Indiana towns were marched to the capitol where Adjutant General Lewis Wallace administered the soldier's oath of allegiance. Stepping forward he would close harshly by saying, "You are no longer citizens, but soldiers!"

On the next morning they were ordered to "fall in," and marched to Camp Morton (named for the current governor) on the old state fairgrounds. Here they made their quarters in horse stalls, full of fleas. It was cold in the last of April, but no blankets were at hand. No preparations had been made for their reception. So the good citizens of Indianapolis contributed blankets and comforters—several wagon loads of them. Each soldier was allowed one cover, but some were rather thin. More companies arrived and then the fun began. There was plenty of fiddling, dancing, singing, acrobatics, and each evening a minstrel show.

When the ranks were filled (there were 782 men in all) the Sixth organized and elected its own company and regimental officers! Thomas T. Crittenden of Madison was chosen colonel and

[98]

John Gerber, major. There were 10 regimental officers, among them Horace Bell serving as quartermaster sergeant. The Sixth had many tall men. One out of every ten stood at least six feet, some even six feet, six. (Whence came the vitamins for these Hoosier giants—from the virgin soil?)

Eventually the men received arms and clothing. Their uniform included pants and a close jacket called a roundabout, both being of inferior gray (!) cloth, a big hat and stogy shoes. Each man was given a rubber blanket to lie on or to use for a night's cover. On the march it was rolled up in a knapsack, but not one soldier in a hundred ever learned the art of doing it up properly. For six weeks they stayed at Camp Morton, drilling and being disciplined for the battlefield. Bell's Nicaraguan reputation and title of major had arrived with him. He was conspicuous for his knowledge of skirmish drill and expertness with bayonet and sword.

Their training completed, General George Brinton McClellan came to Indianapolis and reviewed the Sixth Regiment with other troops in his command before they left for western Virginia. It was there they were most needed, for the Confederates controlled that area, although the western part of the state was mostly Federal in feeling. Southern soldiers already occupied Grafton, the junction point of the Baltimore and Ohio railroad, an important thoroughfare in northwest Virginia. On the last day of May the Hoosiers departed for the battlefields by way of Cincinnati.

When the train was starting off Charlie Gavitt hopped on the rear end with his knapsack strapped on his back, covering his quilts and rubber blanket. They were rolled up full width, extending on either side about two feet. The cars being in motion the soldiers were sitting forward. Coming up the aisle from behind, Charlie made a clean sweep of hats with the ends of his bundle, knocking them off in the tobacco spit heavily spattered on the floor. He reached his company seated near the front of the train, but not without receiving the fluent curses of his comrades whose hats he had soiled with tobacco juice.

It was pleasant, riding toward Cincinnati. The men, being in good spirits, chatted and sang. Arriving at five in the evening they paraded proudly through the Ohio town. Citizens crowded the sidewalks and from nearly every house ladies waved handkerchiefs. Marching up Fourth street the regiment came to the home of the brother of Major Robert Anderson, hero of Fort Sumter. The major stood watching at an open window. At once Colonel Crittenden called a halt and facing his men toward the house, he ordered, "Present arms!" The honored officer returned the salute. Then Crittenden spoke out, "Major Anderson, this is the tribute Indiana pays to a brave and deserving officer!" Whereupon a sequence of hurrahs arose from the 800 men. They passed on to another depot and entrained for Camp Dennison, where they bivouacked, not attempting to pitch their tents, merely pulling the canvas shelters up over them for covering.

In the morning the regiment continued across southern Ohio toward Marietta, all along the way receiving ovations. Word was telegraphed ahead that the Indiana boys were "on the warpath and needed cooked provisions." In response people turned out by thousands carrying to the depots basketfuls of bread, butter, pies, sliced ham, dried beef, and great cans of hot coffee which were served by fair young hands. The Sixth stuffed itself and its haversacks. Many of the boys exchanged addresses with these Ohio girls and later received letters from their new friends. At a point on the state's border the train stopped for the night.

On the morrow the Hoosiers bade farewell to Ohio and were ferried across the great river to Parkersburg where they took the Baltimore and Ohio railroad for the interior of western Virginia. On the way thither they rode through many tunnels, one soldier counting 25. The engine stopped once while a trestle destroyed by the enemy was being repaired. Reaching Webster, 100 miles from the Ohio river, the regiment detrained and encamped, attempting for the first time to put up tents.

But the regiment was hardly ready to sleep when four companies were ordered out on a night march, Bell being among them. Under Crittenden's command they left for Philippi, a town 20 miles distant where Colonel G. A. Porterfield's Confederates lay encamped—2,000 of them. They had been burning railroad bridges in that part of the country. Other detachments of Indiana regiments joined Crittenden's men bringing their number up to that of the enemy. They took with them a battery of artillery. Another column of Federals under Colonel B. F. Kelly of western Virginia moved simultaneously from Grafton, not far away, intending to reach the rebels by another road and so prevent their escape. The attack was planned in two moves. Kelly would engage the enemy in their rear while the Indianians struck at their front.

It was a nasty night for a march. A cold rain poured down the whole time. The way was muddy, slippery, and so dark that the soldiers could tell each other apart only by their voices. Leaving his horse at Webster, Colonel Crittenden walked, sharing his men's hardship. They became sorely fatigued in carrying their blankets and quilts which grew heavier, soaked by the rain. One by one these burdens were thrown down. In silence the Hoosiers trudged through the storm, the mud and darkness so checking their progress that when they reached Philippi it was almost dawn. Four was the hour to attack, but Kelly had not come. Anxiously Crittenden awaited him until daylight. Then from his position on a hill he saw the Confederates packing up and opened fire with his battery. Soon Kelly's men arrived on "double-quick." Panic-struck, the rebels broke and ran, leaving everything but their muskets behind.

Now Crittenden hurried his companies down the hill. They passed through a long covered bridge over the Tygart river and reached the courthouse yard where the Southern soldiers had been cooking breakfast. What was left the rugged boys from Indiana ate. This engagement was called the Skirmish at Philippi. Occurring on June, the third, 1861, it was probably the first field action in the Civil War.

It was well for the Northerners that their enemy retreated, for there were not 10 muskets in any company that could have been fired—so wet they were you would have thought they had been thrown in the river. All the people of Philippi had fled. Many left their houses open, so that the hungry invaders walked in and devoured what they could find.

Colonel Crittenden now returned with his men to Webster and on the fifth of June the reunited Sixth Regiment boarded the cars and rode a few miles north to Grafton. On a hill overlooking the place they pitched their tents, naming the camp Madison to honor the Indiana town which had furnished three companies to the regiment. Here they were joined by a unit of artillery. While the Sixth lay at Camp Madison the men ran out of money. Alas, there were no coins to bet on chuck-a-luck. Someone telegraphed the sad news to the governor, who went at once to the bankers of Indianapolis and borrowed money for the Hoosier boys. He sent them each five dollars, deducting that amount from their pay. At once morale picked up and all day long until taps you could hear the rattle of dice in the chuck-a-luck box.

Another inconvenience was the rattlesnakes. The country was full of them. Soldiers on guard in the woods back of camp had to stand on logs or stumps to keep from being bitten.

When the last week of June came the regiment moved back to Philippi. In their new camp on a hill near town they celebrated the Fourth of July. Congressman William Dunne of Indiana honored the soldiers with a visit and delivered a patriotic address. On learning that postage stamps were scarce he graciously franked a few packages of envelopes for the boys before leaving.

Shortly after, a detachment was ordered to go on an expedition to the Buckhannon bridge about 10 miles southwest of camp. Their objective was to ambush a party of Confederate cavalrymen who regularly crossed the bridge on their way to a mill. They carried grain to have it ground into meal to furnish General Garnett's army with bread. Major Gerber headed the Indiana detail, Horace Bell being under his command. Hidden behind laurel bushes that grew at its hither end the Hoosiers waited to annihilate the party whenever it crossed the bridge. They lay there in perfect quiet until well past midnight. Then one restless spirit could endure waiting no longer.

Suddenly Horace rose up from the shrubs exclaiming, "This is all damned foolishness—squatting here. I'm going down the road and drive in Garnett's pickets!" He persuaded Charlie Steele of

Madison to go with him and when the pair was within a few hundred yards of the enemy's picket lines Bell, as his partner afterward told the story, yelled out, "Battalion, halt!" Continuing his commands he marched Charlie back and forth through the brush as though he were a whole battalion. The pickets peered out into the darkness, and not being able to tell the number in Bell's command discharged their guns and ran into camp. Instantly pandemonium broke loose in Garnett's army. Above the din could be heard the voices of officers calling their men into battle formation. Soon regiment after regiment came rushing out across the bridge, artillery rumbling, the hoofs of cavalry horses beating the road. Meanwhile the Hoosiers hid behind the laurels, quaking. It was almost dawn when the last of the Confederates returned to camp, convinced of a false alarm.

In the morning Major John Gerber went back to his colonel, thoroughly angry. Because of Bell he had failed in his mission. So Horace was placed under arrest. In defending his conduct he made matters worse by starting a fight with his own superior officer, but Gerber was too big for him and gave his sergeant a thorough thrashing. This affair put an end to Bell's career in the three-months' service. Fearing his impulsiveness and insubordination Bell's colonel would not allow him to go farther with his regiment on its military adventures. Presumably he was not allowed to leave camp.

But briefly what was the action, the excitement, which Bell missed in not being permitted to accompany his comrades—that for which he must have sorely pined?

The Sixth Regiment of Indiana now marched toward General Garnett's camp 14 miles away. With the rest of its brigade the Sixth pitched its tents on a hill running out from Laurel mountain. It was a central position overlooking the surrounding valleys and hills. Daily their pickets skirmished with the Confederates sheltered below the village of Belington. But though the Indiana batteries gave Garnett's men a terrific shelling, no pitched battle occurred.

Soon General McClellan took over the Federals in western

Virginia and began to drive out the Confederates. He moved on Colonel Pegram's army posted at Rich mountain, compelling that officer with hundreds of his men to come in and surrender. This defeat caused Garnett to evacuate his position and on the night of July 11 decamp with his 6,000 men.

At once the Sixth moved down the hill, possessed his late camp, and being augmented by another regiment followed the retreating army. Rain fell in torrents, turning the road into a bed of mortar. Onward pressed the men of the Sixth, almost at double-quick, while the enemy strained every nerve to outrun them. Over hills and rocks, across creeks and through dense forests Garnett's men fled. Coming to Cheat river the Indianians plunged in, glad to wash off the mud plastered all over them. The stream was crooked and the road through the mountain pass crossed it every few miles. The water came up to their shoulders. The rocks on the bottom were so slippery the worn-out Hoosiers could hardly stand against the swift current. Arm in arm many waded through in couples. Not far ahead they could hear the shouting of Confederate teamsters urging their tired mules onward.

At length General Garnett crossed Carrick's ford at Cheat river and on a rocky bluff stationed his cannon. Covered by thick foliage his men crouched behind a rail fence on the hilltop. When an Ohio regiment came down the road the soldiers in ambush opened fire from the bluff, then turned their artillery upon the Sixth Regiment halting on an elevation just across the river. Though surprised, the Ohioans replied with a volley that sent their enemy again in retreat. Farther on, Garnett made a last attempt to rally his men, but failed. Almost alone in a wheat field, the brave chief lay dead on the ground, shot by some Hoosier's bullet. Near him reclined the lifeless form of a lad from Georgia who had refused to leave his commander. Unfortunate General Robert Selden Garnett! From the first everything worked against him. In the region where he fought, public sentiment opposed the Confederacy. Worse than that—he lacked cavalry, guns, supplies. Yet by a masterly withdrawal he saved his little army outnumbered by McClellan's men six to one.

On the following day Bell's regiment turned their steps northward. At noon they halted but not for dinner—there was nothing to eat. Close by they found a farmhouse but not the kind they knew back in Indiana, for here they could not get a "square meal" for "love or money." A soldier offered the farmer's wife standing by the stove cooking corn cakes a half-dollar for one the size of his hand, but all were sold. How these Indiana boys sighed for their home pantries stored with baked ham, eggs, fried chicken, cakes, and pies! But fortunately not long after, someone drove in a steer. Then Major Gerber, a butcher by trade, shot it with his revolver. Before he could tear the hide fairly off the carcass the soldiers were at work with their knives cutting out great chunks of the warm, quivering beef. There being no salt they sprinkled a few grains of powder over the meat as a substitute to take away the taste of freshness and after broiling devoured it like wolves.

Thus refreshed they rested an hour and then set out for their camp beyond Laurel mountain 20 miles away. During the three days of pursuing the enemy they had traveled 70 miles over the worst roads in the country. A week later they packed up and started for home. Passing through Philippi they reached Webster. Here their hearts turned sick, for they heard the dismal news of the battle of Bull Run! Depressed in spirits they took the train at Grafton which carried them to Bellaire on the Ohio river.

Here Horace Bell was permitted to rejoin his regiment. He accompanied his comrades to Indianapolis and there he was honorably discharged on the second of August, 1861, no word being recorded of his forced inaction during the last weeks of the campaign. Bell never told anyone of his anticlimax—naturally. And we would know nothing of it but for a history of his regiment written by a none-too-friendly comrade.[1]

The campaign in western Virginia brought about certain results. Its prime purpose, the expulsion of Confederates from that area, was accomplished. Incidentally it heightened the military stature of McClellan. In time it led to the admission of a new state, West Virginia, into the Union. As for the hero of our story—he learned a lesson at Buckhannon bridge near Philippi.

[105]

In the month following its mustering out the Sixth Regiment reorganized at Madison, Indiana, for three years of service. Colonel Thomas Crittenden still its commander took the men who remained in camp—about 500—to Louisville, where they entered Kentucky as the first body of troops from the North.

But Horace Bell did not re-enlist with his regiment. His bitter experience had taught him not to serve as a subordinate in the infantry. Rather he chose to be a mounted scout, for as such he would be subject to little discipline. He usually wore no uniform, he had no title, and no close attachment to an organized group. He could act on his own initiative and be as reckless as he pleased— the kind of work adapted to his genius. "I preferred staff service as a scout," Bell wrote later. "It suited me better. I had no small-fry bosses. I had but one boss and he was a general."

CHAPTER VI

Saddle and Spurs

A hurry of hoofs in a village street,
A shape in the moonlight, a bulk in the dark,
And beneath from the pebbles in passing a spark
Struck out by a steed flying fearless and fleet;
That was all! And yet through the gloom and the light
The fate of a nation was riding that night.

LONGFELLOW, *Paul Revere's Ride*

News from Corinth

As a scout of General Lew Wallace, Bell took part in the capture of Forts Henry and Donelson on the boundary between Tennessee and Kentucky. Losing these strongholds General Albert Sidney Johnston concentrated his Confederate army at Corinth, Mississippi, the Union forces following after. Sherman pitched his tents near Shiloh church close to the Mississippi border, Grant settled down not far away, Wallace's division camped at Crump's Landing farther south on the Tennessee river.

In his present situation General Wallace's greatest need was knowledge of the country. His communications with the main Union army being closed, he feared that if he were attacked by a superior force his men would be isolated. So he sent a troop of cavalry toward Purdy, Tennessee, to look for Confederates. In a narrow pass his horsemen were waylaid by bushwhackers and driven back. This convinced Wallace that the bridge on the Mobile and Ohio railroad which he had broken up was now repaired, making it easy for the enemy to attack him from Purdy. Such a possibility required him all the more to keep informed of movements beyond his lines. The work of scouting he gave to Horace Bell, assisted by a soldier named Carpenter. Near sunset on the fourth of April 1862, Bell stepped abruptly into the general's tent, worn out by hard riding.

"Sir, I bring you news," he panted.

"Well, what?" said the chief.

"I picked up some prisoners coming in and turned them over to the provost."

"Oh, is that all?"

"No," answered the scout, "The whole rebel army is on the way up from Corinth."

"How is that?" Wallace asked, rising.

"It is so, sir. They set out this morning early. By now they are all on the road."

"The whole of them, you say? Batteries and all?"

"Batteries and all, sir!"

The general felt the roots of his hair grow hot.

"How strong are they?"

"At least 50,000, sir. There are four corps: Hardee's, Bragg's, Polk's, and Breckinridge's. Hardee has the front, Breckinridge brings up the rear."

The tent grew confining to Wallace. He walked out for air, Bell following.

"Where is General Johnston?"

"With them, sir."

"Whom do you think they have in eye?"

"They are pointed toward Pittsburg Landing, sir."

"And not here?"

"No—Pittsburg Landing. I rode part of the way with some friends in Hardee's corps."

"And they may be looked for—when?"

"One of the bridges on the main road is down and in places the corduroy is afloat. They can't, with all they have to carry, make the distance before tomorrow night."

Wallace then cross-examined Bell, who met him squarely on every point. Yet the general did not believe his own scout, for Johnston he thought could not be ready to fight so soon. In the midst of the quizzing Carpenter rode up to the tent looking excited.

"Good evening, Carpenter," greeted Wallace, "what do you bring?"

Then followed a verification of the first report. The general looked at Bell, who remarked, "Now you see, sir."

Ordering the two scouts to their quarters General Wallace went inside his tent. Dusk coming on he lit a candle and began a note to Grant, reporting the dire news. Suddenly from the outside he heard angry voices. Going to the door of his tent he saw Bell and Carpenter face to face, pistols in hand. He reached the rivals just in time to separate them. Later the general wrote in his auto-biography, "They were desperate men and unflinching. What they quarreled about I never learned."[1]

As soon as Grant received Lew Wallace's note—the former being only three miles away on the opposite side of the Tennessee river—he sent back an order for Bell to verify his report beyond the shadow of a doubt. So the next morning Horace set out, taking with him two companions, a cavalryman and Sanders, a native refugee. Both assistants had volunteered to go, the soldier for adventure, the latter because of his knowledge of side roads and trails. Crossing Snake river they were soon on the enemy's advance line of communication. North of Corinth they talked with solitary soldiers and teamsters, gaining desired information. But Bell wanted further proof. So the party taking still greater chances rode to the rear of the Confederate army and sized up its strength. Luckily they escaped detection. In high glee over their success they turned homeward, crossed Owl creek, and trotted their horses to the Purdy-Shiloh highway.

Sanders had an uncle, Tom Beck, whose plantation touched the road two miles away from Shiloh church. He wanted to stop at his uncle's place, see his relatives and procure a horse. (Beck, a Southern soldier, was away with his company.) While the others went up to the house Bell stayed on the road. Soon a smart-looking mulatto boy slipped up to him, eyes big with fright.

"Is you a Yankee?" he whispered.

"Yes, why?"

"Look at dem 'rebs' down dar!" he warned and disappeared behind a cabin.

Bell looked and saw, not a pistol shot away, an enemy picket resting under a clump of trees, and facing Shiloh stood their vidette. Without thinking he dashed into the grove, firing right and left. Quickly the guard scattered. But one man mounted his horse and was joined by the incoming vidette. Together the pair raced to the woods five miles away with Bell hot after them, Sanders and the cavalryman soon following. Horace had the best horse of the five—Fred Kneffler's big iron-gray. Fred being afraid of him had lent him to Bell to tame. Oh, what a beauty he was! Soon his rider had a revolver at the closer Confederate's back. On command he halted, threw down his arms, and was turned over to Sanders. Before the scouts were halfway to the woods they captured the other picket. Then they recrossed the Snake river and at sunset delivered the prisoners to General Wallace at his headquarters on the steamboat *Diana*.

In the morning Bell had an interview with General Grant and confirmed his first report. Giving the scout a pocket compass to guide him through strange country Grant sent him at once to Jackson, Tennessee, 70 miles away, to discover what Beauregard was doing. Bell learned that this Confederate leader had joined Johnston at Corinth. Spurring his horse he reached at noon the field of Shiloh while the great battle was on. Finding himself at the enemy's rear he flanked the gray army on the left and not being in uniform was taken in by his own troops as a rebel. As a reward for his reconnoitering both Grant and Wallace gave Bell on his request their photographs, which are still preserved; and the future president let him keep the pocket compass as his own. On accepting their praise for his successful expedition Horace replied with his oft-repeated proverb, "Fortune favors fools as well as the brave."[2]

The War Bride

Not long after, Horace Bell for an unknown reason left General Grant in Tennessee and made his way to General George McClellan's army in Virginia. For his service at the battle of Antietam in September 1862, the latter officer procured for him an interview with Edwin M. Stanton in Washington. The Secretary of War proposed sending him to New York City to recruit sharpshooters for General Banks' expedition in Louisiana. In accepting Stanton's offer Bell made a momentous decision.

When he arrived in New York he had with him a letter of introduction written by a comrade to his parents in the city. After this was presented the new friends gave him a party to which they invited among others a young lady named Georgia Herrick. She was 17 years old and being an orphan lived with her uncle and aunt, Mr. and Mrs. Cornelius D. Robinson. Their house displayed its brown stone front on Thirty-fourth street between Eighth and Ninth avenues. The uncle (related by marriage) was a commission merchant, who had his place of business at 598 Broadway between Broom and Bleecker streets.

In preparing for the party Miss Herrick had penciled her eyebrows to make them more striking, and in so doing she unwittingly gave Bell a chance to tease her. During the evening he slyly remarked, "Excuse me, miss, but you have a little soot on your forehead." Then he soberly drew forth his handkerchief and gently wiped off the make-up. Naturally this made the lady of fashion indignant. But her anger soon softened into interest. For Horace now in his thirty-second year fell quickly in love with Georgia and a cyclonic courtship followed.

The Robinsons, however, vigorously objected. Being people of means they wanted their niece to marry an established and well-to-do New Yorker, not a poor Westerner from the recruiting station. The aunt had habitually impressed her social views on her charge by saying, "Position is everything, my dear!" and bringing her palms down in a characteristic gesture she would repeat, "Position is everything!" It was not strange that she felt as she did. For when Albert Edward, the Prince of Wales, visited New York late in 1860 as "Lord Renfrew" and was entertained by the fashionables of the city he had danced with her niece, and the prince then in his nineteenth year had snipped off one of her long black curls.

It was because of Mrs. Robinson's managing that Georgia was now engaged to marry an aristocratic Knickerbocker named Eugene Townsend. He was a member of the Zouaves, the city's crack regiment of volunteer infantrymen. At the outbreak of the Civil War they had been organized by Colonel Elmer Ellsworth, who drilled his men in the manner of the French Zouaves, specializing in the use of the bayonet. Their brilliant uniform was adapted from that of their Gallic prototypes, who dressed much like the fighters of an Algerian tribe. The dash and valor of the New York Zouaves, their masterly precision and unanimity in drill, as well as their unique costume, fascinated the public. More than 1,000 brave fellows joined this unit, which went to Washington to be mustered into combat duty, becoming one of the first three-year regiments entering the war.

An old photograph shows Eugene Townsend wearing his gay dress uniform. A score of brass buttons on his coat spread open to display as many buttons on his vest, loops and diamonds of broad bright braid on his sleeves, a jaunty flat-top cap encircled by gold braid, a sword at his hip, and wide blue trousers all combine with a long drooping mustache and goatee to make him appear as the ideal romantic hero.

But no amount of buttons and braid could match Bell's Spanish gallantry. And so the debutante lost her heart to a Californian. The problem of opposition the lovers solved by running off to St. John's Methodist church on Forty-first street a few blocks away where they were married in secret. This was on the fourteenth of December 1862, the day of the battle of Fredericksburg.

When Georgia left her room forever she laid on her pillow the marriage license, which the maid carried in the morning to the foster parents at breakfast. They were furious—particularly the aunt. They would not let her come back. Never again did she see them. This was a lifelong sorrow for Georgia.[3]

Somewhere in the city Horace found a boarding and rooming house where he placed his war bride and left to where duty called him. Because of his fluent Spanish and his service in Nicaragua with Cubans, Stanton sent him to Cuba as a secret agent. Having run the blockade at Savannah, the Confederate cruiser *Retribution* was supposed to have gone to the West Indies to receive armament from an English vessel. His task was to ascertain where the transfer of guns and ammunition would be made. Finding no clues after two weeks in Havana he boarded the steamer *Columbia*, sailed down to New Orleans now held by the Federals, and reported to General Nathaniel Prentiss Banks.

The Bridal Tour

In April 1863 General Banks made his sweep through western Louisiana. Leaving his location at New Orleans he led his army westward to Brashear City (now called Morgan City). Here they crossed Grand lake and marched up bayou Teche and the Opelousas river to Simmesport on the Atchafalaya. From this leisurely stream they passed to the Mississippi river north of Port Hudson and settled down to a siege of that great Confederate stronghold.

On this expedition Banks captured great spoils—thousands of hogsheads of sugar, barrels of molasses, bales of cotton, multitudes of horses and cattle. These were all sent to the rear, transported from Berwick's bay over Grand lake, and distributed at points along the Southern Pacific line in vast quantities until they could be carried by rail into New Orleans. The general sent Horace Bell to a place called Tigerville, 60 miles west of New Orleans and 20 miles east of Berwick's bay, to take charge of this captured property. The 176th New York regiment of nine-months' men was camped at Tigerville on the railroad to guard the booty.

In the meantime his bride had followed him to Tigerville where he found a house near bayou Black. So after only a few months of separation the young couple was reunited. They were having a pleasant time in a lovely country among friendly people. Some were Anglo-Saxon planters, others were Creoles, many were Cajuns, descendants of the Acadian French in Louisiana. Work on the plantations had been resumed, trade with New Orleans was free, and except for a few military camps one would hardly think a war was in progress.

To relieve Port Hudson and recapture the spoils that Banks had taken, Confederate General Richard Taylor now swooped down on the shores of the Mississippi, marched farther south to

[113]

the towns of Grosse Tete and Plaquemine, thence eastward to Donaldsonville on the great river. All the earthworks along the Mississippi at this point were garrisoned by Negro soldiers, who made almost no defense. Taylor's army then swept the railroad from where it crossed bayou Lafourche over to its junction with Berwick's bay.

One Sunday morning news came that a Confederate army had come in between Tigerville and New Orleans. So panicstruck were the Northern troops along the railroad that they gave up at first summons. But Horace did not intend to surrender if he could help it.

Accordingly he procured a crew—all good Negroes—and an adequate boat. With his wife and her servant, a strapping Irish-woman named Ellen, he started out from bayou Black hoping they could get to Berwick's bay and there board a Northern gunboat. The first place they reached on their journey was a Federal forti-fication within three miles of the bay. It was a large earthwork defended by Negroes. Bell thought he would stop at the fort and take part in its defense. But just when his boat reached the shore a fusillade opened on the opposite side of the bulwark and a great rebel yell split the air. At once the colored troops threw down their arms and came pouring out of the place headed for the water. In a few minutes the Confederates appeared on the parapets open-ing fire on the fleeing guardsmen and on Bell's party. The bullets flew thick and fast over the boat, sometimes splashing the water near it. But its occupants got away as fast as they could, heading their craft to a shelter on the opposite shore and around the point of an island. Except those who were killed or drowned all the gar-rison was captured.

Pushing on to Berwick's the Bell group got there just in time to see the last departing gunboat go sailing down the bay at top speed. And then the battle of Brashear City began. Having cap-tured the fort at Boeuf the rebels pushed rapidly forward and killed or captured all the troops at Berwick's bay. They were white men, most of them belonging to the 176th New York regi-ment, whose gallant commander, Captain Trotter, made a bitter resistance and lost his life. Some Connecticut soldiers escaped in *pirogues* [canoes] and fled after the gunboats. The action of the sailors was contemptible, since they could have saved the garrison. But they steamed away to New Orleans, not even attempting to pick up a single refugee.

Such was Georgia Bell's bridal tour. It was the first time she had ever heard a hostile cannon fired or even a whistling bullet—and for nearly five months she had been pregnant.

The campaign ended and Taylor possessed the railroad and Tigerville. The gunboats being gone Bell was now left to his own resources. So he ordered his crew to row back to bayou Black to the plantation of Mr. Boudro, a Cajun. As the Negroes preferred to return to the plantations where they belonged, Horace picked up another crew. This was composed of three Confederate deserters who wanted to go with him, three other men, and an old German familiar with the water course, who conducted them down to Shell island at the mouth of the Atchafalaya river. Here was a lighthouse station where Captain Jacobs, an old Norwegian seaman and Union sympathizer, lived with his wife in a comfortable house. Late at night the Bells knocked at his door and were warmly welcomed. How good it was to enter after being in the skiff for 20 hours!

The island was a shell mound of two or three acres. In front of the house glittered the great bay of Atchafalaya. Behind, a swamp covered with high grass stretched afar. In the morning three large *pirogues* arrived filled with Union soldiers escaping from Berwick's bay. They were nine-months' men having only six weeks more to serve in the army. They landed and made themselves at ease. Horace was glad to welcome them. It would not be long, Captain Jacobs told his visitors, before the rebels would send a boat down to pick up stragglers. Consequently Bell laid a plan to capture their vessel. The landing on the island was an open space of less than a hundred feet, flanked with swamp grass over 10 feet high and with timber. Seeing that they had arms and plenty of cartridges he proposed to the fugitives that they construct some barricades behind the high grass. Then when the steamer came to land they could open fire and demand her surrender. This should be easy, for probably her guard would be small. To this scheme the soldiers agreed and constructed two little forts in the grass.

But during the night the runaways held a conference and decided to go back up the bay and surrender. So early in the morning, after having their coffee and hardtack the men started to pack their things in the *pirogues*, preparing to leave. Horace begged and protested and Captain Jacobs assured them the capture would be easy, promising to pilot them afterwards to New Orleans. But to reason was hopeless. They had determined to give up. Then came Georgia Bell, who was only 18, and tried to shame them. This too was futile. Then she threatened that if they did the cowardly thing they proposed, she would report them to General Banks when she reached New Orleans and he would send them to Ship island, the military penal camp. But the nine-months' soldiers could not be deterred and as the tide was running in, away they went, paddling up the river.

There were now eight men left on the island. One of them assured the rest that he knew the coast so well that if he had a good craft he could conduct the party safely to New Orleans. There was a large bateau, Jacobs assured them, concealed in a slough about a mile up toward Vermilion bay. If they could get that he thought it would do for such a voyage. As the hostile vessel had not yet appeared, Bell took the pilot and another man to find the flat-bottomed boat. While they were gone, a stern-wheeler came in, about nine in the morning, bearing a guard of six Confederates. They were making a reconnaissance to pick up boats and soldiers. Hiding in the high grass the men on the island escaped capture. When Bell and his friends returned with the bateau the steamer had left after taking on board Captain Jacobs as pilot and also Mrs. Bell and Ellen as prisoners. The sailors, as it was later revealed, were bound for Caillou bay 30 miles southeastward, intending to capture certain Northern schooners loaded with sugar.

On hearing of his wife's absence Horace was naturally annoyed, but not greatly worried. For he believed that the American crew would treat their captives respectfully. He recalled that during all his experience in the war he had never known of a woman being mistreated by either side. "Americans," as he afterwards wrote, "don't war on women. They always protect them." The Southerners had taken the ladies on board, so he learned from Mrs. Jacobs, to prevent information from getting out regarding their steamer's course.

In three days they returned to Shell island having captured and carried some sugar to Berwick's bay. The steamer landed for a few minutes to allow Captain Jacobs to greet his wife and let Georgia and Ellen get off. While it was there Horace hid in the tall grass to escape capture. Fully three weeks were the refugees on the island. Every day or two the steamer piloted by Jacobs would come down and watch at the mouth of the river for Union gunboats. Sometimes it would lie at the island all night and whenever it docked Jacobs would tell his wife all the military news from Berwick's bay, which she passed on to Horace.

One Saturday afternoon Bell could see gunboats in the offing, but they were not coming in. Apparently they lacked a pilot for the mouth of the Atchafalaya. Formerly the channel had been staked; piles driven down and surmounted by barrels had marked the crooked channel running through the mud flats. But these the Confederates had pulled up, leaving nothing to mark the way. As the boats were not coming in, Bell concluded he would go to them. Stepping into a skiff he rowed to the mouth of the river a mile away expecting to see the lights of the gunboats. They were still a mile off. Because of the current he could not get back to the island in the darkness. Therefore on finding a stranded cottonwood tree lodged on a mud flat he drew his boat beside it and tied up for the night.

Early in the morning he espied a gunboat, so he thought, and rowed toward it. But when he came alongside, it turned out to be an enemy blockade runner. How she had slid past the gunboats and reached the river's mouth was a mystery. Bell went to the captain and told him that he was a Southern picket stationed at Shell island—that Union gunboats were lying within a mile and he had been out all night watching them. He stayed on board and while the runner was sailing past Shell island he cut his boat loose and rowed home.

It was then daylight and from the lookout station he saw the Northern gunboats in the same position of the day before. After breakfast he hopped into a skiff and pulled toward them. They were floundering in the mud flats. Reaching the flagship he reported to Captain Johnson. Many of the crew were in the cockpit suffering from wounds caused by sharpshooters when the boat recently ran through a blockade on the Mississippi. Bell informed the captain that General Taylor had immense stores of captured supplies which he was trying to get across the Atchafalaya. He urged him to push on and save all that had not been crossed over.

As Captain Johnson could not find the way into the river, Bell told him of a pilot named Bill Ridden living on the coast 10 miles from Shell island. He was a Union man and lately had visited in secret the lighthouse station. If the captain would give him a crew Bell promised to bring back the pilot. This being done, the next morning at sunrise with Ridden at the wheel of the flagship the gunboats entered the river, stopping long enough at Shell island to receive the latest news. Mrs. Jacobs relayed the report of her husband that great consternation prevailed at Berwick's bay. The enemy lacked transportation to cross the river and they had heard that Union gunboats were coming. Accordingly Captain Johnson pushed forward with all the steam he could raise and at three o'clock he saluted Taylor's rear guard with some well-directed shots.

From the gunboats the sailors could see the disordered ranks of his retreating army, also white flags floating over Brashear City and smoke pouring out from some of the buildings which had been ignited. Said Captain Johnson to Bell, "I will appoint you provost marshal if you will go on shore and organize a guard to save the property." Before dark this was done and the flames extinguished.

Early the next morning Horace mounted a horse and started from Brashear City to the fort three miles off, the place where a few weeks before his boat had been fired upon. On the way he met a column of 250 Texans who had been cut off from the army.

Their commander carrying a white flag said they were going up to surrender, for they knew Union gunboats were in the bay and they could not escape. Bell told them he had purposely come down to accept their submission. But actually he had not even heard of them. He did not intend to have 250 mounted and armed Texans ride into Brashear City and make prisoners of all the Union men as they could easily do. Therefore he compelled them to leave their guns on the roadside and led them into town. He then hurried over to Captain Johnson, who sent two crews to carry the stacked carbines to the gunboats.

Since there were 100 paroled prisoners on the police force and 400 disarmed rebels at freedom in the same town, the Union soldiers were in grave danger. Accordingly Bell procured horses and started for the Lafourche crossing on the railroad, the nearest place to any Federal center. On the following day he returned to the bay with sufficient reinforcements.

During Bell's absence Captain Johnson had sent a light tug down to Shell island and on his return he found his wife and Ellen. They rejoiced over their reunion and the protection of Federal guns. The thrilling adventure had now closed. Though it was a strain on all concerned everything worked together for the good of the Union cause. Bell's escape from capture and his forced residence on Shell island resulted in his finding a pilot to bring the gunboats in. Otherwise they could not have reached Brashear City. Bell's knowledge of affairs at the bay caused Captain Johnson to push forward and not only save the town from burning but to capture it with huge military supplies.

Vividly for the rest of her life Georgia Bell remembered her bridal tour. In telling the romantic story she never failed to praise the Confederate officers of the steamer that took her away. She warmly declared that she had never been treated with more delicate courtesy than she received from these Southerners.

A Message to General Banks

Against his better judgment General Nathaniel Banks was ordered early in 1864 to move up the Red river of Louisiana and invade the cotton-growing sections of that state, as well as those in Arkansas and Texas. By the middle of March his army had taken Fort DeRussy and occupied Alexandria in central Louisiana. At Mansfield farther west the retreating Confederate troops under General Taylor halted and turning on the Federals drove them back in confusion. So ended the expedition.

Out from Washington had hurried General Edward R. S. Canby to relieve Banks and endeavor to save his army from ruin. With less than 2,000 troops scraped together from the defenses of New Orleans Canby now lay at Acklen's plantation opposite the mouth of Red river with gunboats and a fleet of transports. Banks was supposed to be at Alexandria with his unarmored vessels anchored above the rapids, the water being too low for them to pass over. Far down on Banks's line of retreat Polignac, a Confederate general commanding a Texas division, had seized and fortified a position, his object being to intercept Banks, place him close to Taylor's army, and thus bring about his surrender or the destruction of his force. For two weeks the trapped general had not been heard of. As events later showed he was well advanced on his retreat, being harassed on all sides by the victorious troops of Taylor. It was now the middle of May.

Hearing that Horace Bell had been in central Louisiana Canby asked him if he could find someone who could make his way to Banks with a message. "General, I am the very man to do that," responded Horace and on the next morning he started. He carried a paper signed by the military police permitting him as a civilian to go up Red river for the pretended purpose of buying cattle. Wearing a Mexican hat wrapped around with a silver snake he took with him a Mexican saddle, bridle, and spurs, as well as a revolver, expecting to procure a horse later. The message he bore to Banks was that Canby would take his flotilla to Simmesport, the point on the Atchafalaya river that the former would strike on his retreat to the Mississippi. Under no condition was Banks to give up and Canby would assist him in crossing the river. The latter was gravely apprehensive that the harassed general would surrender his army of 30,000, his gunboats, steamers, and transportation trains, thus ruining the Union cause in the southwest.

Going on board the Natchez packet *Reindeer* Bell crossed the Mississippi and debarked at Red river landing. He had scarcely stepped off the boat when a squad of Confederate cavalry seized and led him to their camp nearby where the rebels were watching the enemy across the river. Bell showed his pass to the captain and told him he was a Californian buying cattle for the New Orleans market. The officer being himself a Californian believed his story and was ready to let him go when a civilian coming into camp remarked that he had seen Bell in the gulf city wearing the uniform of a Federal. This changed the situation. So the captain after apologizing for not being able to furnish a horse sent him under guard to Confederate headquarters at bayou Yellow.

It was 15 miles to Simmesport and three miles more up bayou des Glaises to the main camp. The two troopers rode their horses while Horace tramped through the dust. With profuse regrets they lamented subjecting a gentleman of polite bearing to such hardship and inconvenience. After crossing the river the older guardsman returned and the other, named Pancoast Rochelle, went on with his prisoner toward bayou Yellow.

Bell was determined to take any chance to escape. Accordingly he tried to ease the fatigue of walking by resting his hand on the pommel of his keeper's saddle, intending to fling himself on the horse behind its rider and tumble him off. But Pan was too smart for that and kept the captive's hands off the saddle. In the moonlight the two reached the bayou, which was about 70 feet wide, shallow, and sluggish. From the opposite shore they could hear the rumble and rustle of a great military encampment. On the hither side lay a small flatboat. At the command to get in, Bell walked to the far end and sat down on the gunwale. Pancoast led his horse aboard, cast loose the moorings, and commenced poling the boat across. On reaching the middle of the bayou the guard came forward and in setting his pole found the water deeper than he had expected. His carbine bothered him. So he unslung it and laying it near the prisoner's feet, he commenced poling toward the other end of the boat.

In a flash Bell picked up the rifle. He could easily have tapped his keeper on the head with it. But he did not. He would be ashamed all his life if he struck the young fellow without positive necessity. Instead he whispered to Pan as the boy turned his back toward him, "If you open your mouth I'll knock your brains out! You push this boat back and if you hesitate one instant, you're a dead man!"

Rochelle obeyed. Bell ordered, "Get out and hold the rope. Pull the boat up until I get ashore," all the time menacing him, lest he should fail to comply. The guard held the boat while Bell led the horse on shore, still keeping him covered with the carbine. Stepping back some 15 feet the scout mounted and Pan exclaimed, "For God's sake! Mr. Bell, you are not going to take my horse and carbine both, are you?"

"Why, sir," said Bell raising his voice above the noise of the camp sounding in his ears like the roar of Niagara, "I am the biggest Yankee that ever went through these woods. Do you suppose I would let a contemptible little 'Johnny Reb' like you march me into camp?" At once he waved a good-bye and rode off toward the Atchafalaya. Then Pan began to bawl. Being still in his teens the boy had committed the blunder of not making his captive do the work.

But Horace did not go far toward the river. Instead he cut across the field to the edge of a swamp where he was safe for a time and able to reflect on what to do. But soon he moved on. Feeling his way in the dark past the marsh he reached bayou Yellow, crossed over it by swimming 20 feet, flanked the great camp of General Polignac, and came out on the road to Alexandria. By good fortune he had surmounted all obstacles and was on his way to find General Nathaniel Banks in his condition of threatened disaster.

Pushing along the Alexandria road he met several courier parties during the night and when challenged he would dash past with the answer, "A courier for General Polignac! The Yanks are coming!" Shortly before dawn Bell ran against a camp and consequently flanked out into the swamp, wrapped his hands and face in moss as a protection against mosquitos, lay down at the foot of a tree, and slept. At daylight he was awakened by firing. It was Banks pushing his way against the obstructing Confederates. Horace waited until the Federal flank had passed sufficiently to let him drop into the rear and be picked up as a rebel. Bell told who he was, demanding that he be taken at once to the general. To him he delivered his message. Banks was greatly pleased, for he had no idea of meeting assistance at Simmesport.

Two days later at four in the afternoon the retreating army reached bayou Yellow where a terrific battle followed. It was insignificant as compared with the great military dramas of the war, yet many men on that beautiful May day lost their lives. General A. J. Smith's Sixteenth army corps loaned to Banks by General Sherman (they were all Western fighters) carried the position and held it until Banks' bedraggled Nineteenth corps plodded its weary way to the Atchafalaya river, arriving near sundown. According to his promise General Canby was there and formed a bridge of steamboats over which the retiring troops passed in safety.

At the western end of the line of boats stood General Banks with his staff and Horace Bell, when Canby presented his order to remove the unsuccessful leader. Seeing Bell, Canby remarked, "Well, you seem to have made the trip," and Horace answered proudly, "Yes, sir, I delivered your message to General Banks and he can tell you when, how, and where." On returning to New Orleans Canby assumed command of the military division of the gulf. He made Horace Bell an honorary member of his staff and chief of his Trans-Mississippi scouts.

Matching Wits with Magruder

It was now September in 1864. Grant was fighting in Virginia, Sherman preparing for his march to the sea, and Canby struggling to gain the division of the Trans-Mississippi. This comprised all the states bounded on the east by the great river from St. Louis to New Orleans, and also Texas. In Arkansas General Fred Steele had an army to protect the road to St. Louis against a northern advance of the rebels.

On the Confederate side General Kirby Smith with headquarters at Shreveport commanded the Trans-Mississippi forces. General Simon Bolivar Buckner established at Alexandria controlled western Louisiana, while General John Bankhead Magruder, the great strategist, faced Canby on the eastern front and Steele on the northern.

The Atchafalaya formed a line between the opposing armies. Running parallel with the Mississippi out of Red river it empties into the Gulf of Mexico about 120 miles west of the Mississippi, passing through in its course Grand lake. The western bank of this dividing stream Buckner covered with a cloud of cavalry to prevent communication across the line and to mask Confederate movements.

At the post of Morganza, about 20 miles down the Mississippi from the mouth of Red river, hard-fisted General Lawler of Illinois commanded 12,000 Union soldiers, mostly colored. Of white troops there were the Second and Fourteenth of New York, the First Texas cavalry, the Twenty-fourth Indiana, and a Kentucky regiment of infantry—also Marlin's field battery and many gunmen for the large cannon in the earthworks. All these men made a formidable army. They comprised Canby's disposable force to be sent wherever occasion demanded. In and near New Orleans he had only a sufficient number of troops to occupy defenses and perhaps 8,000 men besides.

The object of Magruder, the Confederate strategist, was to pretend an assault on New Orleans so that Canby would weaken his support of Steele in Arkansas. Then the Southerners could crush Steele and move on St. Louis. Rumors came to the Federals that an enemy force using skiffs would pass over Grand lake, go through bayou Plaquemine into the Mississippi, row down the river 50 miles, land a short distance above the city, and enter it from the rear by way of the railroad. Magruder played to make Canby believe that such an expedition was in progress. All over western Louisiana there were many Union spies, but so vigorously did Buckner guard the line that it was impossible to learn from them if the rumors were true. Numerous men and women in the guise of smugglers, cotton buyers, and Southern sympathizers were sent up Red river but never came back. Some were shot, others imprisoned.

Being extremely worried about the situation General Canby sent for Bell. "What can be done!" exclaimed the distressed chief. "No one can go beyond the Atchafalaya and return, and the case is urgent."

"General," responded Horace, "I will go to Alexandria and will come back and tell you all about it."

"But how?" queried Canby. "Just as soon as you put your foot on the west bank of the Atchafalaya you will be arrested and that will be your end."

"Sir, if you will send a sufficient force to pass me beyond the enemy lines, I will take my chance. My tactics are different from those of other scouts. I never try to talk my way through—that means failure. My tactics, sir, are to ride as far as possible and if molested, then to ply boot and spur. That was my way when I scouted for General McClellan and General Grant and I have never failed."

Whereupon Canby sat down and wrote this order still to be found in the archives of the War Department: "To go to Morganza, pass beyond the lines, proceed to Alexandria, observe the military situation, and then fall back in and drift down with the rebel army on its march southward. And when you reach their front, pass through the lines as best you can and report to these headquarters as soon as possible."

Canby also ordered General Lawler stationed at Morganza to furnish the scout with sufficient force to place him in the rear of the enemy's lines. Lawler gave him the First Texas cavalry and Marlin's Massachusetts battery. At once they started to Simmesport on the Atchafalaya, reaching there an hour before sundown. They opened a lively firing at the enemy across the river to distract attention and kept it up till pitchy darkness dropped a concealing curtain.

In the First Texas cavalry there were two companies of Mexicans. Near midnight Bell took one of them and rode about a mile

[125]

down the stream, made a raft on which he placed his riding gear, and launched himself alone and without a horse on the dark bosom of the turbulent river. On the opposite side ran a road along the bank through heavy cottonwood timber. Beyond the road and woods he would be safe for the night.

Before crossing Bell had arranged with Captain Falcon, who commanded the Mexicans, that when he got safely over and under cover he would light a match as a signal, which Falcon, if he saw it, would answer in like manner. There was grave danger that the enemy would follow the cavalry down the stream and quietly bag the scout upon landing. Noiselessly he passed over. Silently he removed the saddle and bridle, then laid them on the ground. For 10 minutes he waited and listened and then recrossed the road. Not a sound disturbed the stillness of the night—not even the clank of a saber or the tap of a horse's hoof from the Mexicans across the river. He thought they had ridden away while he was crossing the water. He stepped behind a large cottonwood, struck a match, and held it forth. It blazed brightly and was answered from the opposite bank. Softly he stole to his saddle beyond the road. Soon there came to his ears the clatter of cavalry moving. It was the Mexicans riding back, cheering his first success with one irrepressible *viva*.

Alone in the dark woods Bell prepared to pass the time until morning. Placing a piece of mosquito netting about his face for protection he fell into a doze, forgetful of the enemy nearby. Daylight came. After a meager breakfast on hardtack he picked up his riding gear and walked obliquely through the woods toward Red river. This would bring him to the rear of the supposed rebel troops on bayou des Glaises. In an hour's time he struck open country, a large abandoned plantation lying a half-mile in width. Standing with his back to the woods and facing the bayou along which ran the road to Alexandria, he discerned obliquely to his right a camp of Confederate cavalry more than a half-mile away. Alone in the rear of the enemy Bell was fully armed and equipped for action—except that he lacked a horse. For that need he resolved to draw upon the Confederacy. He would take one from the enemy camp.

The nearest point of observation which he could safely gain was about 600 yards from the right of the line of bivouacs. Here he hid all day. The time passed slowly, seeming like 10 years. Fortunately there were no guards in the rear of the lines of wagons and picketed horses. Carefully he selected a spot where he could operate. Near midnight he took up his things, moved to that place, halted, listened, observed, then laid down the saddle and bridle. Into the group of horses he tiptoed. In the darkness he picked out a good one, guided only by his sense of touch. Unobserved he led the horse out and very deliberately bridled and saddled him. All this was done as calmly as a farmer harnessing an animal to a plow. But when Horace was ready to mount he was startled by a great thumping noise—the beating of his own heart. It alarmed him.

Mounting he rode off and was soon on his way to Alexandria, following the bank of bayou des Glaises. It was 40 miles to a town called Moreauville and about 50 more to Alexandria. There was, however, a cut-off road through the swamp passable at low water, but inundated when the Mississippi ran high. Over it General Banks had marched when retreating. Bell proposed to shorten the distance to Alexandria by taking the cut-off. But in the darkness he missed it and was well on his way when he noticed his mistake. It was highly important to get beyond Moreauville before daylight. In this he failed and nearly lost his life.

Warm and cloudy was the night and sometimes a drizzle of rain fell. He became intensely sleepy. And he had no made tea. Always he carried a package of tea in his saddle pocket and on finding a chance prepared a strong brew, filled his canteen, and as long as it lasted he was proof against sleep. But tonight he did not dare either to stop or to light a fire for boiling water. For his life's sake he could not keep awake. Spurring his horse into a full run he would still go to sleep. Dismounting he strove by rapid walking to shake off the stupor. He tried chewing dry tea leaves. No use. He slept and slept as he rode—couldn't keep awake. Then he dreamed. Suddenly he awoke from a nightmare of apprehension so horrible that it dispelled all desire for sleep.

How far on his night journey of 40 miles he had ridden he could form no idea. But when daylight came he had reached the ruins of a sugar plantation burned by Banks in the previous May. A solitary cabin was inhabited by a lonely Negro. Bell woke him up and learned it was four miles to Moreauville. Fortunately the old man, who was talkative and friendly, had some corn and fodder. Taking the horse into a corner of the ruined sugarhouse they fed and watered him. He was a fine animal and but for his rider's overpowering sleep could have carried him 60 miles through the night instead of 35. The horse being cared for, the colored host made a fire and started the pot to boil, while the scout lay down on a rude bench. In two minutes he was sound asleep. An hour later he woke up, the sun was shining bright, and a breakfast of eggs, corn bread, and strong tea was ready. When Bell had barely finished eating there came a sudden clatter of horses' feet. Right then his recent nightmare ran across his mind and there fell upon him a great sense of danger.

Drawing one of his revolvers he stepped to the front door, opened it. At the same instant six men entered the cabin by the back door. There must have been a dozen troopers in this squad of Confederate cavalry. But for the moment's advantage gained by the premonition of his dream he would have surrendered. In front of the cabin were three or four mounted men and as many riderless horses. With a tiger's spring Horace landed astride a horse, drove spurs into his sides—dashed away like a thunderbolt. Before the troopers could recover from surprise and fire a shot Bell was 40 yards off. Then began the clatter of pursuit and the whistling of bullets past the scout, but as usual in a chase high in the air. It sounded like sweet music to his ears, for he had escaped a great peril.

The horse he had leaped on was a thoroughbred, a racer and lean—but without a saddle. For two miles up the road, the bayou on one side, a board fence on the other, the distance growing greater every instant between pursued and pursuers, the race kept up. Finally Bell came to an intersecting lane into which he plunged, a minute later entering a jungle of trees and canebrakes—for the present safe. He drew rein and rode leisurely for perhaps a mile through the woods until he struck a trail and met a bright-looking mulatto riding a Confederate cavalry horse with saddle and trappings.

Horace arrested the astonished young man, marched him into the woods out of sight of the road, and asked him who he was and where he was going. He answered that he was a body servant belonging to a Confederate officer and was going to a still house to have some canteens filled with rum, that his master's company was at Moreauville and since the day before had been hunting Yankees. "De country's full of dem, dressed in Confederate uniform, and whenever dey is caught dey shoots 'em!" This remark explained to Bell the danger which he had eluded. Resolving to make the most of the situation Bell whispered to him:

"See here, I'm a Yankee!"

"For de Lawd's sake! Is you one of dem?" he gasped, his eyeballs protruding.

"No, my good fellow, I am not a spy but a Union scout, come all the way from New Orleans to find out what the 'rebs' are doing and I want you to help me. We are fighting for your freedom and you ought to help us."

"What is it you want me to do for you? I'd just die to help you," said the mulatto.

Bell then told him what had happened and that he wanted his saddle and canteen and his guidance through the woods to the Alexandria road far beyond Moreauville. He readily assented and Bell changed the saddle to his own horse. The new-found friend led the way, the scout feeling safe in his guide's hands, for when he said, "Cap'n, you can trust me, I'se Union to de backbone," such honest intelligence beamed from his face as gave perfect assurance.

For more than six hours they pursued their way through the woods, skirting Moreauville, crossing several roads, one leading to Confederate headquarters at Evergreen. At about three o'clock in the afternoon the colored man placed Bell safe on the Alexandria road 12 miles beyond Moreauville, right where he could have been had he not slept and loitered during the night. But this may have been fortunate because, according to his companion, the Confederates were so vigilant that he could not have passed through Moreauville. On parting from Bell the generous guide remarked, "Now you's safe, suh. None of dem fellows who jumped you will come dis way. You can go right along."

Horace ambled on 10 miles farther, but became so fagged out he decided to rest overnight and reach Alexandria on the following day. He was dreadfully hurt from his ride on a barebacked horse, so much so that the blood had run down into his boots from the lacerations on the inside muscles of his thighs. Procuring some tallow and raw cotton he plastered his wounds as best he could, got a poor supper at a plantation, fed and groomed his horse, and went to sleep.

On the road the next morning his suffering continued. For the first mile or two it was like sitting on a red-hot stove. But a man never knows what he can endure until he is subjected to ordeals from which there is no escape. After riding five or six miles farther he began to feel better and started galloping along growing jubilant over his prospects when he came to a squad of Confederate cavalrymen who had halted for breakfast and were going in the same direction as himself. He rode up to the officer and bade him "good morning." The lieutenant wanted to know where he was going and to what command he belonged. The Union scout of course would not tell him; consequently the Southerner said he would have to take him to headquarters unless he gave a better account of himself. (Bell was riding armed like a soldier but wore no uniform.) He would not lie for fear of being caught in a falsehood. Instead he answered, "That is just where I want to go."

The squad jogged on with the stranger until a long-haired Texan suggested, "If we go by the still house we may catch a deserter and also get some Louisiana rum." So making a detour the group came to a place where a vile kind of liquor was made from sugarcane. Then the question arose as to how to get the rum as none of the detachment had any money except Confederate bills and it would take a thousand dollars' worth of them to buy a canteenful. Horace had some coin, more than it would have been good for him had these fellows found it out.

The soldiers began dickering with the owner of the still but could effect no trade. "Suppose," said Bell, "you could get coin, how much would it cost to fill a canteen?"

"Four bits," replied the liquor merchant.

"How much for two Mexican dollars?" the scout again asked.

"Well," added the salesman, "if I could just set my eyes upon two silver dollars you could have all the liquor you want. How many canteens?"

"Six," was the answer and Bell handed him the two coins.

Had those thirsty Texans possessed the power they would have made him a brigadier on the spot. "You must have been smuggling cotton across the Rio Grande," remarked a man in gray after a long pull at his canteen, and he began talking to the donor in Spanish by way of finding out. When Bell answered in Spanish so fluent that the Texans could not understand it, everyone concluded the stranger must be a smuggler of cotton into Mexico. The rum started the troopers' tongues awagging. Horace pretended to drink but not a drop passed his lips. Before the party reached Alexandria he became satisfied that there was no movement toward New Orleans, but that Steele was the game the wily Magruder was after. They rode provokingly slow and at midafternoon halted for a rest and to feed. It was almost dark when the cavalrymen drew rein on the outskirts of Alexandria. Not a word was said about taking Bell to headquarters. The liquor had done its work. So while they were disposing of their horses Bell galloped off. Soon he came up to a teamsters' camp, stopped, bought corn from them, and fed his horse.

In Alexandria the Union army had sympathizers, among them a man who was a paid member of the secret service. Bell was familiar with the town and from talking with men on the road had learned where the agent lived. But to get to his place without running against a picket guard or riding into an enemy camp presented a great danger. After feeding and resting his horse again he supped on cold corn bread and tough Texas beef, then rode away in quest of the man on whom he relied for perfect knowledge of the military situation. He found his house and him at home. The agent told Bell that the whole bent of the Confederate generals was to crush or capture Steele's army in Arkansas. Two days before, he said, a brigade of Louisiana cavalry and a division of infantry had moved northward toward Arkansas. But another gray brigade had gone to the Atchafalaya line—why, the agent did not know, unless it was to carry out a false idea of a movement against New Orleans.

Horace now saw the light. His mission was accomplished. His next problem would be to get back to the Union lines. This was the third night out from Morganza. He determined to return by a southern route almost to the town of Opelousas. The distance was greater by far, but he had two objects in view—to avoid the perils he had encountered on the way up and to ascertain positively the truth or falsity of the story about skiffs crossing Grand lake. The pretty little town of Washington on bayou Cortableau close to Opelousas lay 85 miles southward. From there it would be 18 miles over to Lyon's ferry on the Atchafalaya. Thence he would pass up the river for 12 miles and cut across 13 miles of country to Morganza, making a trip of about 130 miles. Starting from Alexandria at two in the morning he could reach Washington the next afternoon—that is if he could endure the ride in spite of exhaustion.

His horse was watered, fed, and groomed, and a fair supper set before him. At 10 he was sound asleep to be roused at one-thirty. Neither the secret service man nor his wife went to bed. When he was called, a good breakfast awaited him and the hostess filled his canteen with tea so strong that no one could sleep after drinking it. Having eaten, Bell saddled his long lean horse, mounted and started on his homeward journey. As he drew rein to say his last thanks the wife exclaimed, "God speed you, sir! You are the most adventurous man in the world!"

Wanting to get the most out of his horse he took the road for a mile or two in a walk. Then he let him out in a slow canter, sometimes drawing rein for a moment's walk and after riding this way for more than an hour he tickled him with the spur and let him go off into a long sweeping gallop, holding him up for breath every half-hour. By sunup Bell had made half the distance to Washington. On the way he halted at a farmhouse to get corn and fodder.

The noble animal did not show fatigue in the least. No troops had passed either way, the old farmer said, since Vincent went south with his Louisiana cavalry. For three hours Bell remained at the farm, resting and giving every attention to his horse.

Just as he was about to saddle, a Confederate courier rode up rapidly on his way to Colonel Vincent. He wanted to feed his horse and ride on to Opelousas. He desired Bell's company and Bell desired his. A good thing it was to ride with couriers; they were always in a hurry and were never halted. Therefore the Union scout waited for the rebel messenger. Horace proposed stopping at the plantation of Prescott, a captain in Vincent's cavalry. But he did not tell his reason for pausing—that the Federals had a secret service man living there. Near four o'clock they reached the plantation, but the courier galloped on. After finding the observer Bell turned his horse over to him and dropped off to sleep. About dark the agent awoke him with the news that Vincent's men were marching past to Alexandria. So from one of Captain Prescott's windows Horace reviewed the brigade. He was now convinced there was no truth in the story that 1,000 Confederates would cross Grand lake in skiffs to attack New Orleans, for troops were moving northward, not to the south. Thus the goal of his mission was once more attained.

Now he must hurry back to General Canby to prevent his withdrawing troops from the north. He knew that from Prescott's plantation a straight road led through the swamp, now dry, to Lyon's ferry where a rebel picket camped, and on the way there, at the cabin of old man Eddy, a courier station intervened. On this road the danger of capture would be highly probable. Consequently he resolved to make the remainder of the journey on foot.

Next morning at daylight he struck across the swamp, leaving his horse with the agent to be used again on some future occasion. At noon he reached the river. Parallel with the Atchafalaya and about 30 yards from the bank ran a horse trail. For a few minutes he watched it up and down. All was still. He stole to the water's edge, found a light dry log, rolled it into the water and with its aid swam safely over. He slipped into the woods, partially dried his clothes, drank tea, and struck out for Morganza, reporting to General Lawler before sunset. He had left Morganza on Tuesday noon. On Sunday he was back. Away five days he had journeyed fully 300 miles in hostile country—44 miles of which were covered in one day and on foot.

An hour after Bell reached Morganza a fast steam tug was carrying him down to General Canby in New Orleans.

Double-Check

The chief of scouts had been at home with his wife and babe about a week when late in the afternoon an orderly called telling him to report at once to General Canby. "I am not satisfied," the commander said, "with the situation on Red river and beyond the Atchafalaya. General Steele telegraphs that the enemy has withdrawn from his front and is marching southward." Bell replied that this was certainly a *ruse de guerre* to weaken Steele—that *he* was the game they were after.

"On your report of a week ago," the general continued, "I ordered every available man and gun to be sent to Steele. The reinforcement is on transports at Morganza and will be held in readiness to go either way. Can you go to Alexandria immediately to make absolutely sure what the enemy is doing?"

"Yes, sir," answered Horace on the instant.

"Be ready in 15 minutes. An order will be made out to General Lawler to aid you. A fast tug is waiting to carry you to Morganza. Go and get back as soon as possible and let there be no mistake."

"There has been no mistake so far, General," Bell remarked and hurried away to his rooms to change his clothes, pick up his arms and equipment, and kiss Georgia and little Charles good-by. At five o'clock he was steaming up the river and at daylight reported to Lawler.

Bell had an order for the best horse in the army at Morganza. With Quartermaster Ward he was examining a few when Captain Falcon of the Mexican cavalry proposed to show him one. It was

a Texas barb. In the early settlement of that state a drove of
Andalusian horses was imported, pure scions of the old stock
originating in Barbary, whence came the name. These noble
animals were famous for their speed and endurance. Ah, a perfect
beauty was this one!—a blood-red bay with white feet, a blaze in
the face, and a mustache.

"Whose is he?" Bell asked the captain admiringly.

"He was mine. Now he is yours," said the Spaniard with the
graciousness belonging to his people.

Bell accepted the generous offer and Falcon ordered him
saddled. In one hour under escort of the First Texas cavalry the
scout was on his way to Burton's ferry on the Atchafalaya. On
the opposite bank of the river they saw the enemy's cavalry. At
once a lively skirmish at long range began. Then with Captain
Charley Bonnet's company Bell proceeded through the woods far
enough back to escape observation to the point where he had
swum the river a week before, a few miles above the ferry. Two
Mexicans quietly constructed a raft upon which Horace placed
his riding gear. Then he ferried himself across the river. One of
the Latin pair swam the barb over and helped him in saddling.
With his hat the scout waved *adiós* to the captain across the
stream. He pressed the hand of the noble Mexican boy, who said,
"*Vaya con Dios, valiente!*" [Go with God, brave one!] He
mounted, rode up the bank, crossed the trail, and plunged into the
woods—safe at least for a while. It was now two in the afternoon
—just 22 hours from the time General Canby had sent for him and
he was 200 miles from New Orleans.

Bell started through the swamp on the same route he had traveled on foot a week ago—most difficult in riding. How he enjoyed
his barb! Besides being handsome he seemed to have human intelligence! At dark they reached the Prescott plantation where lived
the secret agent. The scout was safe, not the least tired, and 41
miles from Morganza. He groomed and fed his horse, ate supper,
slept two hours, mounted and pushed forward to Alexandria.

Since it was moonlight he rode all night making a detour westward by way of Chicoville through the piney woods, leaving the

[135]

main-traveled road at a point about half-way to Alexandria. He
did this because of information received from the agent at Prescott's that General Bagby had moved his rebel troops from
Alexandria about 30 miles south to Cheneyville. Naturally Bell
wished to avoid them. At daybreak he passed through Chicoville
and stopped at a poor cabin on the edge of a small prairie where
he found a war widow and a big boy dressed in Confederate uniform. The family was almost destitute, yet they had some corn
and fodder, corn bread and low-grade beef. The lad remarked
that the jayhawkers had just made a raid on Ville Platte, 20 miles
from Chicoville, and that Colonel Hill's regiment was down there
hunting them.

This was good news for the scout, for with Bagby at Cheneyville and Hill at Ville Platte, the road would be open to Alexandria. So giving the poor widow two silver dollars he mounted
and pushed on. The distance to Alexandria was yet 50 miles, this
road being 15 miles shorter than the one previously traveled.
About noon he met John Knight, a soldier of the Second Louisiana
Confederate cavalry, whom he knew intimately. The winter
before, Knight was a prisoner on parole and boarding at the same
house in New Orleans, eating at the same table with Mr. and Mrs.
Bell. Knight stared but failed to recognize him in this strange
environment. Horace asked him some questions, which were
readily answered, then spurred his barb and rode rapidly off.
Having gone about 200 yards the rider turned his head and
glimpsed his acquaintance standing stockstill in the road gaping
after him. He seemed dumfounded.

About five miles from a hospital Bell had to cross a bridge over
a wide deep bayou. Here he found a cavalry guard of four men,
but luckily they had treed a coon about a hundred yards above
the bridge and did not notice him until he had passed over. So he
galloped on, pretending not to see them.

It was only six or seven miles to Cheneyville when Bell fell in
with a Confederate captain, who was going up to the hospital. He
quizzed the officer and learned that Bagby was collecting all the
cavalry in the district and in a day or two would move to the

front to join Magruder, who he said was "going to get Steele sure." But the unsuspecting rebel never asked the stranger a question.

The pair separated at the hospital and Bell rode on a mile or two and stopped at the house of a well-to-do planter, one who had a good log dwelling, but no slaves. He went down to the cotton gin house, where he foddered his horse, conversed with the old farmer, suspecting him of being a Union sympathizer. He explained vaguely to the Southerner that he was "going up to report." He got a fair lunch, talked with the wife and daughter, fed his horse on corn, curried and rubbed him down. All the time the elderly man talked freely "ferninst" the Confederacy. The scout listened but held his peace.

By half-past three Bell was riding rapidly toward Alexandria 15 miles away. It began to rain. In an hour it was pouring down. Six miles below Alexandria, Bell came to a sugarhouse used as a quartermaster's station. Here a Texas cavalry guard was taking care of a large herd of cattle. He rode under the shed, where some soldiers were cooking and quizzed them. A well-mounted officer in a rubber coat rode out and started on a canter toward Alexandria. Bell asked, "Who is he?"

"That is Major Mouton, quartermaster for General Buckner," came the reply. Accordingly Bell reined out, resolved to ride with the officer and pump him. Fortunately he took Bell for an ununiformed Confederate soldier. In answer to his inquirer he said, "Tomorrow we will be ready to move. In 20 days we will crush or capture Steele."

He had been down, the major added, to see Bagby at Cheneyville. He was affable and communicative, never asking Bell a question. When the two rode up to Buckner's headquarters the officer halted and dismounted. The scout rode along the river front, wheeled to the left, skirted the town, and drew up in the back yard of a Union secret agent.

Only nine days before he had paced away from the man's door with a "God speed you!" The surprise of the agent and his wife was unbounded. The first duty being to the barb, they cared for him. The next thing was to talk over the situation, which was unchanged since the last visit. Bagby, the man said, had been delayed for lack of equipment, but the program was the same— "to crush or capture Steele."

From two reliable sources the scout had again verified his earlier information. A second time his mission was accomplished. So at dark he started galloping homeward, determined to spend the night at the house of the Union sympathizer who lived in the piney woods near the hospital. The world looked absolutely black and rain fell in a downpour. But the moon would rise at 10 or 11. Despite the darkness his barb showed no inconvenience. He was a perfect nighthawk. Neither did he seem jaded. Near 10 Bell reached the farm, shouted, "Hello!" and the old gentleman came to the door, the rest of the family having not yet gone to bed. They were not much surprised by his reappearance and welcomed him with typical Southern hospitality.

First the horse was cared for, a bright fire started, a good supper laid. Then the scout's boots were pulled off, his dripping outer garments hung up to dry, and all entered into conversation. Horace talked "Secesh" and the old man, mother, and daughter talked "Union." The mission so important and perilous thus far had been a success. A one-and-a-half day's journey might take him into Morganza, that is if he escaped capture. What worried him most was the ride over the broad bayou where yesterday the guard had deserted their post to catch a raccoon. How to pass or avoid that bridge and guard was the problem. If he went down the other road Bagby would be in the way.

The host asked his guest's opinion as to the outcome and dura- tion of the war. Repeating the common wishful thinking of the South he replied:

"If McClellan is elected he will at once recognize the Confed- eracy. But if old Lincoln should be re-elected the North will revolt and this will insure the recognition of the Confederacy."

"Nonsense!" broke in the host, "you don't believe such stuff! Don't you know that McClellan in his letter of acceptance pledged himself to wage war for the preservation of the Union? And don't you know that Lincoln *will be* re-elected and that he will carry the war to a speedy and successful ending? All this Southern talk about revolt is foolish!"

"Sir," replied Bell, looking at the old gentleman straight in the eye, "you must be a Union man!"

"I am a Union man," came the quick answer. "My name is William Dye and I've got a son who's a soldier in the Second Louisiana cavalry—Union cavalry, sir!"

A light now flashed upon Horace Bell's mind. "Well, sir," he avowed, "I am a Yank and came all the way from New Orleans to find out what the 'rebs' are doing. I am a Union scout."

"I knew you were not a rebel soldier," remarked the farmer, "and when you went away I said so to my wife."

"How did you come to such a conclusion?"

"Because of your horse. No rebel soldier would be permitted to ride so fine a horse. The big officers would take it away from him."

It was now past midnight. Horace felt safe and happy, warm and comfortable. He went to bed, slept soundly until late morning, and woke up rested, brave and confident.

Having placed his life in the hands of William Dye the guest told him of his fears concerning the bridge and the cavalry guard. At once his host offered to guide him around the place, saying that the detour would be 15 miles out of his way, but after he had gone beyond the bridge the road would be clear to Washington. It was another rainy day, but they started out, the guide walking. Entering the woods they passed the hospital, continued in a southwest course for two hours as though they were going to Texas, and then changed their way toward the southeast. Here Mr. Dye stopped, saying, "If you will stay on this road for about seven miles you will strike the Opelousas road five miles beyond the bridge."

Taking leave of the generous old patriot who served on foot because the Confederates had taken his last horse, Bell now spurred his barb into more speed and was soon on the main road feeling pleased with his success. In about two hours he met an armed guard. The only thing to do was to ride past hastily, which he did without even a question being asked. The troopers turned their heads, supposing probably that he would be challenged by the commander a quarter-mile farther on. But he would not be caught this way. So off he galloped into the woods in time to review the main body and a company or two guarding a supply train and prisoners. When the command had passed, the Union scout hurried forward obliquely from the road.

Not a person did he see during the rest of the day. Near night he reached the cabin of the war widow where he had recently breakfasted. The woman was at home, also the big boy in Confederate gray. Without removing the saddle Bell had fed his barb and was inside eating when he missed the young man. So he stepped outside, but did not see him anywhere. Alarmed, he bridled, mounted, and galloped in the direction of Chicoville. After riding into a grove of small trees not far from the widow's place, he saw in less than three minutes a squad of Confederate cavalry dash up to her cabin, halt for a moment and then ride on toward Chicoville, passing within a hundred yards of where he was watching. What a narrow escape! The boy had orders, Bell later learned, to watch for him on his return and had slipped over to a neighbor's house where the squad was stopping for the night.

Horace rode right along after the troopers, expecting that they would stop at Chicoville to ask about him. He thought he might be able to pass through the place unobserved or if seen make a run for open road. When he entered the village it was dark. He succeeded in getting through unquestioned, but a mile farther on he was challenged from a house near the roadside. He refused to answer and was threatened with, "Hey, Yank! we'll git you yet!"

It was now still darker and the rain fell in a misty drizzle, making it still harder to see. He came to where the road forked—one branch going to Washington which he wanted to take, the other leading to Ville Platte, the one he desired above all things to avoid. As bad luck would have it he took the wrong road. His error was not discovered until it was too late. The country was wooded, almost wholly unsettled. Not a house intervened between the fork in the road and Ville Platte, a distance of 15 miles. Apparently his pursuers had followed the road to Washington.

For nearly an hour he galloped on when all at once there burst forth on the misty night air the sound of human voices singing. He halted and listened. He could hear the clanking of sabers and the trampling of horses. It was a company of Southern cavalry coming north from Ville Platte to Chicoville. Instantly he reined his horse out of the deep-cut road up on the side of a bank in the edge of the brush and halted. His barb stood stockstill. A stone horse could not have been more quiet. In the pitchy darkness the company of cavalry was actually patrolling the road, bent on Bell's capture. So close they passed him he could have knocked the nearest on the head with his revolver. They were singing a popular war ditty:

> In eighteen-hundred and sixty-three
> Ol' Lincoln set the niggers free
> So we'll all
> Drink   stone   blind
> Johnny   fill up   the bowl.

The barb stood still as death. But Bell's heart beat a devil's tattoo, as loud he thought as the drumming of an Oregon grouse. The troopers passed by and he rode on with a great sigh of relief. By now he had become intensely nervous. His eyes felt as though they were bursting out of his head. He drank cold tea and pressed forward, knowing by this time that he had taken the road above all others which for worlds of gold he would not have dared to travel. He knew he was riding into the jaws of capture and death.

But he could not turn back. He could not veer to one side. Only one thing could he do—press forward, run the gauntlet of Ville Platte and then on to Washington 15 miles farther. If he were captured as a jayhawker (the current name for a guerrilla) instant death would follow; if as a deserter no better treatment; if he were found to be a Union scout he would be shot as a spy!

The moon had risen and he was entering the outskirts of Ville Platte expecting trouble. It came. Soon the sharp cry of "Halt!" rang out in front and he drove his spurs into his barb and shot past the picket like a meteor. Bang! went a carbine and the bullet whizzed past like music in his ears. The town was more than a half-mile long and a row of small houses with porches lined each side of the road. As the weather was rainy the Confederates were sleeping on the porches, having picketed their horses in the back yards. He had progressed through the defile for about a hundred yards when bang! bang! bang! came the fire from the porches as he rode like mad down the street. The bullets zipped high as they usually do when the target is moving. His barb flew like the wind and Bell had almost got to enjoying the excitement. He was about to reach the end of the town and felt good when—hell!—a bright bonfire blazed up in front of him and there stood posted guards waiting his coming. The pickets were supplied with pitch pine for fuel and had just replenished their camp fire. It flamed up instantly making all as clear as day.

The scout's blood was up. He was warmed to his work and when the sentinel barked out his fierce "Halt!" he felt no more like stopping than if women with broomsticks stood barring the way. The soldiers raised their guns and Horace with a yell let fly with his revolver. Then came a volley. His noble horse staggered, stopped stonestill, braced himself, and quivered in every muscle. Bell leaped off on the side opposite the guard, bounded over a fence, sprinted across a back yard filled with picketed horses, cleared the rear fence at a jump, ran across lots, got out of the glare of the bright campfire, crossed to the opposite side of the road and found himself out of town and in a cornfield.

The agony was over, the great danger past. The terrible gauntlet had been run. He was 15 miles from Washington, on foot. His beloved companion that had carried him through this dreadful peril was gone—shot. The canteen of cold tea was tied to the saddle. But he had a watch, as well as General Grant's pocket compass. After going some distance through the cornfield he halted, struck a match and found it was half-past 12. Could he reach Washington before day all would be well—otherwise not. A moment's thought induced him to take the road before a chase would be made. It turned out, however, as he later learned from the sergeant of the picket, that when he jumped from his horse the soldiers thought he had fallen off killed. When they found out their mistake they expected him to be lying dead or wounded nearby and after a brief search made no pursuit. Had they done otherwise, he might have been driven to the woods, hunted down, and captured.

Horace Bell had read in history books that Napoleon's army retreating from Moscow slept while on the march. But this he had never believed. Now he could. He reached his haven of safety at daylight after swimming the Cortableau, but he slept as he walked for the greater part of the way. Only when he stumbled would he wake up, yet he made the trip. He reached the Prescott plantation where lived the secret agent to whom he had committed his long bony race horse on the last expedition.

After changing clothes and eating breakfast he was soon fast asleep to be called at noon. He resolved to take his chances and push through to the Atchafalaya before night, swim his horse over and go on to Morganza. The difficulties ahead seemed trivial to what he had been through. He could ride around the courier station at old man Eddy's in the woods, then make a clean run for the Atchafalaya, leaving the road and riding through the woods to a point on the river a mile or two above the picket at Lyon's ferry.

Oh, he was sore! He bathed and rubbed himself with Louisiana rum, drank strong tea, felt better, ate a good dinner, had his horse saddled, and at one o'clock was riding like wild on the road to the ferry. As the alligators were quietly composing themselves for a night's slumber in their muddy beds at the bottom of the Atchafalaya, Bell rode his horse into its murky waters and soon was in Federal country. He crossed the line where Captain Bonnet had dropped him 78 hours before. Long before tattoo he was safe and sound within the fortress of Morganza. He telegraphed the situation to General Canby and went on board a transport waiting to carry him to New Orleans. He had been gone from Morganza 81 hours. In that time he had traveled 322 miles or an average of four miles an hour for three and a half days of almost continuous riding.

On board the steamer he bathed and went to bed and in the

morning when he tried to go ashore he was too weak to walk. The intense excitement being over, relaxation had come.

Horace had the satisfaction of assuring General Canby that there had been no mistake in judging the situation—the Confederates wanted Steele and would make a desperate effort to get him. So the troops waiting on transports at Morganza were at once pushed forward to Steele and thus ended the Confederate plan of crushing or capturing his little army in Arkansas. And thus was Magruder outwitted and the Northern commander came out master of the situation.

But during Bell's absence Canby had become so anxious concerning the enemy's movements that he himself went scouting on a small steam tug. Going up Red river within range of Fort De Russy he was shot by a bushwhacker, though not fatally.

Among the Guerrillas

Along the Teche and other bayous reaching northward to Opelousas and Alexandria lay the richest sugar and cotton plantations of Louisiana, their owners being strongly Secessionist. On the prairies west of those streams lived the Acadians, or Cajuns as they were commonly called. They were descendants of French exiles long ago deported from Nova Scotia, whose story is told in Longfellow's great poem. In contrast to the other side of the line theirs was a cattle-raising country where wild game abounded, the lakes and bayous teeming with alligators, fish, and water fowl. Broad prairies, groves of live oak, jutting pine forests, and cypress brakes made this land of Evangeline a beautiful region to live in. But compared with their wealthy neighbors eastward these people were generally poor. They hated the Confederacy and held a bitter resentment toward the great planters because of their spirit of arrogance and contempt.

For instance a Creole passing along the Teche in his *pirogue* would be denied the privilege of tying up in front of a plantation during the night for fear he might trade with the slaves. Neither was he ever permitted to approach the house of these lords; if he had business, he must go hat in hand to the overseer. Even Confederate troopers passing through the country or encamped near-by found the gates of the mansion barred against them. A poor soldier in gray would be denied a cup of water if he asked for it at the manorial halls of these parvenus grown rich from slave labor.

After its defeat at Shiloh, the Confederacy began conscripting soldiers. But when the levy came to the prairies of western Louisiana most of the men refused to be drafted, remaining loyal to the Union. Two of the Cajun leaders, Carrière and Guillory, resolved not to be inducted and also to prevent their unwilling fellow citizens from being taken. At public meetings many decided not to join the Southern army and if necessary to die in resistance. As stock-raising was their principal business these people were perfect in horsemanship and handy with firearms. Consequently they waged a guerrilla warfare on the gray army and in the parlance of that day were called "jayhawkers."

Two weeks having passed since his last scouting trip Horace Bell felt fully restored in nerve and muscle. He decided to attempt a mission of his own. He would take to the jayhawkers ammunition and other supplies which he understood they sorely needed. So without orders or even a suggestion from any superior officer he set forth from New Orleans with one man to go up the Mississippi to Morganza. Here they spent two days making a skiff. Under cover of darkness it was conveyed westward on a quarter-master's wagon, an escort of cavalry going along, to the Atchafalaya. They filled it with powder and balls, pistol cartridges and caps, plenty of quinine, needles, thread, coffee and tea, and finally lucifer matches. At that time a box of matches within Confederate lines was worth $1,000 in Southern money. On the somber muddy river the pair floated down about two miles, entered a bayou, and after rowing all night came to Half Moon lake, only nine miles from the Prescott plantation where Bell had previously stopped.

At the head of the lake the two men carried their cargo into the canebrake, concealed the skiff, made camp, ate a sumptuous breakfast, then spread their blankets and slept until noon. After waking they carefully concealed their cache, obliterated their tracks from the water's edge, and struck out through the woods and canebrake. Long before sunset they were in the edge of the woods behind the plantation awaiting darkness. At night they advanced to Prescott's place and learned that all the Confederate troops had left the country except the reserve corps, which were few and scattered.

Fifteen miles to the west lived Guillory, one of the guerrilla leaders. A runner was dispatched to tell him of the arrival of the welcome supply and invite him to come for his share. He was not at home, however, for he had to be constantly on the move lest he be surprised and killed in his own house. But he was found with some jayhawkers at a rendezvous where they were considering an attack on the Confederate reserve corps. On the next morning Guillory and a dozen mounted men were snugly camped in the woods between Prescott's place and Half Moon lake, eager to find the cache of powder. Bell's comrade joined the party as guide while Horace remained at the plantation. After dark the cavalcade rode to the rear of Prescott's, each trooper carrying a portion of supplies. At midnight these Louisiana guerrillas went scurrying westward over the prairie and through the timber until dawn, Bell going with them. In a thick growth of underbrush they pitched camp, posted guards, and sent out scouts to invite the rest of the faithful to come and get their part of the secret treasure.

Bell had met Guillory before. He was a French Creole, small, dark, wiry, and nervous, about 35 years old. He owned a small plantation and six slaves, three of them being men, stalwart mulattoes, who were with him as jayhawkers. The day passed pleasantly and quietly. To wash down their ration of corn bread and boiled beef the guerrillas had been receiving a home-made substitute for coffee, which every one execrated in French. They now cast loving eyes upon the half-sack of genuine coffee brought by Bell in the skiff and parceled out to them. To see these coffee-starved fellows brew and drink during the day delighted him, for to be without that beverage was a Creole's greatest hardship.

By sunset all of Guillory's men were in camp and what a motley crowd they were! French Creoles, free mulattoes who owned property, and mulattoes who were slaves. All spoke French, some knew no English. Each man carried two double-barreled shotguns tied one on each side of his saddle, while a brace of Remington revolvers filled the holsters at the waist belt. A parley followed and each jayhawker was given powder and ball, buckshot, caps and pistol cartridges, quinine, and coffee. A fair quantity of these supplies was placed aside to be sent to Carrière, the other guerrilla chief in the neighborhood of Lake Charles in the Calcasieu parish (county). To Bell it seemed remarkable that these men cut off from the Union could have escaped capture at the hands of the angry Secessionists. But such was the case, although many were slain during the two-years' effort of the Confederacy to exterminate them. But for every jayhawker killed by the Confederates probably three rebels bit the dust.

One hundred fifty guerrillas were now present. They decided to go in the morning to see Carrière and give him the ammunition and supplies for which he had long been suffering. Near midnight on the root of a venerable tree serving for a pillow Horace fell asleep. At daylight the winding of Guillory's horn aroused the camp and soon everyone was busy. Fires were replenished and preparations begun for breakfast. Cold corned beef filled the wallets of each man; there was a sufficiency of coffee pots and plenty of sugar. On convenient boughs hung the parts of a fat steer which had been killed on the plain. But before any man ate, a good feed of corn and a bundle of fodder were given to the neighing horses, most of which bore the brand C.S., giving proof to Guillory's declaration that "when the 'rebs' come down here on the prairies many of them stay and we get their horses."

Guillory was supreme commander of this band of 150. There were no lieutenants, sergeants, or corporals. His only adjutant was his long curved cow's horn which he used for a bugle. It was strange what melody this nervous descendant of the Acadians could draw on his primitive instrument. He alone gave orders. He detailed all guards and sent out all scouts. There was no drill and on the march the column rode without order, the captain sometimes being at the right or left, or passing here and there discussing plans with his own slaves, sometimes with a neighbor who like himself was a slaveholder but hated the Southern aristocracy.

When the sun's rays had illumined the tops of the tall pines the guerrillas were breakfasting. In the midst of the meal Guillory got up and gave one blast on his horn. At once 10 jayhawkers arose, saddled their horses and rode off. They were to relieve the pickets that had been out in pairs during the latter part of the night. For an hour breakfast continued with the slow sipping of coffee and the smoking of the long-lasting American cob pipe. Then the relieved guards came in and it took them an hour to eat and smoke. Horace thought to himself: "Surely these are the slowest-going fellows I have ever had the misfortune to meet." He was tired of waiting, having spent only five minutes at breakfast and twice as long in smoking a cigar. He wanted to be moving. Another blast from the horn and five fresh jayhawkers galloped away to order in the pickets.

At last the whole camp was saddling up for the day's ride. In another half-hour (it was now 10 o'clock) Guillory with Bell riding at his side emerged from the timber and struck out westerly across the prairie, followed by his band, all conversing at once in the Creole language, making a confusion of strange sounds that seemed to the Californian like a modern Babel.

On this morning two other columns broke camp. On learning that the Confederate cavalry had departed from southwestern Louisiana Carrière left the fastnesses of his swamp in the Calcasieu region for a raid on Opelousas and the lower country in quest of ammunition and supplies. The other column was Captain Sam King's Confederate cavalry that had ridden out of Ville Platte farther north, hoping to surprise and strike Carrière. After one hour's ride on this morning Guillory's troopers reached Ville Platte and found the fresh trail of King's column. This caused a brief halt and a parley in French. At such a movement Bell's friends were astonished but agreed to follow the tracks and give the Confederates battle.

The prairie was alternated with patches of timber, bayous fringed with wood, and stretches of open country many miles wide. Near one o'clock while crossing a bayou and emerging into the edge of a prairie, Guillory's party could discern in the distance the gray column far over the open tract about to enter a spur of timber. The jayhawkers halted until the last rebel was clear of the prairie. Then Guillory led off in a fast gallop. On the way he informed Bell that just beyond the timber was a plantation and he thought the enemy would stop there and he might surprise them unsaddled. The pursuers entered the narrow strip of timber, drew rein, and Guillory was in the act of sending scouts forward when firing opened about a mile ahead.

King going west had struck Carrière coming east. Each had surprised the other at the plantation on the western edge of the prairie which King had passed over just as Carrière emerged from the woods near the house. With nearly a hundred men Carrière had discovered King before being noticed and made the attack. To Guillory's men a mile away the fighting seemed lively, but they could not see because of the plantation buildings intervening.

"It's Carrière!" shouted Guillory.

"It's Carrière! *Sacré vive!*" responded each jayhawker and away they galloped for the fray.

On being pushed back by Carrière and blocked by Guillory, Captain King took possession of the plantation house and out-buildings. But the cotton gin house on the east side Guillory reached in time to occupy. Now began a brisk battle never before described on the pages of the great war's history. There were four persons extremely surprised. Sam King was surprised by Carrière, who in turn was surprised by meeting King; Guillory was equally astonished at the unexpected encounter; and Horace Bell was as amazed as anyone, for he had not bargained for other than a pleasant ride over beautiful country—he had not counted on a fight.

For a while the shooting ceased. Carrière occupying the west woods and Guillory the gin house on the east put the Confederates in a tight place. But they lost no time in fortifying. They barri-caded windows and doors, made bastions and lunettes on the outside with fence rails and rubbish lying around the place. Dur-ing the lull the two guerrilla leaders met and consulted. King was their old and merciless enemy. They wanted to get him, having

[149]

recognized his company from the first. They agreed on a plan of attack.

In the gin house there were some 20 bales of cotton and three Creole carts. Beneath the bed of each cart a cotton bale was swung. Two bales were then placed upon each cart; thus a movable fortress was improvised. At the sametime, bales were rolled toward the house within easy range and a barricade was constructed. Then two of the carts were each manned by two guerrillas pushing their vehicles forward, guiding them by the pole to the opposite sides of the house while a lively firing opened on each side. When the carts were placed in position the house was entirely surrounded.

Now Bell perceived the use of the third cart. It would be used to fire the house. At once two men, protected by a concentrated shooting from their comrades, commenced to back it up against a shed close to the dwelling. The top bale was cut open and a match applied. Soon a bright blaze reached and ignited the roof of the shed, and the two jayhawkers started on a run for cover. One was shot dead, the other escaped without a scratch. The larger roof now catching fire made the house no longer tenable.

In a moment all the entrapped soldiers sprang on their horses, which were stationed inside, and charged toward the cotton fortress blocking their escape. Such prompt action found their enemies unprepared, for having surrounded the house they expected a quick surrender. Revolver in hand King led the way out, the guerrillas closed in on each flank, the five men from the side where the roof was fired came in on a dead run to get in their shots. As the fleeing men reached the barricade two fell from their saddles and two horses dropped, leaving their unlucky riders on foot. A momentary tightening of the rein and the discharge of a dozen revolvers left the four jayhawkers dead at the cotton fort, and the rebels were free, flying like the wind for the tall timber.

Before the guerrillas could mount for pursuit the Confederates were gone, except a half-dozen hapless fellows who were captured when their horses were shot. Seven bodies wearing gray uniforms lay stretched on the ground, marking the bloody road opened by their leader, who, had he hesitated for one minute and given Carrière and Guillory time to mount, would have been lost and his men sacrificed. Of the six prisoners taken five were shot on the spot. Horace had time to intercede and save the sixth and a desperate effort it was because no Confederate had ever spared a jayhawker. Begging the poor fellow off he sent him home on a promise never to return to the Confederate army.

To Carrière and Guillory the disappointment in not bagging King was great and the spoil insignificant. To capture only a dozen horses with as many carbines, revolvers, and half as many sabers caused them to cry out, *"Sacré Dieu!"* in their rage.

Sam King was a bloody and merciless scoundrel, but cutting himself out of the trap into which he had fallen showed him to be a man equal for any crisis. No pursuit was made and such laxity of discipline and confusion followed that Bell feared that King might return on a charge and cut his foes to pieces.

As soon as the excitement of the escape had passed, men rushed for the household effects and saved them, although in a short time the structure was a pile of smoking ashes. Protesting regret for the loss the jayhawkers promised to help in rebuilding the house for the owner, a Union Creole. A small detail was now sent on the trail of Sam King not to pursue but to see that he was in full retreat. By midafternoon campfires were started and preparations for dinner begun. The supplies and ammunition for Carrière were duly delivered and a contribution of coffee and other valuables was taken up for the burnt-out Creole to whom the coffee seemed a full compensation for losing his house.

Bell found Carrière to be a handsome, gentlemanly Creole of about 40, rather stoutly built, highly intelligent, talkative, and possessed of that easy elegance of manner peculiar to his race. He was a great terror to the Confederates, a thorn in the flesh which they never did extract, the Francis Marion of western Louisiana. Sorely disappointed at not roasting King alive he told how on a former expedition to the Calcasieu country the escaped officer had captured five jayhawkers, tied them together neck and heels, shut them up in one of their houses and burned them alive in the presence of their wives and children. Had he bagged King he would have served him in the same way and then drawn lots for four other victims of retaliation.

Near sundown the scouting party came back, reporting that King was well on his way to Ville Platte. There could be no more fear of his return. A discussion followed in French as to what steps should be taken, offensive or defensive. One thing all agreed upon: Guillory's band should no longer risk themselves in this range of country. The battle just fought would so arouse the resentment of the Confederacy that jayhawkers exposed on the prairies would be hunted down without mercy. Late in the night Bell was called to the conference. He advised that Guillory and his men should go with him to Morganza. All assented, but on one condition: that each man should have a day to spend with his family before departing. Bell made them all promise that if any rebels were captured they would not be harmed. Such mercy he said would commend them to humane General Canby.

Two nights later they moved in a fast gallop and drew rein at Prescott's plantation where Bell picked up his comrade. The band hurried onward, not on the main-traveled road, but through the dried-up swamp by a cut-off trail to old man Eddy's place, a courier station eight miles distant. They intended to surround his cabin quietly and capture the guard. But when the six Confederates found themselves in the hands of jayhawkers they made a break for liberty and were riddled with buckshot. Horace was sorry for this, but his guerrilla friends rejoiced at the mishap. The party pushed on toward Lyon's ferry, reaching it by daylight. They surprised a company of cavalry located there and had a lively skirmish, but the Confederates escaped, leaving only three dead bodies to mark the trail of the jayhawkers.

The next problem was to cross the Atchafalaya. Luckily they found two skiffs and a large *pirogue* concealed at the landing. In these they ferried across their saddles and equipment. On the last trip their weapons were transported, less one revolver retained by each man, who rode into the river and swam his horse safely over. Now they were out of the Confederacy on neutral ground.

Horace Bell breathed freer than he had for the last six days, a period of intense physical and nervous excitement. When he led his motley escort into camp at Morganza he was satisfied with what he had accomplished, but he felt that he had more than enough of independent service.

The Famous Stranger

It was fall in 1864. Magruder still confronted Steele in Arkansas and Canby remained alert. Horace had been at headquarters in New Orleans only a few days since the last trip when his general sent for him. Canby asked for more information regarding the enemy's movements west of the Atchafalaya and north of Red river. So in a fast tug the scout steamed to Morganza and from there passed northward and up Red river to a point opposite Moreauville. Landing at night he reached the little town where lived a secret service man, a young Creole called Moreau (the place had been named for his family). On being supplied with coin the intelligencer furnished him with military news and a horse.

From here Bell rode southward in one night to Washington, Louisiana, the home of one of his informers, Kendall Carey, a young quadroon who had graduated from a Northern college. Thence he went to Prescott's plantation, where he had stopped several times before, and sent for Carey to come. The two breakfasted together while the agent from Washington revealed the movements of the enemy.

It was still their plan, he declared, to send every possible man to assist Magruder in northern Louisiana. Moreover there was only a thin line of pickets on the Atchafalaya down to bayou Teche. These soldiers on the dividing line were fearful, said Carey, that Bell might lead a cavalry raid from Simmesport southward to the Opelousas country and capture or kill them. For since Horace's adventure with Pancoast Rochelle last May the Union scout had become well known to the Confederate officials.

"They don't know what to make of you," remarked Kendall.

[153]

"They hear of you now and then, but never see you. They regard you as a phantom—a will-o'-the-wisp. And they have offered $2,000 as a reward for your capture. So, my good fellow," warned Carey, "be on the lookout!"

Having acquired the latest news Bell after resting started back home by the way he came. He knew how to cross the Atchafalaya river at Simmesport and thought that after getting over it he could make his way through the swamp to the bank of the Mississippi. From there he would float down to Morganza on a log. After riding all night from Prescott's he came in the morning to a place near the village of Evergreen, which had little more than a store, a tavern, and stable. A small detachment of Southern cavalry was camping there. Stopping for breakfast at a house near the roadside he met a Confederate trooper who asked, "Which-a-way?"

"Oh," said Bell, "I am going on to Evergreen and then down to bayou Yellow where my company is. Where are you going?"

"I'm carrying the mail to McCalla's crossing on the Mississippi," replied the man in gray, "and I wish this mail was in hell because I want to go home. My father lives only 25 miles from here. I want to see him and I want to see the girls. Won't you carry my papers and this mail sack for me? What would you take to relieve me? You know you cross Red river just beyond bayou Yellow. Then you ride across the country and strike the Mississippi about 15 miles above the mouth of Red river."

"Well, yes, I'll do it," said Bell hesitatingly, "if it will accommodate you."

"Will you come back?" asked the trooper.

"Yes," promised Horace, "if you will tell me where to find you."

The Confederate then gave the location of his father's place and the scout agreed to meet him there and hand over the receipts for the mail. At that time the faithless postman would give him another horse for the favor and go back to Alexandria whence he came. The papers and pouch were now handed over with directions as to the road. The trooper left for his home and Bell rode on to Evergreen.

When he reached there he found that a party of gentlemen with a military escort was leaving for McCalla's crossing on the Mississippi. As a mail carrier he could go with them, for they were just starting to ride off. So remarkable was the attention paid to the group by the villagers that Bell wondered, "Who can they be?"

Though all were dressed in civilian clothes they were heavily armed with revolvers and bowie knives. They had an abundance of canteens, haversacks, and equipment, and even some handsome Negroes for body servants—a most elegant set of soldiers.

"Who can they be?" pondered Bell.

After the party had set out and all were cantering down the road, Horace inquired of a corporal, "Who are these great men that you are escorting?" The Southerner was amazed at such ignorance.

"Why, don't you know?" he replied. "This is the admiral of our *Alabama*—our *Alabama* that swept the Yankees from the sea— our *Alabama* that lighted up the skies from the West Indies to the frozen ocean. Yes, damn them, they sunk our *Alabama*. They sunk her, the treacherous scoundrels. And the admiral is going to Richmond and there he will get another ship and sweep the last Yankee from the sea. Just see if he don't!"

"But who is it you are talking about?" ventured the scout.

"Why," declared the corporal, "it is Admiral Raphael Semmes of the Confederate States navy—the greatest sea fighter the world ever knew. We are to see him to the Mississippi and across."[4]

"Well," thought Bell, "this is adventure sure enough!"

He rode along until he came up to the admiral. He looked at Semmes and Semmes looking at him asked, "Have you ever crossed at McCalla's?"

"Oh, yes, several times," answered the Union man casually, "several times."

"Any particular danger?" inquired the great man.

"Oh, no," assured Bell, who had never heard of the place before, "Captain McCalla is the safest man in the world and the shyest. He has managed that crossing ever since the fall of Vicksburg, and the Yanks don't even suspect him."

In midafternoon the party reached bayou Yellow where a

[155]

squad of cavalry, ragged and hungry, was camping. The travelers next crossed bayou des Glaises and rode on to Red river which they passed over in daylight, for very seldom did Union gunboats ascend this stream. It was now about 15 miles to the Mississippi, and as they must reach it by nightfall everyone plied his spurs and pushed forward. Near the water away out in the darkest recesses of the cypress brake they ran upon a little camp where three or four pirate-like fellows took the party in charge. As blackness fell they stood on the banks of the great river.

A red lantern was now exposed on the end of a pole and within five minutes a like ray appeared on the other side of the water, whereupon the admiral's party retired to the thick timber and halted. Everybody dismounted except three or four sentries and Bell, who concealed themselves at the bank awaiting news from across the river. Within 20 minutes Bell and his companions saw something approaching the shore. It looked like an alligator creeping silently, stealthily along. Suddenly a match burned up from the thing whatever it was and one of the sentries struck a similar light. Then a little *pirogue* was gently drawn on the sandy beach and one of the men in waiting gave a low whistle. A dark figure in the canoe answered and the two met. "How many of you?" whispered the boatman.

"About 20," answered the sentry in a low voice, "but you come along and tell us about McCalla and how soon he can be over."

"Oh, he's all ready," said the emissary. "I have to go back and tell him you are here and how many, so that he can plan to get you over."

At this the admiral's spokesman took the dark figure in charge and the watchmen retired to the rendezvous in the woods—all except Bell, who hung back and was left alone in a prospect of glory. No sooner were his companions out of sight and hearing than Horace tiptoed down to the *pirogue*, slipped it into the water, laid the Confederate mail in the bottom, and dexterously maneuvering it from shore paddled out to the strong current.

What a golden opportunity for high service was his!—the capture of Raphael Semmes, the terror of the seas, who had swum from his sinking ship, the *Alabama*, to the British yacht *Deer Hound* off the coast of France, thus saving himself from falling into the hands of the victorious Yankee, Commodore Winslow. Semmes and his party had found their way into Mexico and passed through Texas. Attempting to return overland to Richmond, the Southern capital, they had reached the Confederates' secret crossing of the Mississippi.

It was 25 miles from here to Morganza and early night, nearly seven. Bell knew that the current of the river ran about six miles an hour. In three hours he could cover 18 miles. Could he give the canoe an additional speed of four miles an hour, he would reach Morganza by 10 at the latest. As swift tugs were always kept under steam ready for emergency, he could take one on his arrival, get back to McCalla's crossing by midnight, and perhaps bag the whole party. He plied his paddle for all he was worth. He was not tired yet. His breath did not fail him and his muscles seemed like spring steel. He went faster than he thought he would. At length he heard drums and bugles sounding tattoo and knew that he was nearing the great Union camp at Morganza. In less than an hour after taps he stole in among the transports anchored by the shore and stretched his legs on dry land, took up his sack of Confederate mail, and started toward what he thought would be the headquarters of General Lawler.

"Halt!" cried out a sentry, and he was confronted by a Negro soldier looking as if he would like to drive his bayonet through Horace's tired body.

"Call the sergeant of the guard," requested Bell.

The sergeant came and the sentry explained, "I've got a 'reb' here, sure. How he got into camp I can't tell, but jes' look at him."

The colored sergeant rushed the scout off to the guardhouse. Bell told him who he was, whence he came, and that he wanted to see General Lawler at once.

"De general's done gone to sleep and I don't dare disturb him. I means my general—General Ullman—don't know General Lawler."

"Call the officer of the guard," demanded Bell.

"He's done gone sound asleep too and told me not to disturb him."

"Where's the officer of the day?" asked Bell becoming exasperated.

At this the sergeant laughed hilariously and added, "You can sleep here in the guardhouse until mornin'. Nothin' 's goin' to hurt you. I'll take that bag of yourn."

Drawing forth money from his pocket the scout said, "Look, sergeant. Here is a five-dollar gold piece for you. Go and call any officer you choose. I don't care who it is, just so it's an officer."

Guffawing again the sergeant took the coin and left, but no one came. Shut up in the guardhouse Bell fretted and fumed all night. In the morning the officer of the guard arrived to query him. He wanted to see the rebel who had sneaked into the camp last night.

"Captain," requested Bell, "will you take me to General Lawler?"

"Why, certainly," promised the officer.

"Where were you last night," inquired Bell, "when I was brought in?"

"I was making my rounds of course," he replied. "I was not asleep. An officer of the guard is not permitted to sleep."

"Didn't the sergeant tell you that he had captured a man and the man demanded to see General Lawler, the officer of the day, or any officer?"

"No, the first I heard of you was a little while ago. The sergeant said a 'reb' had stolen into camp and that he had captured him."

By this time the sergeant appeared and restored the mail sack and Bell was taken to Lawler's headquarters farther down the river. He saw what had happened. Last night he had landed by mistake in front of the camp of General Daniel Ullman, commander of the colored phalanx at Morganza and had been seized by one of his sentries. When the scout made known the situation how that hard-boiled general raved and swore! Within 15 minutes Lawler, Bell, and a strong white guard were steaming up to McCalla's crossing. No one had ever heard of the place before.

Behind them followed a transport bearing two companies of cavalry.

Reaching the point they landed on both shores. Evidently the admiral's party had crossed over. But they found no sign of a boat. On both sides of the river the Federals scoured the country—with no results. How the Confederates had got over or what they had done with their boats no one could guess. All the searchers could find were hoofprints where horses had entered the water and where they had clambered out on the opposite bank. How strange it all seemed! Great was the scout's disappointment! He telegraphed his report on the Red river country to General Canby and in the afternoon sailed down to New Orleans.

Thus ended Bell's adventure that brought him face to face with Raphael Semmes, escaped commander of the Confederate ship *Alabama*. If only he could have caught him what a fine feather it would have been for his cap! So nigh to glory!

The California Spirit

At long last the great war between the states had ended, the agony was over. Lee had surrendered at Appomattox; Richmond had been burned and evacuated; Jefferson Davis with his cabinet had fled toward McCalla's crossing hoping to escape into the Southwest.

Breathing a sigh of relief the people of New Orleans relaxed into a festive mood. Every hotel and rooming house in the city was filled with soldiers from both Northern and Southern armies. Leaves of absence being easy to get, officers and men of the rank and file could be seen at all hours of the day or night walking the streets in their brilliant and burnished-up uniforms. Tens of thousands of paroled Confederates, mostly those who lived in Louisiana, had come to the metropolis of the gulf and they had all dressed up. Some wore their uniforms and others new civilian clothes. Texans, Arkansans, and Mississippians were especially bent on having a good time before they returned to the plantations. What a crowd they all made! In general the Southerners were good-natured, the exceptions being mostly the returned roughs of New Orleans, who might insult wearers of the blue uniform. Then would follow a knockdown and a bloody nose. But happily such unpleasantness was infrequent. On the other side the victorious Yanks did not as a rule exult over the defeat of the Johnny Rebs.

In the late spring of '65 a pleasant incident occurred as one of the closing festivities. During the last days of the war a Californian had come to New Orleans as a commission merchant. He had lately received a consignment of California wines from the Stearns wine house of Los Angeles. By one act he endeared himself to hundreds. Wilder inserted a notice in the newspapers saying that he was a Californian, a newly established merchant in the city, having a warehouse full of California wine. Every Californian in New Orleans he invited to come to his place and partake freely of the wine, especially Californians who had served in either army:

> Those who wear the blue
> And those who wear the gray
> Come one and all
> Renew old friendships
> And drink California wine.

At four in the afternoon of the day appointed, almost a battalion stormed Wilder's warehouse. In a large room stood improvised tables loaded with lunches. Oysters were out of season, but cold meats abounded and all kinds of relishes. And of course the wine flowed like water through a Mississippi crevasse. In all his dignity General Canby was present. He came as a Californian, for he was stationed at San Francisco in 1854. He drank sparingly, lit a cigar and made himself socially agreeable. In numbers the Union and Confederate soldiers were just about equal. And what a renewal of fellowship there was! Such inquiries as to old friends! Before long the general making an excuse of the pressure of hard work took his leave. Then the fun began!

During the war it was Bell's observation that Californians on either side had more brotherly love for each other than any group

Elizabeth Wright Bell,
mother of Horace

David Williamson Bell,
father of Horace

Horace Bell, age 35

Horace Bell, age 17

of Freemasons. When a Californian in the Northern army captured a Confederate Californian or met one in distress, he acted as a brother, and so far as Bell knew, it was the same way on the Southern side. Such having been true in wartime one can imagine the spirit that prevailed at Wilder's symposium. Every man turned himself loose. Everybody talked at once. There was reminiscing, shaking of hands, back-slapping, yes, even hugging and pledging of future brotherly love, regardless of which side the other fought on.

But the wine proved to be a deceitful thing—more deceptive than a siren—and when the banquet closed there were many Californians lying under the tables. At midnight Horace found himself in a room at the St. Charles hotel, but he gained sufficient steadiness to find his way home and explain his absence satisfactorily to Georgia. Wilder stayed all night and took care of the "fallen heroes." In the morning he sent them on their way, each carrying a box of cigars under his arm and a bottle of California wine looking like a big revolver stuck in his hip pocket.

Jim Shattuck was a Californian. His father had been judge of the county court at San Francisco in the early 1850s and later lived in Sonoma county. Jim was not at the party because as yet he was with his company of Confederates in the rear of Port Hudson and bayou Sara, his headquarters being Jackson, Louisiana. Shortly after the Wilder frolic Bell was sent to Jackson to conduct Shattuck's company to Clinton, Louisiana, and have them paroled. When the two officers met they exchanged compliments and Shattuck said to Bell, "Do you expect to go back to California?"

"Why, certainly," answered the Union scout. "Where else would I want to go? Just as soon as I get out of the service I'm heading straight back to Los Angeles. Are you returning to California?"

"Yes," replied Jim, "or rather I want to go back. But I will not go like you will. Being on the winning side with the money bags you will travel in grand style. Well, I walked most of the way from California to Missouri to join the Confederate army and now I guess I'll have to walk back."

Bell stayed overnight at Jackson. Forgetting national animosities the two men talked about the Golden State and old times there, of Californians Horace had known in the Union army, and Californians Jim had known on the Confederate side, and what became of them. They talked on until it was well past midnight.

Said Jim, "During the Grierson raid I was taken prisoner and as I was being passed to the rear and had reached the guard conducting several other prisoners I called out, 'Is there any man in this crowd who is a Californian?'

"A man rode out of the ranks and said, 'Yes, I am a Californian.'

"Did you ever hear of Judge Shattuck of San Francisco?

"'Oh, yes!' he says, 'I know of Judge Shattuck.'

"Well, I am his son!

"So we rode along together, all the time moving through a piney wood—I being on horseback just as I was captured except that they had taken my arms away.

"My California friend said to me, 'I'm going to give you a chance to escape, if you have the sand to do it. The first time we come to the top of a hill or the side of a hill I will give you the wink and then you bolt, but be sure you go down hill. They will fire on you, but the bullets will all fly high above your head. I do this, my boy, just because I like to help a Californian.'

"So when we came to a favorable position my friend gave me the wink. I reined off my horse and down the hill I bolted. They chased after me and they fired at me. I heard the bullets whistling over my head. But I made my escape. And so much for California chivalry."

The Good Samaritan

After breakfast the next morning Horace escorted Captain James Shattuck and his company 10 miles east of Jackson to Clinton, Louisiana, where the Confederate cavalrymen were released on parole. He lingered there for a couple of days and then set out on another mission to Opelousas. He left Clinton early to reach bayou Sara, 25 miles west on the Mississippi, before the heat of day. After riding three or four miles he overtook a Confederate soldier walking on crutches. "Where are you going, my good fellow?" inquired Bell.

"I've been paroled and I'm going home."

"Where is your home?"

"Sixty miles west of the Atchafalaya," answered the man in gray. This was 120 miles from where the two were pausing.

"For goodness' sake!" exclaimed the rider. "You don't expect to go all that distance on crutches, do you?"

"What else can I do?" replied the cripple. "I can't stay here and starve. I have nothing to ride, and I'm going to try to get home." At Mobile he had been wounded in the foot.

"Here, my friend," said Horace dismounting, "you get up and ride a while and let me walk."

"Well, who are you anyway?" asked the Confederate scanning the stranger's face.

"Oh, I'm a Yankee," laughed Bell. "I have been conducting a company of Confederate cavalry up to Clinton to be paroled. Now I am going across the Mississippi to Opelousas, and I will help you along best I can."

The astonished hobbler refused, but Horace insisted. The walker hesitated, the other entreated. Finally Bell got him up on the horse. It was a hot day in May, but the Good Samaritan tramped every step of the way to bayou Sara, the lame man riding. Every once in a while the Southerner would turn and say, "And you are a Yankee?"

"Why, certainly," assured Bell, "what of it?"

Then in the soft drawl of Louisiana would come the remark, "Well, I nevah expected this kind of treatment from a Ya-ankee!"

On reaching the bayou they went to a tavern. There the disabled veteran was given a good supper, bed, and breakfast, and the kind hostess cleaned him up as best she could. In the morning Bell boarded a transport with his horse and companion. Together they sailed a few miles up the river to Morganza, the location of a large Union camp. Here they stayed overnight. The officers received and treated the ex-Confederate as cordially as they did Bell, and in the morning furnished a horse and escort to Burton's ferry on the Atchafalaya. At that point, however, the attendants turned back with the extra animal. Crossing the river with his mount and charge Bell went on to Captain Burton's plantation.

The owner was an honorable man, a staunch Secessionist during the war, whom Bell had met on his scouting trips. He introduced his young friend to Burton, telling him where he had met him, how he had found him, and requested the captain to furnish the wounded rebel with a mule to carry him home 60 miles or more up Red river. But Burton hesitated about doing this. He had only a few mules, he explained, and to lose one would ruin his prospects for even a small crop.

"Well," urged Horace, "send a Negro with him to bring the mule back."

"No," answered the planter, "I can't do that. I will lose the Negro as well as his mule and also the mule which the soldier would ride."

"Now listen, Captain," importuned the Union man, "you send this young fellow home and send a Negro with him to bring the mule back. I will return here in a few days. I'm going to Opelousas and when I come back if that Negro has not shown up with both mules, I pledge you my word and honor that I will go to Morganza, buy four mules, bring them back, and give them to you, sir."

So the former Secessionist sent the boy in gray on his homeward journey. The Negro came back. Both mules came back, and later Captain Burton thanked Bell profusely for the interest he had taken in the needy one's behalf.

After the war such deeds were done by hundreds of Federal soldiers, at least in Louisiana. They divided their rations, their little money, and even their clothes with helpless, returning Confederates.

"In looking back over my life during those four years of blood and strife," wrote Bell many years later, "I feel more satisfaction in having helped that young fellow than in any other performance I did during all that time. I never told many people about it and never claimed any credit for myself. I did nothing more than I should have done. But had I failed to do it I would feel very mean. Sometimes when one ponders he stumbles over some mean thing he has done and he don't feel good about it. But when he thinks over the good things he has done he feels grateful for the opportunity that gave him such a privilege."

Blessed are the Merciful

Having finished his assignment in the Opelousas country Bell returned to New Orleans. He was now given the opportunity to be a cotton agent for the United States government. The chief of the signal office (the department to which scouts belonged) said to Bell, "Have General Canby make the request for you and the cotton agent from Washington will give you a commission."

About all the cotton raised in the South had been subscribed to the Confederate Cotton Loan, but much of it was still held by the planters. A grower who had, say, a hundred bales of cotton stored in his gin house subscribed a hundred bales to the loan. These the Confederacy became the owner of and could carry away on demand. During the war the subscription books fell into the hands of Union officials and the subscribed cotton was claimed as captured property. The Northerner receiving a commission would take from the planters the promised cotton, transport it to New Orleans (if he operated in the gulf states) and sell it. After deducting the cost of handling and retaining 25 percent of the selling price for his work, he turned over what was left to the government.

"Now this cotton permit," remarked the agent from Washington, "is intended as a reward to you, Captain Bell, for the distinguished service you have rendered our country and," he added dryly, "you will not be held to strict accountability by me or"— he smiled archly—"by the Treasury Department."

So Bell was given the county of Amite in Mississippi to exploit with headquarters at Liberty, the county seat. He went to the

[165]

place, showed his copy of the subscription list, and demanded that on his return the cotton be delivered to him as the government agent. Since Liberty was a health resort in the piney woods and had an excellent hotel, he brought his wife with him when he returned. She needed to get out of New Orleans, for living there for two and a half years had not been good for her health.

On Bell's second appearance at Liberty a committee of citizens, headed by Colonel Hurst, called upon him. At the battle of Shiloh where he commanded the Sixth Mississippi Regiment the colonel was taken prisoner. When exchanged he resigned from the Confederate army. He was a successful lawyer and a generous noble fellow. The colonel spoke humorously of his military career and capture at Shiloh. "I went to war," he said, "feeling confident that one Southerner could lick five Yankees. I thought the war would be a picnic and that all we would have to do was just to gather in those Yanks that didn't run away. But somehow during the mix-up and the fighting in the woods at Shiloh I got separated from my command and was captured by a little Yankee five feet high who weighed about 130 pounds, but to me he looked bigger than Goliath did to David." Here the group laughed as they surveyed the colonel's height of six-feet-two and his weight of more than 200 pounds.

"So that little Yank yanked me in," went on the colonel good-naturedly, "and when I was exchanged I felt that I had had enough and here I have been, a civilian. The Confederacy has not molested me since and I haven't had any more fights."

With this shrewd approach the lawyer and his committeemen now got down to the point of the meeting. They explained to Bell that the cotton in the gin houses was all the exchangeable wealth the people of Amite county had. They had started out to try to raise a little crop. Their county had been raided by both armies, harried, and trodden underfoot. The people were in consternation and despair. If this cotton were taken away from them they would be utterly destitute. "Is there no way of having our cotton exempted from this levy?" they implored, not knowing that its seizure would enrich the agent.

Bell answered that he would go down to New Orleans and see what could be done. He went at once, leaving his wife and little Charles in care of Mr. and Mrs. Wynne, proprietors of the hotel. In New Orleans he sought the chief official of the United States Treasury Department and gave him a clear-cut statement of the condition of the people in Amite county. He pictured the ruin that would fall upon them if their cotton were confiscated. He urged their case with as much earnestness as though he were a paid advocate. Forgetting his own interest he asked that the people be allowed to keep their subscribed cotton.

Horace returned to Liberty and two months elapsed pending the application. Then he took his family back to New Orleans. Shortly after, he got a letter from the Treasury Department giving its decision. His request was granted, the claim remitted. Horace never went back to Liberty and so never received the thanks of the Mississippians, but he never reproached himself for not making a fortune at the cost of their impoverishment. At the current price of cotton his commission on the levy would have been about $60,000.

Homeward Bound!

Horace Bell's service in Louisiana was ended. For his scouting work throughout the war the government had paid him more than $10,000. But he was quite poor now, being always incurably free-handed. To refill his purse General Canby appointed him as agent of the Treasury Department, sending him in September 1865 to Victoria, Texas. Here his second child was born, Elizabeth Victoria, whose middle name honored her birthplace.

By the following spring the Bells were ready to go to Los Angeles for a permanent home. Hardship and danger awaited those who traveled in that day across the southwest plains. To prevent Bell, his wife, and two babies from being massacred by Indians, Canby gave them a military escort as far as the western edge of Texas. So at the opening of May the party set out from San Antonio on the perilous journey. Ample provisions were loaded in an army ambulance drawn by six mules. Each man had

[167]

his horse and Mrs. Bell took along her own New Orleans pony which she rode when she grew tired of sitting in the heavy wagon. To help with the work of camping and to tend to the children the couple had brought with them a colored man and woman from Louisiana.

Near Fort Clark in Texas the caravan came upon the remains of an Indian massacre. A few white families after leaving the fort had all been murdered except some little children who were carried into captivity. Their wagons were burned, fragments of furniture littered the spot, and dead bodies lay unburied. An affecting sight was the children's playthings and dolls scattered over the ground.

On the Rio Grande a hundred miles below El Paso the Bells came to the wreck of a Mexican train that had been to Salinas on the Texas side of the river. The people had loaded their wagons with salt and were on their way back to Mexico when they were killed by Indians.

At El Paso the cavalry escort headed by Sergeant Mose Kelly of Illinois turned back, leaving the Bells to go the rest of the way alone. About 30 miles east of Tucson, Arizona, they came to the wreck of some government wagons. Evidence showed that the teamsters and a few soldiers had been tortured and killed by savages.

How unpleasant these incidents must have been for a young city-bred woman caring for two small children! Farther on, Indians twice slipped into their camp at night and drove off some of the stock. But after this there were no more horrors.[5]

CHAPTER VII

Mosaic Glimpses

I ask not for the great, the remote, the romantic; . . . .
I embrace the common, I explore and sit at the feet of
the familiar, the low.

EMERSON, *The American Scholar*

Near to Nature

LEAVING Fort Yuma on the western edge of Arizona the little family entered the Golden State by the Butterfield Southern Overland Stage Route and stopped at Willow Grove, a few miles east of their destination. How long the journey had been and how precarious! This day was the thirty-first of July 1866—just 90 days after driving out of San Antonio. To Horace it seemed a strange coincidence that this trip had taken exactly the same number of days as his boyhood expedition to Hangtown.

Willow Grove was the earliest village near Los Angeles to be founded by Easterners. The Americans had named the place for its dense growth of willows, but the Mexicans called it El Monte meaning "thicket." On its eastern side stood the post office and Ira W. Thompson's Willow Grove hotel, which was the local station of the Overland Route—the only tavern between San Gabriel and San Bernardino and the first they had seen for many days. Here they stayed overnight and became acquainted with the proprietor.

In the morning they left for the town where Georgia Bell would spend the rest of her life. Riding into Los Angeles they saw as far as their eyes could reach, the bones of thousands of cattle bleaching in the hot sun. They had died of thirst during the drouth of the last two years. At the corner of Aliso and Los

[169]

Angeles streets Bell drew up his team in front of his uncle's door. (He had written that they were coming.) Here they remained as guests until they could build a house of their own.

Back in Louisiana Horace had told his wife of the beauties of Los Angeles. He promised it would be a paradise. But when the young wife first beheld her new home town she was disappointed. Far away on all sides the lonely plains swept brown and barren. There were hardly any trees in the settled area besides those near the Catholic church and no grass on the Plaza. To Georgia Bell the whole place looked uninteresting. Only a minority of the people she saw were of Eastern descent. Almost the only streets worthy of notice were Los Angeles, Main, Spring, and Fort (later called Broadway). There was not a single house on Fort street south of Eighth and no buildings whatever west of it. On Nigger alley by the Plaza, blacksmiths were making their anvils ring, pounding out spurs for horsemen and gaffs for roosters to wear when they fought to their death in the cockpits a few steps from Uncle Aleck's place.

There were no cool cisterns by shady elms. Water came from an open public ditch called the *zanja*. Twice a week an ox-drawn cart carried hogsheads of the precious fluid through the streets. Stopping at each dwelling the driver dipped out enough to fill the family barrel. There were no gas lights and no fireplaces. Many of the American homes had dirt floors inlaid with stones which required laborious scrubbing. Surely, she thought, the City of Angels had nothing to boast of but its climate.[1]

Six months after their arrival Bell bought 35 acres of farming land southwest of town from Alfonso Tilden (so city records still show) and paid for it $500 or about $14 an acre. This tract was bounded on the north by Pico street, on the east by Figueroa. It had once been a part of the pueblo's communal lands. With his own money he paid for extending a branch of the *zanja* past his place. But this served only for irrigation. For the family never drank from the ditch but from a well which he dug on his lot as soon as it was purchased.[2]

Near the intersection of the two streets and facing east on Figueroa he built a wooden cottage. It was the first house to appear south of Eighth street and west of Charity (now Grand avenue). Here he settled down to a farmer's life. At the corner near his dwelling he planted grapevines which reached southward about 600 feet from Pico and a greater distance from the same corner westward. He bordered the vineyard with walnut trees. On the south side of his place he set out an orange grove and back of his house to the west 10 acres of corn and deciduous fruit trees. A rear driveway from the barn cut the vineyard in half and led to Pico. Each weekday morning he rose at dawn and plowed or did other heavy work before breakfast. Each evening the family went to bed at seven. Such a life promised tranquillity, but Horace Bell was not to have his peace unbroken.

For as soon as he came back to Los Angeles he encountered the hate of Southern sympathizers, mostly those who had not joined an army. During the late war the town had been strongly Secessionist. In fact only two of its citizens had fought on a battlefield for the Union, Bell being one. The other man was Charles Jenkins, whose brother had warned him that if he returned he would be hanged. So now he was prudently staying on San Clemente island, 60 miles off shore from San Diego, until animosity waned. But the former scout had determined to live where he pleased and if necessary defend his right to do so with his two fists.

Shortly after his home-coming he narrowly missed being assassinated by Copperheads on the road to El Monte. Failing in their purpose they set upon him their biggest and toughest fighting man, Wiley McNear, to thrash him into numbness. If he survived the beating they thought he would surely leave town.

One afternoon in 1867 Bell rode up to the corner of Main and Commercial streets, hitched his horse, and walked into Kraemer's store to buy an article for his wife. While he was in the shop a friend whispered that McNear was waiting outside to attack him. Bell thanked the man for his kind information, completed his purchase, and coolly strode out the front door. Close to his face stood a 240-pound giant blocking the way, who was four inches taller than his quarry. Behind him glared a dozen pairs of eyes thirsting for the sight of Bell's blood.

"When I saw the man with a big blacksnake [whip] in his hand, butt foremost, I saw it meant fight!" (So wrote Bell in his manu-script *Saddle and Sword*.) "I caught the gentleman's eye and I said to him: 'My dear sir, is it me that you are looking for?'"

"He bristled up and was about to draw back to strike when I said to him in a low, cool tone of voice, because I was seeking for an advantage: 'My good friend, you are mistaken in your man, but I am not mistaken in you. If you will just go down with me to one of these lanes I will tie you to the first pole I come to and I will take that whip away from you.'"

"By this time the fellow looked absolutely astonished and I threw the strength of a lifetime into one blow and hit that fellow at the butt of the ear, and down he went, measuring his full length in the street, tripping over a boot box in his fall. I stepped onto that boot box and I came down on that fellow with both feet with sufficient force to break three of his ribs from his backbone."

Bell then grabbed the whip and flayed his would-be assailant until the mayor coming up from behind caught his arms and ordered him in the name of the law to stop. As the victor walked away to his horse the prone figure started to rise. Horace then turned, came back, and shaking his finger said, "Sir, you lay down. I am going home and if you attempt to get up while I am in sight I will come back and knock you down again." McNear meekly lay down. The crowd that had now gathered in the street jeered at the vanquished and the returned veteran rode safely home.

But this was only one of many fights with rebel sympathizers. "I never did get the worst of it in any of them," concluded Bell. "The reason was . . . I always got there first with the most force. That is more than half the fight. When a man knows he has to fight he must get there first—never wait to be assaulted."[3]

Early in 1869 the Bells bought more land—35 acres—adjoining their place on the west. They now owned from Figueroa westward to a line which later became Union street, and from Pico to Washington, one block south, except for the south corner on Figueroa belonging to the Hellman family. On the new tract he set out more trees and increased the cultivated area. Later he planted several limes in accordance with the popular notion that one such tree would provide for a child's complete education. He sold his oranges by contract to marketing agents. The local wineries bought and harvested his grapes, carrying them away to huge vats where men trampled out the juice with their bare feet.

At this time raising sheep was highly profitable or at least men thought it would be. So Bell began a pastoral venture. Leaving his wife and children on the farm he placed a Mexican in charge of his crops and went up to the region of Soledad 300 miles to the north. Here he spent lonely weeks with his sheep owned jointly with a neighbor, Colonel Louis Marshall. A letter written in the fall of '69 reveals his new way of life.

My own dear Georgie,

Myself and Polly [the horse] and Fatjack [the dog] came in from our sheep camp yesterday to get something to eat. I am moving slowly down the mountains. It would be impossible to winter up here without shelter. We had one light rain the day after Marshall left and we had two lambs die with cold and wet. I have moved over to the south side of the mountain and it is much warmer. I think I will winter at Cahuenga or some place down there.

Leave the sweet potatoes in the ground, but if it frosts have the vines cut off immediately, and try and get half of the corn crop if I don't get down in time. I will come in and see you after getting to San Fernando.

I hope you have managed to get along well during my long absence —I have never been so long away before, have I?

It will soon be time that father should arrive. When he gets here should his wardrobe need replenishing, you must go to Mr. Goodwin's and get him whatever he needs. Then go down to Uncle Aleck's and tell him about the arrival and that it is simply your duty to tell him, and if he don't want to go to my house to see his brother, then I object to my father going to see him. Be very polite and friendly with

[173]

him. You can have José drive you down, but be careful of the horses, you need not get out.

I suppose Mrs. Widney has a baby now. And what are our prospects?

Ten thousand kisses for yourself. Five thousand for Charley and hug Bessie half to death for me.

Your own true love

Horace Bell

In the next year he returned to full-time farming and Horace Junior was born. On May 15 the Los Angeles Daily *News* printed a story of his quarrel with a neighbor, John Harmon. They appeared in court before Judge William H. Gray. Harmon charged that Bell had committed assault and battery upon his person. Some mules belonging to the plaintiff were trespassing on the cultivated ground of Bell, who caught them and was driving them off to the pound when Harmon coming along tried to recover them. Both became excited and Bell struck Harmon once with a heavy whip. The arrested man defended himself with the argument that "a party taking an animal to the pound becomes invested with the character of an officer and has the right to repel any attempt to impede the carrying out of his purpose." Judge Gray reserved his decision until the following Monday. But whether he fined Bell or not we shall never know, since the *News* did not report the case further.

Then came the fire! In 1871 the cottage burned to the ground, for there was no organized fire protection. While the house was in flames Georgia ran out with her mother's silverware tossed into a tablecloth and saved her most cherished heirloom. Such a calamity would happen then, she said, for was it not the month of May? a superstition she had acquired with many others from living among Negroes in Louisiana. While a new house was being built the displaced family found shelter with their friends, the Louis Marshalls, not far away. During her stay there Mrs. Bell was delivered of her fourth child, whom she named Virginia. On the

[174]

same night across the hall her hostess also gave birth to a baby girl.

The new residence built on the site of the old was larger and more comfortable. As the family increased, new rooms could be added. In keeping with the style of those days they had twin parlors, separated by sliding doors. The one in front was "kept for company"; the other they called "the back parlor." On the wall of the latter, used as a living room, hung a gilt-framed mirror above a green marble mantle. To the left of these appeared a built-in bookcase enclosed with glass doors. On the upmost shelf the Major kept his guns and knives, the compass General Grant had given him, and other souvenirs of war. Below rested his books and materials for writing.

Mrs. Bell insisted on having two fireplaces (one in the parents' bedroom, the other in the back parlor). They were both alike, of dark green marble. She needed them she said to keep her from getting homesick for New York. To have such things people thought was silly, for these were the first fireplaces ever built in Los Angeles. Bell added the comfort of a home-made bathtub. Made of wood and six feet long it was lined with tin. A pipe in the bottom fitted into a hole in the floor through which the drainage flowed to a point far back of the house. A "hired man" filled the tub with water carried in a wash boiler. After being used the tub was raised by handles on the end and stood upright against a wall of the dining room in the corner next to the chimney. Then a curtain was drawn concealing it from view. In those days it was a remarkable contraption, since people generally used wash tubs for bathing.

Georgia wanted a lawn and she loved flowers. After the grass seeds were sown the ground was dampened by means of a hand pump attached to a barrel. These were mounted on a dolly and wheeled about the yard as needed. A man filled the barrel by dipping up buckets of water from the *zanja* flowing down Figueroa. But when the ditch was dry he went to the well. As the distance was far to where Bell stored the apparatus, it was drawn up to the lawn by a horse.

When the grass had grown sufficiently the whole place was

flooded. This was done by placing "slide gates" in the *zanja*, which caused the stream to back up and cover the ground. As soon as the water reached the middle of the lot the gates were pulled out and the *zanja* resumed its onward course. A wooden coping built around the yard retained the inflow which seeped gently down irrigating the grass as well as trees and flowers.

There was one time when the water had been turned on rather late and whoever put in the gates forgot to take them out. The family had gone to bed early. In the morning at five, according to his custom, Bell arose and started out to get the newspaper when he saw his whole place deep in water. At the top of his lungs he holloed out, "Great Jehoshaphat, Georgie! We are flooded out!"

The lady of the house had already planted in the back yard the cutting from a black fig tree brought by her all the way from Texas. She now went to Mr. Stengel, the local nurseryman, and ordered from Australia the first scarlet eucalyptus to grow in Los Angeles. Before long she had a flourishing garden of trees and flowers.

Sometime in the early '70s an unknown person appeared at the place and asked to buy it. Mrs. Bell replied (her husband being absent) that it was not for sale. But the stranger insisted, saying, "Please state your price, madam. General Beauregard of Louisiana wants to settle in Los Angeles and to have a gentleman's home. I am his agent and have come to buy him one. This looks like a gentleman's place." And then he added temptingly, "General Pierre Beauregard is a very rich man!" At once Mrs. Bell blocked the offer. "Sir," she interposed, "the general has not money enough to buy our place."[4]

In 1875 Bell at the instigation of his wife divided most of his land into town lots and sold them to the public, making a profit of $8,000. This was the first subdivision annexed to Los Angeles and on old maps is marked Bell's Addition. After his transaction many others did likewise, producing the first land-boom. To lay off the lots it was necessary to create and give to the city certain

Mrs. Georgia Herrick Bell, age 18

Mrs. Georgia Herrick Bell, age 44

The Bell home on Figueroa street in 1872, built after burning of first house

The Bell home, no. 1337 Figueroa street, in 1885

streets for thoroughfares. He donated all the streets lying between Figueroa and Union within the boundaries of Pico and Washington. He named one street Georgia for his wife (which even to the present time is one block west of Figueroa), another Virginia for his second daughter, and Charles street for his first son. He also gave the site for a public school still used today at the corner of Georgia and Seventeenth. In earlier years it was called the Georgia Street School.[5]

During the excitement of selling the lots the Bell family sat one noon around the dinner table with several agents who were discussing with the parents the progress of sales. Mother noticed that Virginia aged four was making a muss on the red-checkered tablecloth, playing with her knife and food. She spoke sharply. "Jinnie, what on earth are you doing?"

"I'm cutting up my gingerbread into building lots, Mamma."

Gentleman's Profession

It humiliated Georgia Bell, granddaughter of the Crockers of Virginia and the Herricks of Massachusetts, that her husband should be a farmer. Such a feeling was natural to one who in her youth had danced with a future British king. True, her mother's people had been Southern planters on the Potomac river and her father Albert had rented his many acres near Springfield, Massachusetts, for cultivation. But they were not "dirt farmers," men who toiled with their hands and used tools. Her uncle Hiram was a fashionable doctor in New York City growing richer each year from the national sale of his "Herrick Pills."

Her husband should be a professional man, she decided, preferably a physician. So she pled with Horace to give up plowing corn and herding sheep. He had too good a mind for that, she insisted. But he positively refused to study medicine. When a boy in his teens he had served for a short time as a doctor's apprentice and had helped in delivering a colored infant. But the experience was so dreadful that then and there he resolved never to be a physician. That much was settled. Consequently Horace and Georgia compromised on law.

He brought home the necessary books which his wife studied too. Then she coached and quizzed him into the legal profession. In that day there was no college sheepskin to be earned. Instead he capitalized his mental keenness, his Sullivan fluency, and a combative disposition. In due time he appeared before the Supreme Court sitting in Los Angeles, paid the fee of five dollars, and passed an oral examination. He was ready now in 1872 to paint his name on an office window of the Temple Block,[6] and begin a legal career lasting more than a quarter-century.

Soon after he had started his practice and was struggling to get established, the county judge, William Hugh Gray, decided a case against Bell, acting as defending attorney. The Major was angry with the judge, for he took the decision as a personal insult. Sam Bryant, deputy sheriff, reported to Gray, "Judge, you had better carry your gun. Horace Bell has threatened to shoot you!"

One late afternoon when Gray was leaving the courthouse for home, he had come to the top of the stairway on the second floor. Bell waited for him in the hall below. At the same instant they both saw each other. "What do you want, Major?" calmly asked the court official.

"Judge William H. Gray," came the answer, "I give you fair warning. I am going to shoot you!"

"Hold your horses, Horace Bell!" urged the magistrate collecting his wits. Then with no trace of fear or anger he dropped his voice below: "Sir, I have no gun. You would not shoot an unarmed man, would you? If you are a gentleman come up here and we'll fight it out with our fists."

A brief silence. Then Bell started up the stairs. By the time he reached the top step the word *gentleman* had done its work. With soft eyes he said in warm tones, "Why, Judge, you know I would not shoot you, I'm your friend." Then he impulsively hugged him and patted his back in the manner of the Mexican *abrazo*.

"Well, Bell, I see you *are* a gentleman!" remarked Gray. And

[178]

so the two lawyers passed down the stairs and out to Main street, arm in arm. In recounting this incident the judge always concluded with: "The Major may have a legal mind, but he has a lawless disposition."[7]

Always Bell appeared in court immaculately dressed and adorned with a red flower in his lapel. Tall and erect he was the image of assurance. His colleagues still living recall his characteristic manner when he was arguing a case. Excitedly he would walk back and forth straight as a soldier on dress parade. His arms were bent at right angles and pressed against his sides, hands clenched with both thumbs pointing stiffly up.

His quick temper proved to be a professional handicap. When fighting mad as he often was his face turned red, his cheeks puffed out, reminding one—so his friends say—of an irate turkey.

Frequently he befriended young lawyers striving to gain a practice, by giving them cases he did not want. Frederick Baker, an attorney of Los Angeles, still recalls with gratitude the aid he received from the Major. This came after a clash in court. During a suit involving a traffic accident Bell lost his temper and threatened to throw the young opponent out the window, thereby receiving the judge's rebuke. But this was only a social introduction, as it were, and Bell took a great fancy to his youthful colleague.

According to LeCompte Davis, his friend and professional contemporary, Bell habitually let his legal battles descend into personal quarrels with the opposing attorney. Such ways however were common in the '70s when lawyers sometimes fought each other in the streets. Pistols were worn in the courtroom and when tension mounted, the sheriff might remove everyone's gun. But throughout his long practice Bell was esteemed for his integrity; no man ever charged him with dishonesty.

The late Byron Waters, for many years dean of the San Bernardino county bar, did not rank Bell among the eminent lawyers of the state, for he never appeared in famous cases. Explaining this fact the historian George William Beattie remarked: "It is easy to understand that a man who had a part in as much activity and adventure as Bell did might not be a profound student of the law. He did do, however, a great amount of legal work for the old Californians and sympathized deeply with them in their troubles over land titles and their unfortunate contacts with American loan sharks."[8]

A poor man, certainly if he were a Latin, could stop him on the street and obtain free legal advice. In Sonoratown, the Mexican district northwest of the Plaza, as well as throughout the county, Bell was called *el abogado de los pobres* (the poor people's lawyer). There was the case in point of the Serrano sisters, the Señoritas Dolores and Maria de los Angeles, whose story follows:

Lying now in Riverside county Temescal valley stretches northward from Lake Elsinore to the present towns of Corona and Arlington. On its sunset side stand the Santa Ana hills and the morning light breaks over Temescal mountain. In early years before its waters were piped away, wanderers passing through the valley beheld a lovely sight. There were *ciénagas* (marshes) green during the longest drouth and groves of live oaks and sycamores where cattle might rest in the shade. Bordering the streams grew willows and cottonwoods, while among the underbrush ran tangles of wild grapevines. Roses of Castile and fields of Matilija poppies bloomed and in the spring, grasses sprinkled with creamcups carpeted the hills. Near the eastern edge hot sulphur springs bubbled up.

In 1818 the padres of San Luis Rey claimed this valley for their mission and sent a soldier to settle there, giving him only a written permit to graze cattle. He was Leandro Serrano, whose father had come over from Spain with Padre Junipero Serra. The priests had chosen him because his influence over the Indians might prevent trouble for their mission. Building a house by a large *ciénaga* he became the first man of European blood to settle in what would later be Riverside county. After his first wife's death Leandro went up to Santa Barbara, married Señorita Josefa Montalva, and brought her down to live in the pleasant valley. In one way he was

[180]

smart, having chosen a former cook of Father Boscano's, the first parish priest in Los Angeles. Seven children were born of this marriage, the youngest being Dolores and Maria.

Leandro knew that the padres could not officially grant him the land; so a few years after coming to the valley he sent his papers of occupancy up to Monterey to obtain legal ownership. But Governor José Maria de Echeandia never answered. Leandro fully intended to write again. He would do so tomorrow, or maybe the next day—*mañana*. But he never did—and in 1853 he died. When the American government arrived insisting on legal titles, the land commissioners rejected the heirs' claim to every part of the valley. As a result the once great property holders were left without title to even the orchards and vineyards surrounding their house. In desperation they appealed to a higher body, which likewise decided against them. As the last blow to their hopes the Supreme Court confirmed the decision of the lower.

Years after, when the land was opened for settlement Horace Bell as attorney somehow managed to retain for the family 160 acres surrounding their adobe dwelling. By now all the children had left the mother but Maria and Dolores. Their living was scant, for the old servant who raised the crops had become too crippled to work. Consequently all the silks, shawls, and mantillas long stored in the family chest were gradually sold to keep them alive.

In time Señora Serrano died and there was no money for her funeral. As the daughters could not suffer the thought of burying their mother in unconsecrated ground they mortgaged their house to the Corona Water Company and bore her body to the little graveyard at Agua Mansa near Colton.

In a later distress the sisters turned again to Major Bell, who sold their farm and with the money bought them a little place on East Sixteenth street in Los Angeles where they lived for many years.[9]

They adored Horace Bell. Wishing to express their gratitude in a personal way they carried to his family a batch of tamales. After eating one, poor Mrs. Bell almost died. She was allergic to red pepper. Complying with the Major's warning the señoritas had prepared some especially for his wife, omitting the condiment. But alas! in stirring both portions they had used the same spoon.

A Daughter of Old New York

Georgia Bell was a lady—an upholder of Eastern propriety, the acme of Victorian gentility. In some ways she was unlike the more rugged pioneer women. Always quiet and dignified she carried on the aristocratic tradition of her people. She had been reared a patrician, having her own inheritance. She never did hard work with her hands or washed dishes. There was no need to, for there were always plenty of servants to be had, colored or Irish. For a dollar and a half a week Chung Wo for many years did all the family laundry regardless of the steady increase in children's garments and young ladies' white petticoats. Then too Bell would not permit his wife or daughters to clean even an occasional tea towel. "I have never allowed my women folks to do any washing," he would protest, "and I don't intend to let you start it now." So Mrs. Bell's life consisted mostly in tending her flowers, managing the house, and bringing up numerous children.

Whenever she drove in the buggy or rode her pony she would not go past the Washington Gardens. This was a place on the southwest corner of Washington and Main where Germans took their families to drink beer. No lady she insisted would ever go near a saloon or any place where alcohol was sold or drunk. When she left home she always wore gloves and made her daughters do likewise. And to chew gum! ugh! that was a sure sign of coarseness. After they had passed through the Georgia Street Grade School she sent her girls to Miss Marsh's private finishing academy at Hope and Pico.

Good speech and correct grammar she loved. Horace exasperated her when he said, "he don't," as he always did, or used a wrong participle. "Don't you see, dear," she would say, "the subject is singular, so you must use a singular verb to agree. Now try to do that and remember also that a gentleman never says, 'he don't.'" After this admonition Horace would reply teasingly, "You're right, Georgie, he don't."

[182]

In appearance this daughter of New York was attractive. Bell was always convinced of that. Throughout his wedded life he fondly described his first sight of her with the same phrase: "the daintiest bit of fashion you ever saw!" In height she was five feet, four. Her eyes were hazel, her complexion lily-pale. Every morning during her young womanhood she wrapped her blue-black locks around finger-like sticks to make long curls. Being naturally wavy her hair needed no wetting to make it stay in place until bed time.

During her early years in Los Angeles, when she went to town alone or called on friends, Mrs. Bell would ride her pony—the one that had carried her across the plains from Texas. He was dark brown and well trained. When his mistress took her whip and swished it back and forth against his belly, he would kneel down. Then by giving a little spring she could mount or get off unaided. Of course she used a sidesaddle. Made of patent leather it was small and shiny. Her whip was a gift from William H. Workman (or Uncle Billy as the family called him) a saddlery merchant who as a young man had come to California in the early '50s. How proud she was of its beauty! Its ivory handle was inlaid with gold and set with highly polished turquoises. The first recollection of "Jinnie" is seeing her mother on the pony. She came dashing in from Pico street on her way to the barn, wearing a gray riding habit and a bright blue veil tied round her hat. And as she rode, the ends of the veil floated behind her like a cloud.

In religion Mrs. Bell was a Presbyterian. But since the town had no congregation of that kind during the '70s, she joined and attended the Methodist church on Fort street (Broadway). In due time all her sons except Charles and all her daughters became members. When her last two children were old enough she sent them to a neighborhood Sunday School called the May Bell Band. Here Mr. and Mrs. Lewis D. Bell (no relatives), who lived on Pico street close to Figueroa, gathered together the youngsters in that part of town, told them Bible stories, and taught them to sing Sunday School songs. Out of their work with children grew

[183]

the Immanuel Presbyterian church, which was founded in 1888 and first located at the southeast corner of Figueroa and Tenth streets. In 1892 Mrs. Bell transferred her membership to this congregation, whose present temple lifts its noble Gothic tower high above the traffic streaming past on Wilshire boulevard at Berendo.

Throughout her whole married life Georgia knelt each night by her bed and prayed that Horace might be converted and join a Christian church. Almost every Sunday he went with her to the 11 o'clock service. Sometimes he caused her great embarrassment, for on looking over the audience he was prone to make personal remarks. He thought he whispered, but his voice had such a quality that he could not.

"Georgie, see that woman's funny hat," he once said. And then came a ripple of suppressed laughter.

"Horace," Mrs. Bell would warn him while going up the steps to enter, "remember now—don't you try to whisper!"

If she missed the morning worship she went in the evening, and as Papa always wanted to go to bed early she would be accompanied by some of her children.

She loved to go to church; she also loved the theater and never missed seeing a good entertainment, except of course when she was pregnant. Like a true Victorian lady she was embarrassed by this condition and during such periods shrank from public view.

She attended the opening of Child's Opera House in 1884 when Mlle. Rhea starred in Sheridan's *The School for Scandal*. Later she went to see Edwin Booth and Lawrence Barrett play in Shakespeare. Gilbert and Sullivan's light operas, particularly *The Mikado*, she enjoyed. She saw Lillian Langtry in the eighteenth-century drama of Goldsmith, *She Stoops to Conquer*. Joseph Jefferson in his *Rip Van Winkle* and the stage version of *Uncle Tom's Cabin* never failed to hold her interest.

But Mrs. Bell almost missed hearing Adelina Patti, an Italian soprano. People hoped that this famous artist would sing in the opera house, but as it was already booked the only available auditorium was the Seventh Regiment Armory over Mott's store on

Main street. At first she decided not to go, for the hall was above a fish market. To be present in a place with such surroundings would violate her sense of propriety. But the temptation was too strong to resist and so she went with the Major, who paid $20 for their seats.

Being superior to her husband in economic wisdom Georgia Bell was the financial manager of the household. Besides lacking a gift for money-making he had trouble in keeping the dollars he earned. Every morning when he left for his office she would walk with him to the front gate and kiss him good-by. After pinning a red flower in his lapel (red being his favorite color) she would place in his hand a half-dollar and say, "Here, Horace, is four bits for you to spend today—two bits for your lunch, 10¢ for carfare if you like, and the rest for cigars. And remember, dear, if you collect any fees don't give any of the money away." Then when he came home in the late afternoon she required him to deposit with her his pocket cash. Such strict measures were necessary to keep the family out of the poorhouse, for he could never resist appeals for charity.

It was she who persuaded him to subdivide their acres into town lots. The home place was owned in her name, as one can see by looking on an old city map. So were all other properties. In her last testament she left none of the family possessions to her husband, wishing to protect him against loss. Instead she willed everything to her second daughter. "See to it," she wrote to Virginia, "that Papa always has a home and that he and the five youngest children are provided for."

The adventurous rover had married a home-keeper. From the time she entered California she never left it. She never returned to New York for a visit, partly because her elopement had alienated her relatives. As the years passed, Horace grew restless and his mind turned to Nicaragua. Everything in that faraway land took on a rosy glow. He longed to go back. He described it romantically to his wife, painting an ideal picture of its lakes, mountains, and natives. "Why," he would add proudly, "I know Nicaragua

[185]

like I had made it with a pick and shovel." Usually she said nothing. Then he would burst out,

"Georgie, let's take the children and move to Nicaragua!"

He harped on the subject everlastingly. Driven to reply she always gave the same answer. Dropping her needlework in her lap she would look up and exclaim in exasperation,

"Horace Bell, you can go to Jericho!"

Despite her first unfavorable impressions this transplanted flower of New York became adapted to new surroundings. She grew to love the town where her husband had brought her, and caught a vision of its future. It was a common thing for her to say: "Children, some day Los Angeles will be a great city. I will not live to see it, but you will, dears. And it will extend from the mountains to the sea." As she said this she raised a hand, as soft and white as one of her own magnolia buds, and pointing it to Sierra Madre beyond Pasadena swept it westwardly toward Santa Monica.

Little Judy Fitzgerald lived with her grandfather, William Hugh Gray, the county judge, in his home on Fort street at the corner of Seventh, the present site of the Lankershim hotel. Being privately tutored she was never sent to school. So having no little friends to play with she became very lonely. She loved Mrs. Bell because that kind lady mothered her like one of her own. She could stay all afternoon with her if she liked and sometimes she was allowed to hold the baby. When Judy wanted to visit Mrs. Bell she got on her burro and rode alone up from Seventh and Fort to the corner of Pico and Figueroa. Above Eighth street there were no buildings on the way—nothing but a dusty road. If she stayed all night the burro trotted back at feeding time without a rider.[10]

On returning from the courthouse and not finding the child at home the judge would ask his servant, a former slave from Kentucky, where she was. "Oh, she's went down to Massa Bell's. I 'spec' she's gwine to stay all night 'cause heah comes de burro without Miss Judy."

[186]

One day the little girl spoke some naughty words which Grandpa overheard. He explained to her the importance of one's words —how they should always be kind and pretty like jewels. "Judy," he added, "let only pearls fall from your lips." The child mused a moment, then remarked, "Grandpa, I think Mrs. Bell is like that. She never lets anything but pearls fall from her lips, does she?"

"Yes, Judy, I'm sure you are right." And then he chuckled, "But I wonder how she does it—living with the Major!"[11]

The Small Fry

When the Bells arrived in Los Angeles they had two children, Charles and Elizabeth. A year before the cottage burned, Horace Junior was born and not long after came Virginia. Then came seven babies in the decade following 1873: Georgia and Albert, Daisy and Lillian, Walter, Canby, and Maud—in all five sons and six daughters.[12] In the early years of family life so many little pitchers had as many big ears. To guard against prattling tongues the parents in matters of privacy conversed in the native language. Mrs. Bell learned quickly, for Spanish was easy to pick up in a town where the majority of people spoke it. Then too she had received a good start when living with Aunt Nievas, who seldom bothered herself with *el inglés*.

In the '70s a mule-drawn car carried passengers from Washington down Main to Temple street in the central shopping district. The Bell children loved the ride and went frequently. Ordinarily when they walked the streets everyone they saw looked familiar, at least those among the Eastern settlers. But once in a while the little Bells would see somebody who seemed different and on returning home they would say: "Mamma, we saw a strange-looking man and a lady and some children on Spring street. Who do you suppose they were?" Then Mother would answer, "Oh, it was probably some traveling man who brought his family along, or maybe they are Easterners who have come to California for their papa's health."

Grandfather came out from Indiana to visit his relatives. "That cruel old man! I hope I never meet him!" Georgia had said after hearing Horace's story of how David Bell made his children sit in the chestnut trees when they were sick with ague. But when the joke was revealed she grew fond of her husband's parent. During his stay he was sitting one afternoon in the house conversing with his daughter-in-law. Five-year-old Bessie was playing with her doll on the floor. Wanting a drink of water he asked the child to fetch him one from the *olla* [water jar] on the back porch. But Bessie refused to budge, pretending not to hear. Her mother spoke sharply, "Bessie, go get Grandpa a drink and be quick about it."

The little girl rose sullenly and shuffled toward the porch. When she was behind her mother's chair she made an ugly face and stuck out her tongue at Grandpa. He let his eyes follow her through the door to the *olla*. He saw her fill the long-handled tin dipper with water and then slyly spit in it. Coming back she approached him, saying sweetly, "Here's your drink, Grandpa." Without a word he took the dipper from her hand, threw its contents out the window, then laid little Bessie across his knees and spanked her emphatically. Because she was his only daughter thus far, Horace had spoiled her badly. As one of his generation who spared not the rod in bringing up children, Grandfather wanted to see her trained with severity. That was why Bessie disliked him.

Long before his daughters were in their teens Bell made them practice each day carrying a burden on their heads. First it was a school book or two. Up and down the porch steps and over the yard, back to the barn, and out to the front gate the little girls trudged, balancing the weight to keep it from falling, their hands hanging free or resting lightly on their hips. When they had learned to carry the books he replaced them with a small pail containing water. Gradually the amount of liquid was increased. Sometimes the children tripped or attention flagged. Then the bucket fell, drenching their dresses. But this brought no rebuke, only encouragement to try harder.

Their papa told them about the women of Nicaragua—how beautifully they walked and how they acquired their graceful

[188]

posture by carrying water jars on their heads as they climbed the hillsides, or heavy baskets of food in the same way as they came from market. "Practice a little each day," he promised his daughters, "and you will all walk like queens." They did as they were told. And the erect bearing they acquired remained with them even throughout old age. Bell tried to make his sons do likewise, giving assurance that it would make them walk like West Pointers. But they refused, having no desire to look like either queens or soldiers.

The Major took time out from his busy life to instruct his boys and girls in sports. On some warm afternoon they would go with him to the depot at Commercial and Alameda streets, board the Wilmington and Los Angeles railroad and ride down to San Pedro. At Boschke island the water was calm and safe. Here he hired a rowboat and tied a rope around each child's waist. After demonstrating the swimming stroke he shoved each one by turn into the water. When they grabbed the side of the boat to hold on, he gently tapped the little hands with an oar and made them let go. Thus he compelled them all to become good swimmers— certainly an unusual accomplishment for girls in the 1880s. On West Lake, which is now in MacArthur Park, he taught his children to feather an oar.

All the brothers and sisters learned to ride and manage a horse. At first they were taught to go to the field alone, slip a rope halter over the animal's head, and lead it to a fence. Then having climbed up on its bare back they rode astraddle to get the feel of its body. After mastering this lesson they were given saddles.

One day at the county fair being held in Agricultural Park (where the University of Southern California now centers) Bessie then 18 rode her father's big stallion Fred in a contest of equestrian skill. During the exhibition the horse reared and fell back with its rider. But Bessie quickly got up, straightened her hat, dusted off her sleeves, remounted and won first prize. The cheering was loud and long. From the grandstand Bell witnessed the accident and never moved a muscle. That evening at supper Bessie fishing for a compliment inquired, "Papa, weren't you rather proud of me when I picked myself up and got back on Fred?" "Huh," said her father with no show of praise, "if you had not done so, I would disown you."

In 1879 a circus came to town. Becoming insolvent the company disbanded and Major Bell closed its legal affairs. In the show there was a clown named Johnny Bull, who had a small trained burro which he used in one of his acts. As the performer had no lodging place Bell let him come out to his barn and sleep with the donkey. During the day the children had great sport riding the comical creature around in the yard. Johnny had taught his pet a trick. Standing off at a fairly long distance the buffoon would bray; whereupon the burro would lay back his long ears and run madly to his master, regardless of where the voice came from, or who was on his back. When this happened the children usually fell off, having no saddle or bridle—and what a frolic it was!

While the affairs of the circus were being settled, Bull had to appear in court several times; and for long hours he was sorely missed by the burro. One afternoon the youngsters had taken him out of the barn lot into the yard, and eight-year-old Virginia had climbed up on him. As soon as he was free he went searching all over the place for Johnny, who was nowhere to be found. Then as though he were possessed with human intelligence he started off to town with Virginia astride his back. Either by chance or uncanny instinct he headed straight for the court, which was being held on the first floor of a hall on the west side of Spring street. The wooden sidewalk nearby lay about six inches above the ground.

Sitting by an open window the clown suddenly beheld his pet ambling up the street, and regardless of where he was he brayed. Immediately the donkey laid back his ears and dashed toward Johnny Bull. Jumping up on the board walk he ran straight through an open door and into the courtroom, the little girl resolutely holding on. The Major was so startled by the sight that he leaped from his chair, his hands stretched out in utter amazement, and shouted, "Great Jehoshaphat! Jinnie! What brings you here?"

[190]

A picket fence enclosed the home place on the front side facing Figueroa street. The Major wanted it brightened up with a fresh coat of whitewash. His sons refused to do the job even for the reward of five dollars. Virginia now 13 suggested, "Papa, you give me the money and I'll do it." So she put on a brother's overalls and his straw hat, a little too big, and started to work. She was painting away busily with her back to the street when Jerry Collins, a neighborhood lad, came up from behind unobserved. As she did not turn around, the onlooker thought she was his rival, Horace Junior. What an opportunity to even old scores, he thought, his opponent being handicapped by the fence!

"Now I've got you!" he threatened and knocked off Virginia's hat. Quick as a flash she turned, dropped her brush, and slapped the boy's face as hard as she could. Seeing that he had struck a girl Jerry slipped away in shame and did not come near the Bell place for weeks. When the Major came home from his office that evening and heard the story, he paid her double. "Jinnie's a great girl," he said proudly to a friend the next morning, "she's got plenty of spunk."

Bell did not want his daughters to marry. When they were old enough to have beaus he ruled that they should have none. And to keep the young gentlemen away he obtained a bulldog. He was about the size of an Airedale only heavier, and white with black and tan spots. So fierce was Tippecanoe that none but the family dared set foot on the place. When Jebne's deliveryman arrived he backed his wagon up to the rear porch and made the family carry in the groceries. The baker in passing refused to get out of his wagon and placed the loaves of bread on the gate posts. When it came about in due course of time that boys strolled home from town with Virginia, they went no farther than the front gate. Sometimes in passing her house hoping to see her they would whistle the refrain of a popular song which ran: "Wait till the bulldog dies, Jennie!"

Time fulfilled this unspoken prophecy. Tippecanoe passed away, the daughters became older, and the boy friends more persistent. One evening Mr. and Mrs. Bell had gone to their bedroom to retire as usual at seven. The Major had turned off the gas light and his wife was kneeling by the bed in her regular devotions. Suddenly there came the sound of footsteps on the front porch. "Georgie!" exclaimed the Major (he never could whisper), "it's burglars! Where's my revolver?" Stepping into the back parlor he seized a gun from the bookcase, loading it quickly. Two daring souls had come to call on Virginia, then in her seventeenth year. They were young Englishmen: George Hatton, 21 and a reporter for the *Times*; the other, his friend, a son of the Earl of Craven, who was visiting Los Angeles on a tour of the world.

Hearing Bell's words the callers leaped off the porch. It seemed too far to race for the street and leap over the picket fence or rush through the gate foolishly left latched. Instead they ran to the cypress hedge beside the front drive and crawled under. Soon the father appeared on the porch clad only in his nightshirt, revolver in hand. Barefooted he stalked about the yard looking for prowlers to shoot at. He peered behind trees and into fence corners, he beat the bushes, but luckily never thought to examine the hedge by the driveway. Meanwhile the boys shivered in secret, one young fellow wondering no doubt if he would ever get back to London to be someday the Earl of Craven. Finally Bell went back into the house and the boys slid out.

The following afternoon Hatton came as usual to the Major's office in the Temple Block to gather news on his beat. Bell sat him down, told of last night's attempted robbery, and made the reporter print the story in the next issue of the *Times*. As George went out the door he gave a knowing wink to Virginia, sitting at her desk as her father's amanuensis.

One Sunday afternoon the family had just finished eating their dinner and the Major leaving the table started to the front porch to smoke his postprandial cigar. When he opened the front door there stood two young men ready to knock for admittance. Bell glared at them, then blurted, "What do you want?"

"Sir," they said politely, "we've come to see Miss Bessie."

Virginia Herrick Bell

The complete Horace Bell family in the front parlor at home: parents, 11 children, 2 in-laws, 1 grandchild. (Virginia at the piano) In 1888

The Major stiffened. His face turned red as it always did when he was angry. Then he whipped out the words, "Miss Bessie is not on exhibition," and turning closed the door on the young men's faces.

Soon after this, Virginia announced at the supper table that Mr. George Hatton was going to call. At once Bell flew into a rage. "I won't have men coming to see my daughters," he shouted. Virginia waited for him to calm down. Then she softly explained that Mr. Hatton wanted to come—that she would entertain him in the front parlor—that all the family could come in and meet him and talk as much as they liked. "But, Papa," added Virginia firmly, "you must not treat me as you treated Bessie. If I can't have boys come and call on me in my home, then I will meet them outside."

The Major was stunned. Never before had his patriarchal authority been challenged. To the surprise of all he became as meek as a lamb and said nothing. The young man called at the appointed hour and the door swung graciously open.

The other girls were beneficiaries of Virginia's courage. For after her showdown Bell never again objected to men visitors. But he persisted in the embarrassing practice of interrupting Bessie's evening "dates." Regularly as the clock struck nine like a faithful cuckoo he would stick his head in the front parlor and snap out, "Time to shut up shop, Bessie!" And she did.

"Ha!" laughed Virginia many years after, "Papa never said that to me. He did not dare to!"

Eventually there were weddings for all six daughters.[13]

Charles at 16 pined for a mustache. He fretted over its slow appearance. His father like most of the family jested about the fuzz on his upper lip. He promised the boy that a heavy mustache would come quickly if every night for a week he would take milk foam fresh from the family cow and smear it above his mouth. This treatment the boy kept up to the amusement of his father and the other children. When the time had almost expired the Major thought he would play a joke on the youthful aspirant to manhood. So he procured a false mustache, and while the boy slept he gently glued it above his upper lip.

In the morning howls of merriment arose from the breakfast table as Charley, a sound sleeper, came in late from his bedroom, stretching and yawning, still unconscious of his appendage. But Mrs. Bell was not laughing. Completely taken by surprise she stared for a moment at the sheepish boy. Then under their long black lashes her hazel eyes caught fire. This was the only time Virginia can remember when her mother was so angry with Papa. "Horace Bell!" she burst out, her voice cutting like a razor. "Horace Bell! You can play all the pranks you want to on other people. But you can not play pranks on *my children!*" Breakfast was finished in silence.

But Charles expressed his manhood successfully at the age of 20 when on the first of October 1883 he became a postman. That was when free delivery began and Charley's job started on the opening day. Up and down Figueroa street collecting and distributing mail he rode horseback. For the whole town there were only five carriers. Prior to this civic innovation the *Herald* had remarked: "Charley Bell will do duty on the outskirts of the city. Everyone is anxiously awaiting the postal convenience."

In Pursuit of Letters

Along came the year 1881 bringing its great event, the first centennial of the founding of Los Angeles. The fourth of September had been accepted as the correct date for the anniversary, but Major Ben Truman, a local author and editor,[14] claimed evidence that it was a day later and so convinced the city fathers that the celebration was held on the fifth. The day dawned beautiful and clear and a gentle breeze made riding or walking in the sun even comfortable. At an early hour people began to fill the downtown streets. Across Main and Spring swung green festoons bearing the numerals 1781 and 1881. On the lot adjoining the Plaza church stood a rostrum adorned with boughs of evergreen and the national colors. Above the old temple fluttered the Pope's banner, flanked on one side by the flag of Mexico, on the other by the Stars and Stripes.

There were 30,000 people in town that day, so guessed the *Herald*, far more than double the permanent population. The parade forming at two o'clock was so grand that it took 20 minutes to pass under the arch erected on Main street by the courthouse. You could see up-to-date surreys and victorias mingling with horsemen in old-fashioned costumes, seated on silver-studded saddles and displaying gay Spanish serapes.

First came the mounted police ahead of their chief; then the grand marshal, General George Stoneman (later to be governor) with his aides. Following them on horses rode six surviving members of the Los Angeles Rangers, among them Horace Bell. Now rolled into view a creaking *carreta* pulled by oxen, and a carriage exhibiting two Mexican ladies wearing mantillas. One was three years more than a centenarian, the other had attained the riper age of 117. Both were living when Governor Felipe de Neve founded the pueblo. Next in order marched the Eagle Corps or state guard in uniform and the society of California Pioneers. Then arrived as a climax Governor George Perkins, riding with his staff in an open hack; behind him came others: Mayor James R. Toberman, the two superior judges, the board of education, the city council, and the board of supervisors. At the end appeared the ultramodern touch, the fire department clinging to its two horse-drawn steam engines.

After parading through the principal business streets the procession dissolved upon the Plaza where Don Juan de Torro mounted the platform and delivered a Mexican oration. Then Major Horace Bell spoke on the early history of Los Angeles—as the reporter put it—"in the American language."[15]

In leisure hours Bell was an inveterate reader. He had three favorite books which he reread many times. They were *Gil Blas*, a picaresque French novel, in Padre Isla's Spanish translation; Cervantes' *Don Quixote*, enjoyed for its satirical humor; and Bernal Díaz' *Historia verdadera de la conquista de la Nueva España*

[195]

(The True History of the Conquest of Mexico) which he read in the original Spanish. This last work long held his interest because he loved history and enjoyed the familiarity of its setting. When he first came to California it was apparently "a best seller," as well as the other two, for he records having seen it commonly in the homes of the dons. Then there was Flavius Josephus, the Jewish historian. Bell never grew tired of him.

Next to history he delighted in poetry. He relished the *Divine Comedy* by Dante and Milton's *Paradise Lost*. Among the long modern poems he preferred Thomas Moore's *Lalla Rookh* for its Oriental narratives.

He liked nothing better than to get his wife off alone, away from the children, and read to her. And how she enjoyed it! She was an insatiable listener. Every Sunday after dinner, except when they went for a ride, the pair would sit on the front porch when it was pleasant, in bad weather in the back parlor, while he read to her several chapters from the big family Bible. Eventually he completed the whole volume from Genesis to Revelation. It was in the book of First Kings that he learned of Jehoshaphat, who provided his exclamation of surprise. He read to her also a popular book called *Why We Love Lincoln* and all of Robert Burns's works. One Sunday afternoon when Mrs. Bell first heard his poem "To a Louse" she passed a discriminating judgment. "But Horace," she interrupted, "a lady would not have a louse on her bonnet."

More than being an avid reader Horace Bell like many Hoosiers had an urge for original writing. In 1856 he had worked on the staff of the San Francisco *Bulletin*. Later while staying in Tehuantepec, Mexico, he wrote, in Spanish, for the local newspaper. Soon after the Civil War he contributed articles to the *Golden Era*, a literary journal of San Francisco. These were sketches of northern California during the Gold Rush.

The Major was blessed with a phenomenal memory, an eye for picturesque details, and the pioneer's gift for narrative. These traits made personal recollections his natural form of expression. Having enjoyed composing his sketches for the *Golden Era* he was led on to a larger project. He would tell the story of the set-tling of California as he had seen it, down to the present, giving more attention to the southern country.

One day in 1878 he closed all the doors of the back parlor, took paper and pencil, and sat down to begin his memoirs, inspired by his guns and knives in the bookcase. His table stood by two windows. As he made notes he stuck them on a long nail set in a wooden block. The title came quickly, *Reminiscences of a Ranger*. But actually the pursuit of Joaquin Murietta's bad men, suggested by the name, comprised but a small part of his story. He had no time for writing except on Sundays. Rising at five he did much of his work before breakfast, after which he continued until dinner at two, taking time out to go with his wife to church. When the children raised their voices in the house or played out-side near his windows, Mrs. Bell would whisper, "Hush, Papa's writing the *Ranger*!"

A chapter finished he called in his wife to hear it and pass judgment. Sometime in 1881 the manuscript was completed and carried to the print shop of Yarnell, Caystile, and Mathes, who published the *Weekly Mirror*, predecessor of the Los Angeles *Times*—the only job-printing shop in town. There was not enough type for its 450 octavo pages. So the first half of the text was printed, the type taken down and reset for the last half. The book was bound in cloth—part of the edition being in dark red, another in green, a third in navy blue. On the front cover ap-peared, stamped in gold, symbols of early California—a pistol crossed by a bowie knife, a huge cactus growing by a mission, a squad of armed horsemen in action. When the workmen had finished their job Bell's *Reminiscences of a Ranger* was the first cloth bound volume to be printed in Los Angeles.[16]

The Major had composed his opus as an avocation, yet with a purpose. He wrote, as he stated in a private letter, not for money but to record his times as a duty to posterity. Accordingly his book remains an essential source for historians, being the first eyewitness account of life in southern California in the period following the rule of the missions. If LeCompte Davis, his contemporary, be right, "it is the only book about early Los Angeles that will live forever. Other pioneers," he added, "published their annals decades later and erred in putting themselves near the center. Bell wisely kept himself in the background."

In being full of action *Reminiscences of a Ranger* is early Western. Its method is episodical—not tightly coherent—and sometimes provokingly digressive. But such was the mode of frontiersmen telling their story by a campfire—the form to which Mark Twain, another pioneer, was best adapted. Bell selected his material for its liveliness and color and yet his treatment is realistic. He scorned Helen Hunt Jackson's novel *Ramona*[17] for its romantic distortion of the Californian scene, and repeatedly called himself a "truthful historian." The *Ranger* is highly spiced with Western humor — a boisterous merriment loved by the pioneers, which made their hard lives bearable.

His work shows the influence of his three favorite books. Fundamentally the *Ranger* belongs to the picaresque type of literature and is like *Gil Blas* not only in its loose structure but also in having rogues for characters. It is satirical like *Don Quixote*, and like the *Conquest of Mexico* is offered as true history. Bernal Díaz had given his eyewitness narrative of the fighting in New Spain. Horace Bell would do the same for his young state. Finally let it be repeated that these three books, as he himself had observed, were commonly read in the Spanish homes of early California. Wherefore it follows that *Reminiscences of a Ranger* bears the brand of the Latin Southwest.[18]

CHAPTER VIII

The Fretful Porcupine

I was asking for something specific and perfect for my city.
WHITMAN, *Mannahatta*

Faithful, Fearless, and Free

FINISHING the *Reminiscences of a Ranger* was not to mark the close of Bell's career as a writer. Rather it opened the way to an avocation of journalism. In the following year he established a weekly newspaper called the *Porcupine*. This was a journal of caustic nature as the title indicated, designed to reform the government of Los Angeles city and county.[1]

In the first issue appearing on November 11, 1882 he set forth his purpose and policy. He adopted the slogan, *Faithful, Fearless, and Free*, placing it on page one under the animal's name. Heading the editorial columns appeared his motto which read:

> For the cause that needs assistance
> For the wrongs that need resistance
> For the good that I can do

His paper would serve all upright people. He described the lawless conditions of Los Angeles at that time as he saw them. There were abuses in the administration of law and justice— abuses so old and tolerated that to be an official in Los Angeles was sufficient to brand one as being dishonest and a filcher of the public purse. So corrupt had the municipal rulers become, he affirmed, that none but "bummers" and men devoid of self-respect could be found to serve in a city office. If a man kept out of the penitentiary he was good enough to be a Los Angeles official. If he got into the "pen" and out again he was promoted to high office.

[199]

Bell compared present conditions with those in San Francisco in 1856. The *Bulletin*, for which he worked as reporter in that year, was established in the northern city because justice was not impartially administered by the local courts. Only the poor and friendless, he remembered, were punished by the law. Those of wealth and influence escaped. In this respect the editor judged Los Angeles in 1882 to be as bad. Yet in spite of many signs of political corruption, he conceded in his first number: "We will not proclaim the universal dishonesty of our public servants—far from it. We believe that many of our *county* officers are honest capable men."

No people anywhere in America, the *Porcupine* averred, had been so overtaxed as the residents of Los Angeles city and county. City taxpayers paid as high as six percent on assessed valuations and some had lost their property because of the high rate. A chief cause for the burdensome levies was the lazzaroni, a name given by Bell to criminal loafers, who spent their time sitting on the courthouse steps waiting to be called in for jury duty, or lounging on the grass, or leaning many hours on the cannon in front of the building. These hoodlums he declared had cost the taxpayers more coin than it would take to build a new courthouse, a jail, a city hall, a branch penitentiary, and to grade and macadamize every street and road in the county. Their evil influence was increased by selling their votes to villainous officials who could thus keep their jobs and waste public funds.

As the primary goal the *Porcupine* proposed to work for the reduction of city and county taxes. This thought was uppermost in the minds of the sponsors who persuaded Bell to start the paper, John G. Downey, a former governor, and Louis Mesmer, owner of the United States hotel. Both men being large property holders who desired to protect themselves from excessive taxation had agreed to subsidize the publication.[2] But the storm raised by the first number so frightened Downey that he reneged and never paid a dollar. True to his word Mesmer gave his share of the money until the paper was completely owned by the editor.

Another purpose was to correct abuses in law and justice by exposing the evil record of office seekers and the corrupt doings of office holders. Suppose, wrote Bell, a man were a candidate for city treasurer whom an editor knew to be an ex-convict, a murderer, or midnight robber. The people might not know this, many of whom had arrived in town only a few months before. They would expect and have the right to learn from their newspapers all the good and bad concerning the candidate. Was it not an editor's duty to give all information about such persons and not suppress it? And yet there were publishers in Los Angeles who had proclaimed as honest men those whom they knew to be rascals.

As for the *Porcupine* it would pursue the course taken by James King, founder of the San Francisco *Bulletin*, and later by editor Glancy of the Santa Barbara *Press*, and print the whole truth. It would do this in defiance of all the rogues and assassins infesting Los Angeles. Wherefore the *Porcupine* proclaimed that any person seeking public office had better look to his record.

Here the Major acted within the law. For the statutes of California permitted newspapers to print the dishonorable history of men seeking public office. This concession was grounded on the principle that the people had a right to know the character of their officers as a protection to the state. Bell being a lawyer knew that so long as he printed only the truth he was legally invulnerable. It was for this reason that he was never convicted of libeling an official or candidate. But though the law would not touch him he was not exempt from personal violence.

He further promised to hold officials responsible for appointing improper persons as policemen; he would watch the board of supervisors and publish the minutes of their meetings; he would pay attention to judges who perverted justice. Moreover the irrigation system as managed by the city called for scrutiny. So did the sewer system, the cleansing of the city from filth, and the control of prostitution.

Besides giving his general objectives Bell outlined his editorial policy. Though he had always been a Republican his paper would be non-partisan. He would grant to corporations the same rights as to individuals, but no more; while the man who worked with his hands should have the same hearing as the railroad magnate, Leland Stanford. In exposing corruption the editor would of necessity deal in personalities. But when doing so he would confine himself within the bounds of decorum. He would publish scandal only when it pertained to officialdom.

Having flung his banner to the breeze Bell called upon the public to support the *Porcupine* by buying and reading it. With the help of all good citizens it would succeed in the battle for better government.

Such startling announcements brought a response from other newspapers. The *Ledger* of New Albany, Indiana, his birthplace, informed its readers that Horace Bell, now living in Los Angeles, was editor of a new weekly called the *Porcupine*. It added, "If the Major writes as well as he shoots, is as brave in peace as he was in war, the paper will not belie its name." And the Los Angeles *Times*, edited by Harrison Gray Otis, soon to become an enemy, remarked prophetically: "The *Porcupine* made its first appearance last Saturday. True to its nature each quill was on end and deuced sharp. Somebody will be looking for the editor with a shotgun if he doesn't smooth them down a bit!"

Brass Buttons

Bell began by attacking the city police. They were thugs, he charged. Their brutality continued a tradition reaching back to primitive days when Los Angeles, with the single exception of Santa Fe, was the wickedest pueblo in the Southwest. In the year 1853, he recalled, more murders were committed within the town than in the rest of California. There was an average in that blood-stained period of more than one for each day. As time went on good people came and red-handed ruffians moved elsewhere, many to Arizona. But in 1882 the spirits of these bad men still walked the streets disguised as officers of the peace.

He complained of their drunkenness, even when on duty. He described an intoxicated policeman he had seen in Sonoratown. This inebriate had lain down on a street bench and while he was asleep some mischievous Mexican boys removed his star, fastened it on the seat of his breeches, pinned his coat tails apart and waited for the officer to awake. When he did he stood up and exclaimed, "Will be jabers now and where's me shtar?" With sober face and twinkling eyes a little gamin informed him that the chief had removed it while he slept.

"Did he indade! Will thin, that's all right," and away he marched to headquarters followed by a crowd of yelling imps. In almost every block the man of parted coat tails and misplaced badge would turn around and accost the urchins with, "Yez devils, and what does yez mane? I'll arrisht the lasht of yez, yez dirthy blackguard spalpeens." Thus was the paid officer of the law escorted through the streets, creating merriment but little shame, so accustomed were the pedestrians to the disgraceful conduct of policemen.

The editor protested against the manner in which the police force was appointed. They were chosen he asserted not according to ability but for their value as vote-getters on election day.

He accused them of corruption, particularly Henry King, the top man. Bell asserted that the disreputable women remained on Los Angeles street contrary to orders from the city council because of a gold-headed cane presented by them to the chief of police. A former officer who had quit the force in disgust informed the Major a year before that the bribes accepted by the police amounted to the monthly sum of $2,000.

Shortly before the first issue of the *Porcupine* appeared the rumor spread that the editor was going to expose the chief, one of the printers having furnished the police with a proof sheet. On Saturday morning when the press was turning out the first copies a group of men in blue uniforms with brass buttons came to the shop demanding that the machine be stopped and the printed copies surrendered to them for destruction. Instead 2,000 copies were passed out free on the streets. On the next morning some of Bell's friends called at his home on Figueroa and warned him against going to town that day, for threats had been made that he would be shot down. But the Major came to his office as usual.

A month later the *Porcupine* charged the chief with "drunkenness, indecency, bribe-taking, and blackmailing." These allegations he stood ready to prove. Soon a member of the force came to the *Porcupine* office and disclosed a plot to assassinate Bell. The head officer would get a warrant for the editor's arrest and go with a half-dozen others to his home in the suburbs. If Bell resisted they would put an end to him. If he submitted they would kill him on the way to town, then report that because he assaulted one of them they had to shoot him in self-defense.

While more weeks passed the *Porcupine* continued to stick its quills in the blue uniforms. Finally the climax came on June 25, 1883. At about two in the afternoon the editor was sitting at his office desk in the Temple Block. He had just finished writing and turned in his seat toward the closed door a few feet away from his chair. He had picked up a copy of the San Francisco *Wasp*, another journalistic stinger, and begun to read it. Hearing a little squeak he looked up. Quietly the bolt of the door began to turn, so gently that he thought some timid maiden was stealing unobserved upon his privacy. He watched the door as it slowly opened and there stood the chief of police leveling his silver-mounted, self-cocking revolver at his head. Instantly Bell sprang upon his enemy, deflecting the weapon. At the same time, the pistol flashed, its fire burning the Major's right hand. With his other he seized the wrist of King's pistol hand. They struggled, the editor having the disadvantage of weighing 30 pounds less than his opponent of 220.

Charles A. Alward, whose office was just across the hall, gave to the *Express* reporter his account of the fight. After a moment's scuffle he saw the pair drop to the floor and heard Bell call out at the top of his lungs, "Charley, Charley!" The chief had fallen underneath his intended victim. Desperately Bell was holding

King's pistol hand with his own left hand when his son Charles came bounding into the office from the *Porcupine* shop on the third floor, carrying a heavy wooden mallet, the kind used by printers. Young Bell struck the officer two or three blows squarely on the head. At this point Jewell Newell who was standing in the hallway leading past Bell's office and had heard the pistol shot ran in, took the gun away from King, and restrained Charley from delivering more thwacks. Soon Constable Griffin appeared and separated the wrestlers and then came Justice Ling. By this time a crowd of spectators blocked the hall.

Badly beaten up the chief was carried to his home where his wounds were dressed. But he was not dangerously hurt. His blood-stained straw hat and gun were left behind, which for many years hung on the editor's wall as trophies.

In the next week's issue the *Porcupine* gave its readers a full account of the affair, agreeing in essential points with the story as told by the *Express*. To celebrate his victory Bell added an extra sheet which displayed a comic cartoon deriding King.[3]

But this physical encounter did not stop his criticisms of the police. For four years he continued to charge them with wrongdoing. By 1887 Bell began to see results in his battle for reform. He claimed to have rid the city of the worst rascals on the force. He took credit for the dismissal of four chiefs who had been guilty, he alleged, of taking bribes. As time went on his complaints diminished, but to the end of his editorial career he protested against the mistreatment of arrested citizens. In 1888 when the commissioners were investigating charges of brutality Bell wrote, "A policeman is armed with the power of the law, but rare indeed is the case when he should use his club and still less his revolver. Shoot a few of them. That will put them on their good behavior."

A Plea for Progress

The *Porcupine* wanted the century-old town to be made modern. More public buildings were needed, it declared in 1882, including "a big hotel, an opera house, a great big jail, a house of correction, and a branch penitentiary."

It pointed out that the city's fire brigades (there were only two) had no apparatus for reaching persons trapped in the top story of a burning building. Despite progress in other things they were still compelled to jump into the ancient contrivance of a canvas held many feet below. There were as yet—in 1883—no four-story buildings in Los Angeles, but the editor believed there would be some day. Even so at the present time it would puzzle a volunteer fireman to get a ladder, if he had one, fixed against any of the buildings on Spring street. This problem demanded study.

During the land boom the number of new settlers and transients greatly swelled the population. So many new people had come to town that although nearly 4,000 dwellings had been built during the three years since 1882 it was still difficult to procure a vacant house. Yet despite the influx postal facilities had not been increased. The office building was no longer large enough. "Put out the barbers and real estate agents located on the ground floor and give their space to the mail service," suggested the editor, who claimed to be well-informed and no doubt he was, since his son Charles was at that time a postman.

At least three more employees should be added to the staff at the office and paid adequate salaries. It was absurd, the *Porcupine* declared, to expect good service from a clerk who received only $40 for a month of eleven-hour working days.

Then there should be four more letter carriers. The Morris Vineyard Tract was one mile within the city limits and but one mile from the post office; yet mail was not delivered there. One half-mile up Temple street lived a group of 700 people who received their mail only at the general delivery window or in their private boxes. The same condition existed in Boyle Heights and East Los Angeles. "Gentlemen of the post office department," entreated Bell, "these people should not lose in time what in a year would amount to many dollars. Let something be done for them."

In '87 during the boom he warned against erecting buildings too cheaply and hastily. There were public structures in Los Angeles, he asserted, so frail that a light earthquake would tumble them down like toy houses. It was criminal for authorities to permit the construction of such man-traps. This advice had been prompted by a recent disaster occurring on a California desert where a wind storm blew down a hotel built as a speculative project, killing women and children. "How many," he remarked sarcastically, "it would not do to let Eastern visitors know—it might frighten them away." True, Los Angeles had no cyclones, but it did have earthquakes. As a protection against disaster he called for a city inspector of buildings.

The people of Los Angeles were frequently reminded of the need for adequate sewerage. Large sums of money had been collected for sewers, yet the town in '86 had no satisfactory disposal system. In the name of those who would die from bad sanitation he protested against the fraudulent construction of the sewer line on Spring street. He had inspected the cement pipe being laid and found that taking a section of pipe as it lay on the street he could grind it into powder with the sole of his shoe. This was no exaggeration on the part of Bell, for old-timers still remember the poor quality of cement in that day. Some towns even forbade the use of cement made at Colton, not far from Los Angeles.

Before the city could progress much further Bell insisted it must have a complete and permanent sewer system. It would not do to pave a street and then dig it up frequently for repairs or extensions. The main trunk line should be made large enough for all time. It should debouch many miles from town—the ocean would be better, only that water being so precious the sewage should be utilized for irrigating fields and orchards.

There was no place in Los Angeles, in the early '80s, where boys were permitted to swim. They could go to the beaches, but that meant a long drive with a horse and not every boy had a horse. Or they could board a train, one ran to Wilmington, another to Santa Monica, but such a trip took a big part of a day and cost money. The river nearby like most streams in southern California was dry in the summer, except for a few water holes in its bed. Bell tells us that when boys stole out on hot days to the Los Angeles river or to the reservoirs where cattle were watered, their heels were dogged by policemen. If caught in the act of swimming they were brought before the court, fined, humiliated, and possibly jailed. He made a plea for the boys—that a place be provided where they could play in the water unmolested. The greatest pleasure of boyhood he remembered was swimming.

Furthermore a man could not discharge his full duty as a citizen if he were unable to take care of himself in water, for he would never make a perfect soldier. A courier, a scout, an aide-de-camp, an engineer, or pontoon-layer must be a good swimmer. Certainly boys who lacked this accomplishment would never make good sailors. If necessary, asserted Bell, the Federal government should require every lad to learn. But compulsion would be needless—they would learn soon enough—if they had the opportunity. "Our city government," he concluded, "should set aside a place for them to swim and make it as safe as possible for small boys."

Bell called attention in 1888 to the need for a first-aid station. He told of a man whose foot was torn off by a runaway team. "Nothing could be done for him," the editor lamented, "until he reached the county hospital two miles distant over a rough road. Are we merciful to our fellow creatures sending them in such a condition so far away when a city receiving hospital could be so cheaply maintained?" Never did Bell dream that someday Los Angeles would have such an institution located on Georgia street —the thoroughfare he had named for his wife.[4]

Sodom and Gomorrah

Frequently the *Porcupine* exposed the gamblers. For years, it declared, they had ruled the city, once even placing a member of their clique in the chair of the chief magistrate. "They are yet

The Major at home, mounted on his horse, in 1885

Major Bell, about 1901

*Horace Bell as commander of
G.A.R. post in 1884*

a power," it affirmed in '83, "going so far in the last election as to subsidize lazzaroni voters in favor of candidates who in turn will favor the gamesters, all this being known to the public."

The paper called attention to a gambling hall close to the public library and known to the police. It reported that the chief received $200 a month for protecting games of chance going on at a place between the Pico House and his headquarters. Among the bluecoats it had long been understood that he received $35 monthly from each of two fan-tan games running day and night in Nigger alley. The editor favored strict supervision of all gambling games. Minors and intoxicated men should be kept from playing and heavy taxes imposed on the operators. Though many people opposed legalizing this evil, in his opinion such action was the only solution.

Moreover the Major stood for a stricter control of the liquor traffic. "When a vice can not be cured then do the next best thing," he admonished, "mitigate it." One of the greatest evils in Los Angeles he thought was the large number of low-class saloons. These, however, should be abolished. By raising the cost of a license from $10 to $1,000 they could be forced out of business. The better class of saloon-keepers, who alone would be able to buy a license, discouraged excessive drinking and when they saw a customer getting beyond his depth refused further drinks and sent him home in a condition less liable to be robbed. On the other hand keepers of low-type barrooms lured men on to intoxication hoping to obtain their cash. Woe be to the man who commenced to drink at such places! He was sure to get drunk and to lose his money, and if he were a stranger in Los Angeles he was certain to wind up on the chain gang, where to finish his misfortune he was robbed by the police.

Let the city government make such nuisances impossible.

Late in 1882 a news item in the *Porcupine* revealed that a dozen women had been apprehended for keeping houses of prostitution in Nigger alley. A special detective had procured the arrests, but when the madams were brought to trial the policemen swore to their good character. While the city attorney was conducting the prosecution he was so hindered by the chief and his force that he filed charges against the head officer.

In the next year the *Porcupine* demanded the removal of brothels from Los Angeles street. Single-handed Bell fought for this reform until the last house of prostitution vanished and the street became respectable. Later the police grew careless and wickedness won back its old quarters. This street on the west side from First to Requena (now called Market) had filled, it was said, with the vilest set of harlots that ever disgraced a community. Immediately after its cleaning up, Los Angeles street was a popular road for travel into and out of the city. "Now," said Bell in 1887, "nobody will drive along that thoroughfare unless obliged to, and businessmen located in that section suffer in their trade. Why should dens of iniquity be tolerated in the heart of the city? Can and will the police commissioners answer?"

He announced that he was having a list compiled of all ill-famed houses and the names of the property owners. When this was complete he would publish it together with the statute against prostitution, unless the mayor and chief of police enforced the law and closed the bagnios. It was gross hypocrisy, declared Bell, for otherwise decent people, including church members, to treble and quadruple their income by renting their buildings to prostitutes. We will never know if he carried out his threat, since so many issues of his paper have been lost.

The Yellow Peril

Bitterness rose against the Chinese in Los Angeles, many people wishing to see them excluded from the city. Two arguments were used to oppose their presence. One pertained to conditions in Chinatown, the other to the effects of Oriental labor on native workingmen.

Almost as soon as he began to publish his paper Bell set forth his objections. He declared that at least a dozen opium dens were flourishing in the Chinese section, where perhaps 50 Americans had been taught to smoke the drug. The city council, he said, had engaged a detective to gather evidence against the proprietors, but the police had thrown every obstacle in his way. While talking with a businessman on Alameda street, in the rear of Chinatown, the editor saw two young white women leave a Chinese hovel looking as though they had been using the vile poppy, and 10 minutes later an Oriental emerged from the same place bearing similar marks of addiction. Soon after, two white boys entered. Then a pair of young American women accompanied by several Chinese passed through an alley near the temple on their way to the center of the colony. In his next issue Bell called upon the police to protect the young people of Los Angeles from narcotic ruin.

The Major feared also the lack of sanitation in the Chinese settlement. Its crowded, ill-ventilated houses and its filth he regarded as a menace to public health. It was an outrage, he asserted, to have such a plague spot near the post office and hotels. "Remove Chinatown to some other locality and do it at once," he demanded. "Open Los Angeles street clear through and remove this ulcer from the face of the city."

In 1886 the *Porcupine* presented the economic argument. The 30,000 inhabitants of the city paid the Orientals, it figured, almost a million dollars yearly for vegetables, laundry work, and domestic labor. Probably most of this amount was sent to China. If it were paid to French or German citizens fine houses and stables would be built in place of shanties and rookeries. Consequently there would be added a million dollars' worth of property to the tax rolls instead of decreasing the general wealth by making Caucasian workingmen poorer. The situation would worsen, for as the Chinese entered into more occupations more Americans would be impoverished.

Bell printed the resolutions of the local Trades Council to be read and discussed at a coming mass meeting. If these were adopted the citizens in attendance would begin action on the first of May. They would stop patronizing Chinese vegetable gardens and laundries. They would boycott hotels and restaurants where Orientals worked, and all persons who rented or leased ground to the Chinese or who sold goods manufactured by them anywhere in the United States. The *Porcupine* urged everyone to attend.

Since he had championed the cause of labor Horace Bell was invited to speak, in addition to 11 others, including State Senator R. F. Del Valle and Stephen Mallory White, the district attorney. Apparently the meeting accomplished nothing, for Bell reported that he left the hall in disgust before his turn came to speak, along with half of the audience, because of the prolonged oratory.

But the Chinese found a friend at the Methodist church on Fort street. The pastor, Mr. F. P. Bresee, a week later preached a sermon on the Chinese question. Major Bell had to listen to it since he had come with his wife, who was a member of the church. The minister reminded his congregation of a treaty existing between the United States and China, and of California's obligation to refrain from any procedure until it was authorized by Congress. He asserted that boycotting was a belligerent act toward a people whom the United States were bound to protect. As our country had opened her doors to the oppressed of all nations it was inconsistent to violate this policy and un-American to refuse to patronize the Chinese as a class.

In his next paper Bell replied to the ministerial way of reasoning. He confirmed his case by describing the "fortifications" of Chinatown. The place was protected, he said, with iron gates and no one could enter, not even a policeman, without giving a secret sign. Why was it closed to inspection? What did the Chinese do inside? Why should a foreign bastile be allowed in an American city?

What further part the Major took in the controversy we shall never know since at this point there is a break in the files of the *Porcupine*. But the last mention of the Oriental problem occurred in July of '87 with the news of a fire in Chinatown. The entire east side, about one-half of the settlement, burned down. The editor remarked that the atmosphere in that locality now seemed purer.

All Around the Town

Horace Bell has left in his newspaper brief pictures of places in his home town and nearby. They show what life was like in Los Angeles county in the years shortly before and after the land boom of 1886.[5] What he saw and recorded concerned mostly what he wanted to have changed. Other writers have dwelt upon the charm of early Los Angeles, but the Major with the disposition of a reformer paid more attention to its unloveliness. Perhaps it was well that he did, since his realism dispels the glamor of idyllic histories.

From the beginning of the *Porcupine* until the end of his editorship the public ways of Los Angeles were his perennial theme. "The streets are in a deplorable condition," he wrote in '86. "Chuckholes abound everywhere and visitors take no comfort in driving about the city. Many of the streets are so bad that a team cannot pass through them faster than a walk."

He pointed out the worst thoroughfares. There was for example Summit street. This right-hand termination of old Aliso street came down a hill from the east suburbs. Its condition was so bad in the spring of '82 that within a fortnight two citizens suffered broken legs when their wagons turned over because the road had been washed out by the rains.

One summer the Major himself undertook to improve the 542 feet of Figueroa street bounding his place. He claimed to have put it in pretty decent condition, at least for a while. He and some hired help removed the dust from each chuckhole, emptied a bucket of water into it, dumped in a wheelbarrowful of cobblestones and gravel, then filled up the hole with dust from the road, and poured over all buckets of water from the nearby *zanja*. Bell remarked that this work cost him $10 and as the city had just voted the magnificent sum of $100 for the repair and sprinkling of Figueroa, which was three miles long and 99 feet wide, the officials could now deduct $10 from the appropriation and spend this amount elsewhere.

During the winter rains the mud on Spring and First streets

would be 12 inches deep. Over the biggest water holes wise-crackers placed signs which read, "No fishing allowed here." When horses and wagons came splashing through the main business streets the mud, mixed with manure, flew upon the faces and clothes of passers-by and splattered the shop windows of the stores beyond the sidewalk. Even Temple street in the busiest section was full of chuckholes. A subscriber writing to the *Porcupine* proclaimed the inconsistency of heralding to the world the perfect climate of Los Angeles, inviting all to come and enjoy it, then ushering the visitors into a city whose streets were a loblolly of mire.

During the spring of '87, according to Bell, the streets were sprinkled insufficiently. Only on the main business thoroughfares was the work properly done. He demanded that every street which had been graded at public expense be sprinkled and kept in good order and also that the superintendent should see to it that people who dug up the roadway for the laying of pipe should be made to leave it in as smooth a condition as they found it.

And as for cleaning the highways, the Major saw in December of '82 seven ghostly phantoms while away two solid hours sweeping a space 100 feet square on Spring street near the post office. Their painful and languid movements were sad to behold. Two Chinese he thought would have accomplished more in the same time. But then these gentry were employees of a prosperous city amply able to stand such insignificant drains on its treasury.

Bell complained in the same year about the way repairs were made on roadbeds. When they became so uneven as to be almost impassable the chain gang was sent out to improve them. The usual manner of performing this labor was to go to the first convenient place and get a cartful of dirt and rocks and dump the load upon the surface. Instead of having a beautiful street the citizens living on Figueroa had a "miserable, rocky, weed-grown, gopher-infested, swamp-lined dusty road, a disgrace to any civilized community." It seemed to Bell that the city council having graded the streets at enormous expense to the property owners should clean the gutters and cut the weeds from the sidewalks.

[214]

That the streets of Los Angeles would be paved was a settled question in 1886. The money was in the city treasury and many plans were offered as the best method. A letter to the *Porcupine* called for soft, sedimentary rocks to be taken from the natural beds of asphalt or *brea* in adjacent hills. Granite blocks, thought Bell, were objectionable as being slippery, dangerous, and hard on horses. Wooden blocks set on end might be good, but he believed the best material would be limestone macadam, for limestone when it is reduced to dirt will form a hard and perfect cement and it makes a beautiful roadbed, always smooth—never slippery.

"Remove," urged the Major, "eight inches or a foot from the surface of Main street and fill in with crushed limestone and the work is accomplished, and should the necessity arise of excavating for sewers or water pipes, the holes made can be filled in with the same material, which will shape itself until the bed is as compact and smooth as before."

Still dwelling on his dominant topic of streets Bell complained against the railroad company's vexatious practice of standing freight trains at crossings, a daily occurrence at the old depot on Commercial street. This blocked intersecting roads for a long time. Frequently the line of freight cars reached from the depot to a point beyond Aliso, a busy thoroughfare. Bell demanded that the ordinance forbidding this nuisance be enforced. Out on the edge of town sheep were driven into the streets to graze on grass growing beside the water ditches and fences. They became a hazard by blockading the streets, frightening horses and causing runaways, thus endangering school children on their way home.

When the city decided to extend Figueroa street in 1883 the *Porcupine* exposed the fact that a mile or more of this highway from Pico north had been occupied for a long time by "street-jumpers." Many years before and down to a recent time "street-jumping" in Los Angeles had been a lucrative business. The "street-jumper" was an enterprising person who increased the area of his land by enclosing adjacent streets, and when the city demanded the return of the former public way he asked for and invariably obtained from the city 10 times the value of the land he had stolen. Pearl street (formerly a northern extension of Figueroa) was fenced in by "jumpers" and paid for three times from 1868 to 1883. Pico street, Bell recalled, was "jumped" from Figueroa to Main, bought back by the city, and later half of it was again encroached upon. In 1883 a strip of the highway 10 feet wide on the north side of Pico, at the corner of Pearl, lay inside a man's enclosure to whom was previously paid $350 to restore a similar encroachment on Pearl. How many other streets had been thus treated it was hard to tell. As the streets were marked on the city maps whoever bought a street from a "jumper" did so with his eyes open, and he should be required promptly to vacate. Let it be so with Figueroa.

The editor maintained that Los Angeles had the most disgraceful sidewalks in the West, the worst one being on the north side of Commercial east of Los Angeles street, extending as far as the old depot. It was dangerous, malarious, and a harbor for rats. How long would this nuisance of years' standing continue? Was there no board of public works?

Careless contractors were not restrained from monopolizing the streets with their building materials. They dumped sand in piles reaching from the sidewalks to the streetcar tracks. Careful regard was always given to the railroad company, but the rights of the people to a passage were ignored. Downtown merchants freely trespassed against pedestrians by obstructing the sidewalks with their wares. The Baker Block on Main street had a good sidewalk about 14 feet wide, smooth and hard, on the inside of which you could always find high heaps of fresh groceries: sacks of potatoes, cabbages, onions, dray loads of limes, oranges, and apples. Outside the walk, in the street, usually lay a long parallel mountain range of Oregon pine lumber, several schooner loads, surmounted by peaks of chili peppers. Thundering in and out through this long and winding defile would go the heavy iron trucks of the greengrocers. When passers-by stepped off the obstructed sidewalks they would risk their bones in the traffic of the street.

An even more difficult pass retarded the daily march of these old-timers. This was on the east side of Spring street, reaching from Market to the post office, where fruit merchants emptied on the sidewalk dray loads of red peppers and dingy fruit. On this street near the post office stood the largest fruit store in town called Woodhead and Gay's, which caused the most hindrance. About the only place downtown where the walk was kept free from obstruction was the one in front of the Downey Block (at the intersection of Main, Spring, and Temple streets). Other cities enforced ordinances protecting the rights of pedestrians—why did not Los Angeles? queried Bell.

Another unpleasant thing about walking in the business section, in the year 1888, after the great influx of strangers, was having to pass through squads of men loafing on the corners. Some were dudes; others were bums, and crooked gamblers or black-legs, as they were called in that day. A lady could hardly go past without hearing foul language—she might even be insulted—and every pedestrian was in peril of being spattered with tobacco juice. "Let these toughs be run in and fined," urged the Major, "and it is probable that a decent person might be able to walk the streets unmolested."

It was in the year 1882 that the city of Los Angeles installed electric street lights. Two sticks of carbon, each a foot long, when placed end to end and heated by the current produced the illumination emanating from the top of a seventy-five-foot pole. After each night of burning, the carbons were replaced with new ones by a man on horseback. In the whole town there were at first only five light masts. One stood on the hilltop a half-block north of the Normal School, which was at the corner of Fifth and Charity (Grand), the present site of the City Library.[6] Another shed its beams in front of the St. Charles hotel on upper Main street, south of the Baker Block and not far from the Pico House. A third lit up the corner of Ninth and Main. These were the only masts in the town proper. The other two served the suburbs of Boyle Heights and East Los Angeles.

When the city contracted with the light company the people of Los Angeles rejoiced, declared Bell, but in 1883 they began to realize that like everything else connected with municipal government the lights as they were then operated were somewhat of a cheat. Boyle Heights complained, West Los Angeles (which had lately acquired a pole) complained, and Louis Mesmer complained for the whole town. And when highly respected Louis Mesmer complained something must be wrong. The chief charge was that on nights when the company gave its current the lights were turned on at too late an hour and were always extinguished before daylight, thus exposing the city to depredations.

Many people grumbled because on so-called moonlit nights when the planet was obscured by thick clouds the lights were not turned on at all, leaving the citizens to grope their way as best they could. Bell thought the city council should make the electric company comply with its contract and give the people light, and also that two more masts should be erected in West Los Angeles: one at Figueroa and Adams, another at Pico and Figueroa. (Here the Major had an eye for his own welfare, for the latter spot was at the corner of his home place.) By rights, asserted Bell, the people of this flourishing suburb were as much entitled to illumination as East Los Angeles and Boyle Heights, although West Los Angeles was not represented in the city council.

Five years after the first light poles were put up George E. Long and his neighbors asked for the erection of an electric mast at the corner of Date and Macy streets. Bell thought they should have it, for more light was needed in that vicinity. The vineyards, lumber yards, freight cars, and sheds in this neighborhood, as well as the stretch of willows by the Los Angeles river, were the lurking places of tramps, making it unsafe to be out after dark unless one carried in his pocket a good revolver. "Let the pole be put up," argued the editor, "before some honorable citizen is sandbagged, robbed, or murdered in this dark region."

Elsewhere about the town, the *Porcupine* reported, teams collided with each other and with pedestrians because of poor lighting. Bell himself had barely escaped an accident. "Have the lights turned on as soon as night sets in!"

The service must have continued to be poor, for six years after the erection of the first poles the Major wrote that if there was the faintest suggestion of a pale moon the company made it a pretext for not turning the power on. In a short time there would be no lights at all and the operators would say that although one could not see the moon it was still shining behind the clouds.

The *Porcupine* humorously observed in 1882 that the new lights would seriously affect the happiness of those loving couples who were in the habit of whispering tender vows beneath the stately eucalyptus trees in public parks. The city council should have placed the towering mast where its searching light would not fall on the gay and gushing Normal School girls and their thirty-dollar-a-month-we-can-live-without-your-father admirers. It was cruel that the leafy glooms in Sixth Street Park (now Pershing Square) where many sweet sentences had been spoken should now be invaded by the electric light and the romance of young loves blighted. But when the modern reader considers that the light nearest to Sixth Street Park was a half-block north of where the city library now stands and more than a block from the west edge of the park, it would seem that the Normal School girls and their beaus had little need for the *Porcupine's* sympathy.

The editor called the attention of his fellow citizens to the condition of their public parks. In 1884 there were only two: the old Plaza on North Main street and the other bounded by Fifth and Sixth streets and Hill and Olive, now bearing the name of Pershing. The city council, Bell insisted, should put them in respectable order. The Plaza, he admitted, had at the present time a fairly good appearance—the grass was growing well—the trees had received some care. Still the place could be improved. As for the park on Sixth street—it had been wholly neglected. There one could find a few patches of grass, but they were all withered. The trees had not been either trimmed or watered. Along the *zanja* flowing through the park lay piles of dirt. The enclosing fence and the gates were tottering. Altogether the open square was a picture of mismanagement and neglect.

"And the more the pity," sighed the Major, "as this park is now the center of one of the principal residential sections of the town and is surrounded by the homes of families who would make it a plot of recreation for the grownups and a playground for their children if it were kept in decent order and free from filth and hoodlums. For the juniors in daytime, for paterfamilias puffing his cigar at twilight, for the lover and his lass strolling in the soft beams of the electric light or the moon, the park could be made a place of pleasure. In behalf of all we appeal to the city council to provide abundant grass and shade."

Regarding public squares Bell thought that Los Angeles could learn a lesson from the countries of Central America. In every city which he had visited in those lands he had found a plaza where the people gathered in the cool of the evening to meet their friends and enjoy music furnished by the municipal government. "Why can't we have such entertainment here in Los Angeles? Why can't the city hire musicians to play at least two nights a week? Why not improve our park on Fifth and Sixth streets, which henceforth I propose to call South Park, and build a pavilion with surrounding benches, thus bringing our people together in social and harmonious enjoyment." If bands played on Saturday and Sunday evenings, he believed there would be a decrease in the number of petty offenders at the police court on Monday morning.

In the middle '80s the streets of Los Angeles needed improvement, but the roads leading out of town were worse. If you took a buggy at Ferguson and Rose's stable on Main and drove south on this street to the city limits you would pass over a rough road, but if you went east to San Gabriel Mission, or northwest to San Fernando, or south on San Pedro street, it was still worse. "There is not one mile of continuously good road in Los Angeles county," complained a subscriber in the *Porcupine*.

There was no road leading from the Los Angeles courthouse to Pasadena until after the city line was passed. Bell declared that he knew no trip more difficult and hazardous and could not understand why Pasadena people ever came to Los Angeles. When they came in or left by way of San Fernando street and the Arroyo Seco road they must run the gauntlet of·locomotives chugging up and down that street from morning till night, endangering the life of anyone who had the temerity to drive a team of horses upon it.[7] From there to the Los Angeles city line two miles farther on, the driver would find a succession of rocks, ditches, and chuckholes. "What an enterprising lot we are!" Bell concluded ironically.

A gentleman living in Pasadena assured the Major that he suffered great embarrassment when coming to Los Angeles with his wife and daughter because of swimmers disporting themselves in the *toma* (a walled pool) lying parallel to the road. These men he complained would stalk around stark naked with no concern for a passing carriage containing ladies. Unless the authorities put a stop to this he proposed to carry his double-barreled shotgun loaded with mustard seed lead and "give these fellows a peppering they would remember for the rest of their lives." The Major suggested that the chief of police detail Officer Fonck for this job and end a disgraceful practice.

The residents of Savannah and El Monte, two settlements east of Los Angeles, were as unfortunate as the Pasadenans in regard to the danger and discomfort of returning from the city. After wallowing through ruts, gutters, and chuckholes in the outlying streets of Los Angeles they reached the Southern Pacific railroad and drove alongside it, almost touching it for a great part of the way home, in constant peril of their horses being frightened by a passing train with its puffing, whistling locomotive. This declared Bell was all wrong. It was bad for Los Angeles and for her country neighbors. The fault lay with the people of the city and the county board of supervisors.

Before there were any supervisors the drive to Santa Monica was a pleasure, for the roadbed was smooth and hard. In 1883 according to Bell it was so full of holes and knobs that in passing over it in a vehicle the rider imagined himself to be a jumping jack and feared that his carriage would be shivered to pieces, the springs broken and snapped apart. The road to Santa Monica could not be worse, yet there was a supervisor who pretended to spend the people's money on this very road. Why did the liverymen who could derive a valuable trade from excursions to Santa Monica stand for it? Why did the people of Santa Monica, whose beautiful little city could gain so much benefit from a good run out of Los Angeles, stand for it? And why did the farmers whose wagons were damaged and whose horses were jaded in straining over this horrible highway stand for it?

Then as the Major reflected upon his permanent subject of public improvements his wrath rose in crescendo and he burst out: "Where is a city of 20,000 inhabitants, a city teeming with wealth as Los Angeles, a city of fine homes surrounded with orange groves and vineyards, a city with a revenue so magnificent —where is a city that has a government so imbecile as ours and public works so contemptible? We have no parks that would grace a Mexican town and not a street properly graded. In a state of nature the roads leading out of Los Angeles were more useful and good-looking than they are today, after having been tampered with by our corporation asses for the past 16 years, and why is this so?

"The reason is that we have always had a corrupt municipal government—a set of ignoramuses whose sole ambition has been to put up jobs for their own petty advancement, and should it happen that a public-spirited man got into the council he would be driven out by his vicious associates."

Horace Bell has left us also his impressions of what he saw in the settlements close to Los Angeles during the middle '80s. Like candles they throw light on the way of life in those primitive times. In August of 1884, two years before the great boom began, the Major combining business with pleasure took a horse-and-buggy trip to Santa Monica. Here he saw young vineyards flourishing and corn growing without irrigation which would delight an Indiana farmer. The town was crowded, and besides there were nearly 2,000 people camping on the beach. The hotel was so jammed that when the wife of Senator John P. Jones telegraphed for rooms the proprietor answered that he was unable to furnish her any, but he would build her a cottage. Tents were in great demand. William Hull had 50, none of which was without an occupant for more than a day.

Santa Monica, thought Bell, had improved over last year. The trees and shrubs had thrived as plants always do in Los Angeles county when watered and made a pleasing contrast with the surrounding bare plains. He remarked on the presence of many tramps, persistent in their begging. They should not be tolerated. A few special policemen he advised would be "just the thing for the city by the sea."

At the height of the boom the *Porcupine* observed that East Los Angeles was not keeping pace in improvements with other parts of the city. This had been due largely to the uncertain supply of drinking water, but that shortage was now remedied by connections with the Garvanza mains providing plenty of pure water from the mountains. The approaches to the Buena Vista street bridge having been recently completed, this eastern part of town would be more easily accessible and therefore become more populous. The irrigation reservoir was full and fishermen caught good strings of carp, some weighing eight pounds. Charles Robb, the letter carrier, had applied to the city council for the privilege of keeping pleasure boats on the artificial pond. This ought to be granted, thought the reporter, as Robb was an expert swimmer and the water was not fit for drinking. To encourage him to start a swimming school the council should also permit him to rent bathing suits and teach young people to swim.

In the same year Bell drove to the quiet little town of Florence, six miles south of Los Angeles. He observed that the inhabitants did not appear to have been seized with that "peculiar mania for speculation" which he found in other localities. *For Sale* signs were absent, as well as the festive real estate agent. Yet the people looked prosperous and contented. Neat cottages sheltered by shady trees and bedecked with clustering vines gave one the feeling that here were happy homes.

Driving six miles farther south he came to the village of Compton, surrounded by rich farming and fruit country. Each settler seemed to have all the cows, horses, hogs, and poultry he wanted and nearly every farmer owned a fine buggy.

In December of 1885 Major Bell took the train to Santa Ana 30 miles southeast of Los Angeles and spent there a day and a night. On all sides he saw prosperity. Fruits of all kinds proved the presence of rich soil and plentiful water. Pumpkins and corn were abundant, and pigs basked lazily in the sun. He stayed at the Layman hotel, enjoying its clean comfort. After looking the locality over he was moved to suggest in his paper that the people of Santa Ana should first elect Mr. Layman mayor and then grade the streets, lay sewers, and make the growing village ready to become a city.

But two faults marred the perfection of life in Santa Ana. One was that the barbers did not open their shops long before the departure of the noon train—an annoyance to the Major because he always wanted a shave before breakfast. The other was the keeping of hogs in livery stables. Whether these animals were used as coach hogs or saddle hogs he did not learn, but he admonished the residents that this local peculiarity smelled loud for abatement. He did not see any horses in the public stables, perhaps there were none. He hoped not, for the horse is a sensitive animal. Bell could hardly believe that any man would subject a horse to the ignominy of living with hogs. Hogs look pretty grazing in alfalfa patches, but in livery stables they are wholly out of place. With these exceptions he thought everything in Santa Ana was commendable. He advised the community to incorporate and put the swine out of the village.

Six months later when her population was 2,000 Santa Ana followed Bell's advice in becoming a corporate town.

The Double Eagle

The summer of '83 saw Virginia Bell shoot up in her twelfth year like a mushroom. She had grown so fast that when she returned to school in the fall the children did not know her, and making her look still more strange, her heavy head of dark brown hair had been bobbed, since her mother having a new baby to care for lacked the physical strength for brushing it sufficiently and keeping out the tangles underneath. On the opening day at recess the boys and girls were running around and playing together when Dana Burks came up. He was a nice lad, but like most boys he enjoyed teasing the girls.

"Well, well, well, if it ain't Penny Porcupine!" he jibed. "Hello, Penny Porcupine!"

This made all the children laugh hilariously at Virginia. Her face and throat turned pink with wrath. As Dana was standing less than 10 feet away the young girl walked straight up to him and struck him with her fist. He dodged, but the blow reached his neck. To keep himself from falling he grabbed her dress and tore it.

When Virginia got home her mother wanted to know how she had ruined her pretty new dress. She hesitated. Then her brothers and sisters screamed in chorus, "She had a fight with a boy!" Poor Mrs. Bell was crushed with shame and ordered that a full explanation be given to father. What would her punishment be when he returned from the office, Virginia anxiously wondered.

In the late afternoon he came and sent for her. He was in the back parlor sitting in his chair by the bookcase. When she entered he beckoned for her to come closer.

"What's this I hear about you getting into trouble?" he asked sternly, gazing into a pair of big blue eyes. "What did you do, child?"

"I hit a boy at school, Papa."

"Why did you do that?"

"Because he made fun of me and called me a bad name."

"And what did he call you?"

"He called me 'Penny Porcupine.' So I doubled up my fist like this and hit him hard."

There were no more questions. Papa leaned back in his chair, stretched out his long right leg, and put his hand down deep into his pants' side pocket. Virginia was scared. What kind of weapon would he draw forth? Instead he pulled out very deliberately his purse. (Its contents had not yet been collected by the home treasurer.) He opened it and took out a twenty-dollar gold coin. Then he gently placed it in her palm, saying as he did so, his blue eyes twinkling: "Jinnie, you're a chip off the old block."

The child did not know what that meant, but she sensed that all was well.

Hello, Sucker!

Sitting in his office Horace Bell read in the Los Angeles *Herald* the current prices for farming land in Los Angeles and San Barnardino counties. At Pomona, he learned, fields for the planting of citrus groves were selling at $75 to $100 an acre. The Cucamonga tract recently placed on the market ranged upward from $100. Nearby at Ontario, a newly named area, prices were placed at $100 to $200 an acre and sales were lively. Farther east on the "base line" near San Bernardino,[8] a man who wanted to plant orange trees could get a piece of desert by paying $200 to $400 for each acre. At Redlands a few miles south of the last region a tract of sagebrush cost $200 per acre. Crafton lying on the edge of Redlands farther east demanded as much, but sales would be light until the reservoirs and distributing ditches were near completion. Highest of all was Riverside where the figures for virgin soil ranged from $250 to $400 and improved lands ran above $500. Seeing these figures Bell reached for his pen and dashed off an editorial to appear in his next number.

"Hitherto in the history of new settlements," he wrote, "the settlers were poor, being equipped with no capital but strong wills and hard muscles. They grew up with the country, becoming rich as it developed. But in southern California the reverse is the rule. The new settlers bring money with them. But they are

[226]

poor in knowledge of the conditions necessary for successful farming. Wherefore it behooves experienced Californians to deal so fairly with these newcomers as to advance their prosperity."

Eight years before, in 1875, he recalled, there was a large migration to the Los Angeles area. But the booms at Centinela, Artesia, and Cucamonga, with their blueprints of promised colleges and other tricks for deceiving buyers, ruined many people and brought disrepute on the county. He had thought that the public would profit by these sad losses, but no, the same thing was happening again.

Within the last year many Easterners had sought homes in the southern country. "At once they were met by land sharks equipped with maps, pamphlets, fancy place names and high prices. These fellows tried to persuade strangers that waste land where sheep could never live, where there was not enough water to supply the forlorn jackrabbit and disconsolate coyote was cheap at $200 an acre, sand storms thrown in gratis. They would also allege that alkali flats would grow alfalfa. One heard of lands never imagined to be valuable advertised for sale at $100 to $200 an acre!"

To the editor these prices seemed monstrous. They would drive away desirable people and Los Angeles would suffer a setback. Such practices he thought explained the undevelopment of the area lying between the city and Wilmington, where the passer-by saw no new houses or farms. The *Porcupine* promised to inform newcomers as to fair values for orchard lands. Its publisher ought to know something about it, for he had raised oranges for the last 16 years. If he wanted to buy land again for a grove he would hesitate to pay more than $30 an acre for unimproved ground anywhere in the county. "Look well before you pay absurd prices," Bell cautioned the tenderfoot. "Otherwise you are liable to be taken in by the land shark and done for."

Speculators in 1886 were advertising a stretch of land facing the ocean 12 miles southwest of Los Angeles as a natural harbor. They had named the place Redondo and were offering lots for sale at outrageous prices. Bell warned the credulous. The coast near this place he described as a large indentation forming a half-circle about 30 miles long. It included Topanga on the north, Redondo Beach on the south with Santa Monica and Ballona in between. This sea frontage for the sake of having a name was called Santa Monica bay. "But it is no bay, not even a roadstead," he declared. "It is a big bend in the seacoast exposed to all the winds that blow and all the tides that flow."

Attempts had been made to convince people first that Santa Monica and then Ballona were natural harbors.[9] These failing, speculators and subsidized newspapers were now trying to boom Redondo, a place which they discovered and named only a year ago. Though he had been up and down the coast many times in the last four decades, Bell had never known of any such harbor until the last few months. Nor had he heard of any boat anchoring there or seeking shelter from storms, but he did remember a merchant ship having been driven ashore at that point and dashed to pieces. The old Spanish navigators had surveyed and named every roadstead and harbor on the West Coast, but they had not found the Redondo harbor. The United States government had also missed it. How strange, observed Bell, that the discovery and naming of this wonderful port was left to the land speculators of Los Angeles!

He condemned the *Tribune* for using three columns of print to convince fools that Redondo was a better harbor than the open sea. The *Herald* had done the same thing. He would have less objections, the Major said, if these articles had been published as advertisements. Twelve years ago, he recalled, the *Herald* was cursed by hundreds of people for supporting a real estate fraud at Centinela.

There would come an end to all these wildcat schemes for harbors, glassworks, smelting furnaces, wharves, and breakwaters with their paid editorials, as there was in the Centinela swindle. Redondo Beach could be made into a pleasant resort, but claims of its being a natural harbor were false. They should deceive no one. Yet they probably would.

[228]

Too Little, Too Much

In the summer of 1883 the Major met a lady on the streetcar who lived at the corner of Sixth and Flower streets. She was riding downtown she told him "to get a drink of water." Her need was explained by the fact that the local water company had failed to install hydrants in her neighborhood. Even at Sixth and Main, seven blocks east of her place, water for home use was released only during certain hours of the day. Her remark brought forth in the *Porcupine* a spirited editorial. "Is this not a commentary on our city government?" snapped Bell. "To read our daily papers one would think that all is progress and perfection in Los Angeles."

A month later he complained of the drinking water at the State Normal School on Fifth and Grand. He knew girls who chose to suffer all day from thirst rather than drink the filthy compound that flowed from its pipes. The school administrators kept this plight secret, fearing bad publicity might prevent new students from enrolling. Foolish policy! How much better it would be to openly demand pure water and save someone's health or life!

Why, cried Bell, did the water company delay putting in hydrants at points designated by the city government? The resolutions of the council made it the duty of the mayor "to cause all necessary connections to be made with the pipes and mains for the supplying of pure water." Yet this was not done. A shortage could not be the cause, when both reservoirs were full. The reason that the company did not comply, he ventured, was that the mayor being a large stockholder desired to lower its operating costs. Indeed his inaction explained why the company had worked for his election.

In the same summer the editor disclosed the lack of irrigation water in West Los Angeles, where he had lived—at the corner of Pico and Figueroa—for the last 17 years. Having been the first to settle there he had conveyed at his own expense the first supply of water for his neighborhood. During all that time the city government had never spent a dollar in that section for water, although it had taken from West Los Angeles large sums in taxes.

Occasionally winter floods poured down from the northern mountains, overtopping the banks of the Los Angeles river, making it almost impossible to leave town. During the rainy season of 1886 three train loads of Easterners, nearly 500 people, came to tour the Southland. After being blockaded by snow for a week in Kansas they were marooned for another week in Los Angeles by water.

At this time the sandbars on the river's edge and the houses built thereon were washed away. Also railroad tracks and bridges were swept under. In one hour many people lost all they owned and some were drowned. Bell reminded Los Angeles that the city council had long been importuned to take measures for preventing such a disaster. But what was done? The city garbage carts were dumped so as to form an odorous windrow, dignified by the name of levee. When the waters came it also floated away.

The Major offered his remedy. Let the city council, he proposed, lay out a river bed 600 feet wide, commencing at the bluff opposite the Arroyo Seco and running along the embankment of the Southern Pacific railroad to the bridge in East Los Angeles. From there strike a gentle curve to the covered bridge at Macy street, from the eastern end of which measure 600 feet west. Cut away the approach to the bridge and put in another three-hundred-foot span. Then keep these six-hundred-foot spans open and no more damage need be feared from floods. Provided the river bed were marked out and made smooth on the bottom and its gently sloping banks planted with canes and willows no levee would be necessary. If during the deluge of 1884 as well as the recent one of '86 there had been 600 feet instead of a three-hundred-foot space for a river bed, was it not apparent that the waters would have found their way past the city without destroying property or life?

The Quality of Mercy

Underdogs always roused Bell's pity.
Back in 1883 when less thought was given to social problems

than now, the *Porcupine* called attention to the children of Los Angeles who suffered neglect because of their parents' immorality or intemperance. Such youths it affirmed were worse off than orphans, for their fathers and mothers stood between them and charitable care. It commended these juveniles to the Christian people of the city and advocated the founding of an almshouse for homeless boys and girls who were growing into bad citizens.

Bell made public the deplorable plight of farm laborers. On the great ranches there were about three months of work in the winter planting season and the same amount during harvest. These men were expected to toil from four in the morning until eight at night and then in most cases sleep in a barn or straw stack. When these periods were over, the farm laborer had nothing to do unless he could find an odd job. But when he got into the fruit and vine growing districts he had to compete with low-paid Chinese. If such work was scarce as it usually was he had to pick up his blanket and go from place to place looking for other employment. Meanwhile he was liable to be arrested as a tramp by some constable.

The cause of this situation Bell believed was the large estates. Those who had purchased land for speculation did not desire to farm it themselves but rented it to sheep men for pasturage. Such tracts did not furnish a good living to thousands of farmers. As a remedy for the evil he proposed that the railroad companies be forced to survey and patent all the lands to which they were entitled. If this were done then the lands outside the railroad grants could and would be located and legally claimed. There were thousands of acres of arable land in California he declared that were not settled by industrious immigrants simply because no one knew positively whether or not the property belonged to the railroads. After this was done the state and counties should see that not only these lands but all other large holdings were properly assessed. Then the great ranches would be settled by farmers who would rear families and treat their hired men not as dogs but as Christians.

[231]

The editor observed a trial in Justice Ling's court and was shocked at the condition of the prisoner brought forth from the county jail. The man had not been convicted of any crime; he was merely detained for a hearing. Half-naked, his body reeked with filth, and lice swarmed in his hair. When the vermin were swept from his person they scattered throughout the courtroom. Hardened men turned their faces away in disgust, said Bell, and the sheriff was called to remove him from sight. "Our people go to church," he asserted, "and hear sermons on good will toward all men; yet they permit a human being to suffer such treatment! O Shame, where is thy blush! O Decency, draw thy mantle over thy face to shut out the horrid sight!" There was not a town in the Eastern states with a population of 5,000, Bell ventured, that did not have a better jail and every citizen of the county who did not protest against this horrible man-pen ought to be ashamed of himself.

Five years later Captain M. M. Chase, veteran of the Michigan Sharpshooters, wrote a letter to the *Porcupine* revealing his experience in the Los Angeles prison, which the editor published. Two weeks ago, he was notified to appear in Judge Austin's court at two in the afternoon as a witness. Before attending the trial he was reminded that his wife who was sick at home had asked him to send her some medicine. He did as she wished and was 30 minutes late to court. For this delay Chase was charged with contempt and sentenced to five days' confinement in the county jail.

On entering the gateway of its cold walls he was ushered into the presence of Mr. Russell, who divested him of all his money except 40¢. He was then taken to the iron "tank" occupied by 50 criminals of all kinds. Such treatment, protested the captain, was contrary to the laws of California, which declared that a county jail should contain a sufficient number of rooms to keep each class of inmates separate: those detained for trial, those already convicted, those held as witnesses. Here Chase stayed for 24 hours. He regained his freedom by giving up four dollars taken from him at the gate.

[232]

The captain then gave the daily program of the prisoners. At three in the afternoon they had a dinner of two old potatoes, two ounces of boiled beef—poorest quality—and a slice of stale bread. At eight in the evening they were locked up for the night. At six in the morning the doors were thrown open when every inmate rose up and spent 30 minutes picking off graybacks. Then came breakfast—a half-pint of boiled beans, a small piece of bread, and a cup of coffee which would sicken a dog. For the day's menu, the county paid 35¢ per man. It could be supplied thought Chase for five cents. Some of the prisoners told him that those who had money could buy from the officials four onions, the size of walnuts, for 15¢, and a five-cent pie for 20¢. For sending a message downtown they paid a dollar and a half and five cents for each postage stamp.

Bell objected to the working in public places of convicts chained together. No civilized people ever worked men on the streets in fetters. A convict should be hidden from sight and not paraded on streets and highways to suffer degradation beyond the chance of reform. Let all street work be done by free men paid a fair price for a fair day's work. The cell in which they were all crowded together at night swarmed with vermin and the scanty blanket frequently strayed away from its sleepy user. The air was foul. Sometimes a lunatic or crazy drunk was thrown in to walk over the heads of the tired workers. Their food must have been bad, for we read in a *Porcupine* of 1887 that "on Tuesday the chain gang went on a strike for better grub. They were locked up and put on a bread and water diet." In the name of humanity Bell demanded better treatment for these poor fellows.

His mercy reached down even to the city's fallen women. On an April night in 1883, so he told his readers, the police raided the houses of ill fame. By some mistake they invaded No. 60, Los Angeles street. This well-known resort was supposed to be exempt from intrusion, having the favor of the chief of police. Twenty-nine women were dragged out of their beds at No. 60, marched to the police station and forced individually to pay $10, all of which went to the city treasury. The *Porcupine* called the raid unjust. For any crime these women had committed they should have been properly charged and arrested in open day. Was it possible to reclaim them? Surely not by extortion. Harsh treatment only drove them to worse behavior.

When the city was ready to hold a memorial service for General Ulysses S. Grant, the council had misappropriated the funds allowed for the expense.[10] So by order of the council the police went to the houses of prostitution, put the women into hacks which they were compelled to pay for themselves, and drove them to headquarters where under threat of imprisonment each one was forced to give up $10. That was all until the next time. Bell protested against such extortion. "The law should punish and protect all alike. Then why should not the rich people who rent their houses at high prices to the frail women be yanked up to the captain's office and compelled to hand over contributions to the civic fund? Why not have a fair deal?"

His voice was raised in defense of dumb animals. He complained that Angelenos were about as barbarous as Apaches in their treatment of lower creatures. Every day he could see on the streets men abusing horses and mules. Under the cruel lash some were forced to draw loads beyond their strength; some were ridden having galled and ulcerated backs and others were worked with sore shoulders; some hobbled along on crippled legs; some were so starved that their bones almost cut through their skins; and still others stood trembling on sprung knees. "We call ourselves civilized," exclaimed the Major, "bah! we are in that respect on a par with savages. Who will be the first missionary for the enforcement of the law protecting animals?"

Republican Rebel

Fifty years ago, declared the *Porcupine* (meaning 1836), America had only a few wealthy men and not many indigent people. A merchant retiring on $100,000 was called immensely rich. A farmer with $30,000 was considered opulent. There were no monopolists and only a few millionaires. But now John

Jacob Astor and Stephen Girard would be poor compared with such money kings as Leland Stanford, John D. Rockefeller, and Jay Gould, who could if they wished control the whole country. Such a centralization of wealth was going on, warned Bell, that unless it were checked there would soon be three classes of Americans: at the top the millionaires; below them their dependent flunkies including politicians, lawyers, judges, and officeholders; and on the bottom the non-propertied citizens dependent for their daily bread upon the starvation wages the rich might choose to pay them.

How to improve this situation? The *Porcupine* knew the answer—by ballots. But soon the remedy would be useless because of nominating conventions. This device of government was cheating the public. That is, it gave to the political bosses through the votes of the hoodlum element the power of saying who should be candidates for office. The primaries were being so managed as to put delegates into the conventions who would obey the bosses. In Los Angeles there were both Democratic and Republican bosses and the daily press connived with them. They must be broken. The only force that could do this was the trade unions. Organized workers by capturing the primaries could send to the conventions of both parties men who were boss-free.

Oddly enough the Major himself was accused of wanting to be a political master. The unfriendly Los Angeles *Times*, voicing its editor, Harrison Gray Otis, remarked:

Horace Bell, that uneasy spirit who is ambitious to be known as a "holy terror," who is generally in a fight with somebody and who is always contending in the *Porcupine* for "the pure, the good, and the true" has turned up dictator in local politics. It is given out that he intends to run things or break a trace.[11]

In defense Bell countered that he was not a dictator and had no desire to be one. On the contrary he had always made war on the bosses—those whom the *Times* had never failed to support. For years he had worked for the Republican party in southern

California and when at last it triumphed, his reward was to witness its degradation by the *Times'* crowd of political vagabonds. One more thing he had done for Los Angeles: he had shamed the *Times* into seeming decency when he exposed it for taking bribes from corrupt officials in exchange for journalistic puffs.

Bell was now headed toward political insurgency. He complained that the Republicans in 1886 were campaigning on dead issues and living on former greatness. To listen to their oratory you would conclude that his own political party was like a hill of potatoes—the best part being underground. Would "waving the bloody shirt" [that is, boasting of its war record] and straddling the temperance issue win a majority of votes in California? He doubted it. New problems arise. Old parties that fail to meet them die. Then new parties take their place.

In such a frame of mind he easily turned to the single tax program of Henry George.[12] This Eastern reformer, who once lived in California, had responded to the same economic maladjustments of the Far West as disturbed the Major.

Bell wrote in his paper that:

The upper ten of New York are startled at the possibility of a plebeian like Henry George being made mayor of New York City—and by workingmen's votes. The monopoly press calls him a communist. The bitter *Tribune* implores "all good citizens to combine for his defeat." If elected as mayor, as he will be if workingmen stand together, the reforms of George will be as great a terror to the money kings as a blessing to the people.

But he did not accept the reformer's program exactly as it was. Instead of assessing only land as George desired, he would add a tax on large personal incomes. Then there should be a limit to ownership of land and also restrictions on inheritance.

His next step was to join the United Labor Party of California. He printed and endorsed its platform. These new independents proposed a score of changes. They called for the exclusion and deportation of Chinese, legal recognition of labor unions, safety measures in mines, factories, and construction work, the weekly payment of wages, the prohibition of child labor, and an eight-hour working day. For the benefit of the country at large they promised to elect all government officials by direct ballot, to establish a postal savings system, to prohibit extortionate rates of interest, to prevent adulteration of foods and medicines. More startling still for the year 1886 were proposals for state owner-ship of railroads, the telephone and telegraph lines and, most remarkable for that time, profit-sharing by employees.

The new party held its convention in San Francisco, nom-inating for lieutenant governor Horace Bell of Los Angeles. Evi-dently he did not attend, for the *Alta California* reported his acceptance by letter. When the returns of the election came in its candidates stood lowest among the four contending groups. Out of nearly 200,000 votes cast throughout the state the United Labor Party polled only 1,658, or less than one percent.[13]

"Lucky" Baldwin and Libel

The most exciting episode of Bell's journalistic career was his legal struggle with Elias J. Baldwin (nicknamed "Lucky") the millionaire of Santa Anita, California. In his first number of the *Porcupine* he pledged himself to the policy of judging only public officials. But when he attacked Baldwin, a private citizen, he broke his rule and made one of his editorial mistakes. In Sep-tember of '83 Bell reprinted an ugly story from the Portland *Mercury* and charged the rich horseman with wrong-doing.

A year later Baldwin was confronted by a young woman suing him for breach of promise. At once the *Porcupine* became her champion, holding her up as a paragon of innocence. The suit lasted for two weeks in February 1886 and the jury awarded damages amounting to $75,000. But the judge granted Baldwin a new trial on the ground that the indemnity was excessive. Soon after, his lawyers made a settlement out of court for only $12,000. The young woman accepted the money directly and then with-out compensating her attorney, Stephen M. White, for conduct-ing her suit she disappeared.[14]

As another consequence of the trial Baldwin's attorneys filed charges against the editor of the *Porcupine* for libel, the proposed penalty to be $80,000. Bell went on trial before the Superior Court in April of 1887, his attorney being Stephen M. White, then a state senator. How long the trial lasted or what were the dramatic scenes it is difficult to discover. But the records of the county clerk reveal that more than two years later charges against the editor were dropped by agreement among the lawyers. To quote the Major as he related the affair in a letter to the historian Hubert Howe Bancroft: " 'Lucky' Baldwin had several suits against me amounting to $80,000 and I beat him in all of them."[15]

Wiley Wells's Weapon

The battle with the wealthy sportsman brought with it more trouble for Bell. While the Baldwin suits were in progress there appeared in the *Porcupine* a verbal attack on G. Wiley Wells, the plaintiff's chief attorney. Although he and Bell were comrades in the G. A. R. post, the fraternity of Union veterans, each hated the other. For this journalistic assault Wells brought suit against the editor for libel, which resulted in no verdict, three jurors voting for conviction and nine for acquittal.

Though defeated in his course of revenge Wells tacked his sails in another direction. He filed with Judge William A. Cheney a complaint charging the Major with contempt of court. In his statement of grievance he affirmed that while the late case of Wells versus Bell was pending before Judge Cheney, the editor writing in the *Porcupine* "had scandalized the judge to induce delay, to obstruct the administration of law, and influence public opinion." Incredible though it seems Cheney was to try a man for contempt of his own court.

Two mornings after the filing of Wells's affidavit Bell appeared to answer the charge. The courtroom was filled with spectators eager to hear his defense. He arose and addressed the court. He made a motion for the dismissal of the case and gave his legal points. He argued that the court had no jurisdiction over him or over the matter of the charge. Wells's affidavit he said had failed to show that any contempt in the legal sense had been committed, for there was nothing in the charge to show why he might be maliciously disposed toward the court.

The editor then picked up the two articles which had caused the trouble. He read and discussed them. He protested that they contained nothing to justify his being charged with contempt. "I wrote these pieces," Bell continued, "as a public journalist. In doing so I was exercising my right as a journalist. The people have a right to know what is said and done in the courts of justice." He called for the judge to act upon his motion, but his honor postponed the case until nine the next morning and remanded the defendant to the custody of the sheriff.

On the following day the courtroom was again crowded. Bell read his answer to the charge. He declared that the articles printed in the *Porcupine* were not contemptuous—that they were written for the public good and the writer had confined himself within the limits of legitimate journalism when he penned the lines. He asked to be tried by a jury.

The judge then took Saturday off to prepare his decision and on the next Monday morning read it in open court. It was a long discussion on the rights of free speech and the liberty of the press and ended with the conclusion: "If this be not a contempt of court, then the court has never met with a case that was." And he added, "Mr. Clerk, enter the following order."

Here Bell interrupted: "What will you do with my motion for a trial by jury?" To this question the judge replied, "The demand for a trial by jury is denied upon the ground that the defendant is not entitled to a trial by jury. The defendant is adjudged and decreed to be guilty of contempt of this court and is sentenced to pay a fine of $400 and to five days' imprisonment in the jail of Los Angeles county in addition thereto."

Again the editor spoke up: "If the court please I have a word to say. Will the court hear me?" No answer. Bell flushed scarlet and exclaimed, "There will be a come-out!" The undersheriff then touched his arm and told him to leave. Bell started, then drew back insisting with a bow that the officer should precede him. After this courtesy he followed Deputy Thornton down to the sheriff's office.

But the convicted man did not give up. On the morrow he sent to the other department of the Superior Court a petition calling for a writ of habeas corpus. Such a paper if given would permit an appeal; this would be the "come-out." Judge Anson Brunson received the application and wrote above his signature: "Verified. Writ granted. Petitioner discharged."

To reporters standing by he remarked that Bell's case was so important that it should be tried before the highest tribunal in the state since it concerned the relation of the press to the courts.

It is most likely that the suit brought against the editor was dropped. There is no further record of it in the local papers and none has been discovered in the court minutes. So we may reasonably assume that Bell neither paid the fine nor served the sentence imposed on him by Judge Cheney and brought about by Wiley Wells.[16]

Daring the Deputy

In his role as censor of public officials Horace Bell did not approve of Thornton, a deputy sheriff of the county. Knowing Bell's attitude the officer naturally responded in kind. An opportunity came to show resentment when the critic was undergoing his ordeal with Baldwin. On the morning when the plaintiff from Santa Anita started his first suit, Bell was walking from his home to town. Before reaching the Temple Block he was stopped by an officer wishing to serve a paper. The Major protested that he did not like to receive a summons on the street—that he would prefer to call at the sheriff's rooms and get the writ. To this the subordinate kindly agreed.

Bell proceeded to his office and as he climbed the stairs of the Temple building the same man he had met came running up to him and threw the summons at his feet. At once Bell complained of this discourtesy and was later told by Thornton that he had ordered his assistant to deliver the papers in just that way.

[240]

To prepare his defense in the Baldwin trial Bell had obtained subpoenas for a Mr. Ellsworth and another witness living in the former's house. He gave the writs to Thornton on Saturday and pointed out the second man sitting in his buggy on the street. On Monday the deputy reported that after diligent search he could not find the desired witnesses. This seemed untrue, for Ellsworth, a prominent farmer, lived on Tenth street, and his farm lay near the city line. When Bell complained to Sheriff George Gard the witnesses were promptly found. The Major also went to Thornton and told him what he thought. In reply the undersheriff, according to Bell's story, stepped into his private office, buckled on a revolver, threw himself into a fighting pose, and sneered, "Sir, if you want anything out of this office, now you can have it."

The Major retorted: "Captain, I do want something out of this place. I will want you out of it. But I won't come here with a double-barreled shotgun and make a blackguard of myself as you are now doing. I will get you out in a fair and gentlemanly way." Then he turned on his heel and left.

Shortly after, Thornton remarked to J. B. McChesney, a comrade of his in the G. A. R., "I think Bell is going to attack me in his paper, and the first time he uses my name I intend to shoot him." This intelligence McChesney reported to the Major. Nevertheless on the following Saturday the *Porcupine* called for Thornton's dismissal at the coming election, the chief reason being alleged brutality toward prisoners.

The next act in this tragicomedy occurred a week later. Bell was passing in front of the sheriff's place when he heard his name called out with curses. Turning toward the voice he saw Thornton struggling with two men who were gripping his arms to keep him from shooting at Bell. "No, you don't!" insisted the friends. The Major was standing about 30 feet away holding over one arm his linen duster, in his other hand as usual his rattan cane, which he meant to use later to discipline a certain *Express* reporter.

Bell took one good look. He concluded, as he said, "to make a two-sided affair of the business." He walked back to Slotterbeck's gun store (in the Downey Block at the north corner of Temple and Main) and bought a revolver, "one of those beautiful old-fashioned Colts so dear to the heart of pioneers, 13 inches long, and 42 caliber." He had it loaded, laid the barrel across his arm, draped the duster over it, and walked back to the sheriff's place.

He found Deputy Field in the front office and inquired, "Is anyone holding Thornton now?" Receiving no reply Bell passed in front of a large glass window, on the way to the courthouse stairs, and looking into the back office he saw Thornton and faced him.

There was a space of about four feet between the two enemies, the windowpane intervening. Thornton started to draw, but the editor had his gun ready first and ordered him not to shoot. He obeyed. Suddenly two men rushed upon and held Bell, who said he would not shoot unless Thornton did. As his opponent made no move to do so, he turned to leave, remarking that if the deputy was "bent on human gore, they would walk out to the edge of town where people would not be disturbed by their foolishness."

In the next *Porcupine* Bell told his side of the story and reprinted the editorial which had almost caused a shooting. Using capitals he concluded with "THORNTON MUST GO."

The Libelous Biography

More enmity came out of the Baldwin suits with more legal battles. While the struggle with the millionaire was going on, the Major complained that false newspaper stories harmful to his good name were being published by the Los Angeles *Express*. Protesting he went to the editor, who cleared himself of blame and promised "to see Stephens about it," the man referred to as responsible being at that time a reporter for the paper.

Bell met Bascom A. Stephens on the stairway of the Temple Block and took him into his office, carrying in one hand as he always did his rattan cane. In a moment hot words came from

[242]

over the transom. Then Stephens made a lively egress through the hallway straight to the office of the Justice of the Peace where he swore out a warrant against the Major for assault with a deadly weapon. During the examination at Justice Ranney's court Stephens testified that Bell had called him a liar and ordered him out of his office. "He had a cane in his hand and said he would whip me. When I was struck at I was out of reach."

Bell affirmed under oath that he had called the reporter a liar for assertions made in his paper. "But I did not use the butt end of my cane. I did not attempt to strike him. I am glad because I never whipped a dog in my life and I never called a man a liar before." As a passer-by testified (who was in the hallway at the time of Stephens' exit) that he did not see a cane used, the district attorney remarked to the justice, "I don't think on the testimony before the court that I can ask your Honor to hold the defendant to answer." So the Major was discharged.

This affair however was not over, for a few months later Stephens boarded a train for southern Indiana where Bell was born and reared to search for information which might defame his enemy. When the next state encampment of the Grand Army of the Republic met in Los Angeles, that is in February of 1887, the Major was not surprised to see his brother veterans reading an anonymous pamphlet entitled *Life of Horace Bell*. The Los Angeles *Herald* called it "about the vilest and most abusive thing that has been seen in print for years," and added, "If he is guilty of a one-hundredth part of the crimes attributed to him he would be a disgrace to the gallows on which he were hung." To make Bell's embarrassment worse the whole thing was read aloud before the council of the fraternity and of course read individually and discussed by the membership.

To make revenge still sweeter his enemies within the order raised the question in open meeting as to his performance in the late war. They tauntingly asserted that the Major had never held a rank higher than sergeant and only for three months, ignoring his four-year service as scout. Having had a premonition that attempts would be made to discredit his record, Bell had obtained from the War Department an attested transcript of his complete service and exhibited it at the proper time.

The convention seethed with excitement, for some of Bell's bitterest enemies were in the fraternity. Taking note of the disharmony among the brethren the *Herald* commented: "It is sad to see a house so divided and it would be a good idea for the Major to hire Agricultural [now Exposition] Park, since no other place would be large enough, and on his birthday invite all his adversaries in the G. A. R. and the Republican party to a dinner, and let the dinner be a love feast and scene of reconciliation."

His war record after being read from the platform by the adjutant at the convention was referred together with the biography to a committee for examination. This group reported at length that Bell's record was "gilt-edged" and stigmatized the pamphlet as "cowardly." The report was adopted and spread upon the minutes, but late in the afternoon objection was made to the word "cowardly" and with Bell's consent the whole matter was stricken from the minutes.

Another scene in this play of hate. Time—three weeks later. Place—Justice Taney's township court. Following up the distribution of the anonymous pamphlet Horace Bell had filed charges of libel against G. Wiley Wells, A. M. Thornton, and B. A. Stephens. The courtroom was packed to the doors, everybody expecting a lively time. A printer from Pomona named Ellis Vallicel testified that he had set type for the pamphlet in the print shop of the Pomona *Progress*—that the manuscript was given him by Stephens. Lynn Lyman, another printer, affirmed that he had heard Stephens say that he was "going to get out a pamphlet, something about the life of Bell." According to other witnesses Thornton was seen distributing the leaflets. As a result of the trial the justice discharged Wiley Wells as innocent, but held the other two men over to appear before the Superior Court, where they were eventually convicted.

But they appealed their case to the State Supreme Court on the ground of a technicality. While they were being tried in the lower court the jury left the courthouse, in charge of an officer, to eat their supper. On returning, the jurors stepped into the courtroom instead of going to the jury room and there continued their deliberations. During this time one of the jurors picked up the pamphlet in question and read portions of it to the others. The appellants claimed that by his act the jury had received evidence out of court. To this point the judges of the Supreme Court agreed. They reversed the decision of the lower court and granted the defendants a new trial. Evidently the libel case was now dropped, for no records suggest a continuance.[17]

Years later in a letter to Bancroft, an historian of California, Bell attributed the biographical pamphlet to "Lucky" Baldwin's money as the ultimate source, the motive for its production being, he thought, the millionaire's vindictive anger at being beaten in his suits against the *Porcupine*'s editor.

The Curtain Lecture

A certain Union colonel who lived in the house next to Bell's was chief of the fire department. In 1886 he ran for the office of Secretary of State on the Republican ticket and the Major though long an adherent of that party used his paper to oppose his neighbor's election.

On the afternoon of November tenth shortly after his defeat the colonel and a friend were walking up Spring street and on reaching Shrier's cigar store they met the publisher of the *Porcupine* standing beside the wooden Indian. Bell bowed politely and spoke.

"Don't talk to me, you cowardly cur!" broke out the defeated candidate.

"What's that, sir? What's that?" exclaimed the Major.

And the angry man replied, "How dare you talk to me, you cur?"

At that Bell advanced quickly and struck the fire-chief in the face, who as suddenly dealt his assailant a smacking blow on the mouth. It felled him to the sidewalk, for the colonel was big and heavy-set, the Major tall and spare. As soon as the editor had picked himself up Deputy Sheriff Darcy appeared and stopped the scrimmage.

In the following Saturday's issue Bell reported the incident to his readers. His story agreed with that told by the *Express* except that he failed to mention any punch he had taken. He publicly rejoiced in the thought that he had not acted like Harrison Gray Otis, editor of the *Times*, to whom the same insult was given but without the fist's reply.

When the *Porcupine* reached her home Mrs. Bell opened it up with usual apprehension. Her eyes fell upon the lines:

One thousand Republicans scratched the colonel's name and voted for his opponent. Two thousand disgusted Republicans, it is said, crossed out his name and voted for ——

She could read no farther. "Oh," she sighed, "another friend lost!" Then the gentle lady rested her arm and head on the center table and wept.

That night at bedtime she complained to her husband, saying, "Horace, why do you print such awful things in the *Porcupine* about people? Think how it must make them feel."

"That's not the point, Georgie," he explained. "Such things have to be said for the good of Los Angeles. They deserve it and I print only what I know is true."

"Oh, but don't do it, Horace. It is so unpleasant. And you don't have to."

"Yes, but Georgie, I've got to! I've got to!" he answered excitedly, pacing back and forth in the bedroom.

"But why do you have to do it?" insisted his wife painfully.

"Because it's my lifework, it's my ——"

"Yes, yes, I know," she interposed. "It's your duty. How many times have I heard that before—it's your duty! But what about our children and me? Don't you realize, Horace, how embarrassing it is to us all? Oh, I wish it could be somebody else's work and duty!"[18]

[246]

A Lawyer and an Honest Man

Though Bell was himself a lawyer, having practiced since 1872, he dared to expose in his paper the transgressions of the bar in Los Angeles. He never acquired an occupational loyalty which protects with silence the faults of a colleague. His observations on law and attorneys were not made hastily. Instead they followed an experience of more than a decade.

The lawyers of Los Angeles, he affirmed, were on the average about as good as any other class of citizens. There were many local attorneys who were equal in purity of character and fair dealing to any men in the trades or other professions. But to his knowledge there were some whose sole aim was success, whether won by honest witnesses or perjured testimony. Money they would have, if it could be wrung out of their clients or those of the opposition. To illustrate this point Bell printed the letter of a subscriber who charged that his attorney, giving the name, accepted his money as retainer in a suit, obtained his statement of the case, and then took the other side. "The bar," commented the journalist, "has permitted itself to be smirched by such characters. Litigants who suffer from such malpractice should complain and they should be redressed."

Another reader of the *Porcupine*, signing himself as "One of the Dear People," wrote to the editor protesting against the expense of litigation. He could see no reason why legal work should cost four times as much in California as elsewhere unless it was that there were four times as many lawyers, since supply and demand did not seem to regulate the fees. It was a question often asked by strangers, continued the subscriber, how so many lawyers could make a living in Los Angeles. But let the new arrival purchase real estate and his eyes would be opened. He would learn all about it in a short time when he paid $10 to $25 for a transcript of title and three dollars to record a deed that he had been accustomed to have done in the East for 75¢ or a dollar.

In another issue Bell lamented the high cost of probating wills. The law as it stood on the statute books was good for the lawyers, he thought, but unfair to the public. It needed revision. The man who left at his death a little property brought upon his heirs heavy expenses which might eat up the estate before settlement. However small the inheritance was, the same legal forms had to be followed. Lawyers must be feed, the attorney *ad litem* appointed by the court and paid, bonds filed, appraisers chosen, notices published and posted. And should there be the slightest error the whole proceeding became null. Was this not an absurdity? inquired Bell.

To cite an example he told of an old woman who died in Los Angeles owing not a dollar. She left a house and lot both worth $500, and $400 in cash. She provided a will and an executor. There were two grandchildren, one a man of 21, the other an infant. They should receive the legacy after the funeral expenses were paid, which amounted to $37. Her estate went into the probate court and ran the usual gauntlet for almost two years. Then the young man employed legal aid to procure whatever might be coming to him. His lawyer went through the record, cut down the costs, and his own service fee, saving in all $200, only to find that his client's estate was gone. In fact he was in debt $18. "This was a nice little job for the lawyers," concluded Bell, "but pretty hard on the old woman's heirs."

But he did not see how the public could get along without lawyers. For in such times of enlightenment as the 1880s, when many persons could read, they needed lawyers to tell them the meaning of what they read. The trouble was that no two lawyers would agree as to what a law meant, and so the people were befogged.

To add authority to his remarks the editor cited John Wesley, the founder of Methodism, as saying of lawyers:

[They are] bred up from their youth in the art of proving according as they are paid, by words multiplied for the purpose that white is black and black is white. [They also have] a peculiar cant and jargon of their own in which all their laws are written and these they take special care to multiply, whereby they have so confounded truth and falsity, right and wrong, that it will take 12 years to decide whether the field left me by my ancestors for six generations belongs to me or to one 300 miles off.

Downey Block, north corner of Temple and Main streets, Los Angeles, business center in 1880s. In middle of left side is Slotterbeck's gun store, where Bell bought his gun when threatened by a deputy. On second floor back of window farthest to the left "Reminiscences of a Ranger" was printed.

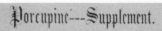

The Chief of Police as he thought he would appear in squelching the PORCUPINE.

The Chief of the Mollie Maguire Police as he appeared after his encounter with the PORCUPINE.

Cartoon in the "Porcupine" following attempted assassination of the editor by the chief of police.

PERTINENT PARAGRAPHS.

Column heading from the "Porcupine"

Front page of a "Porcupine"

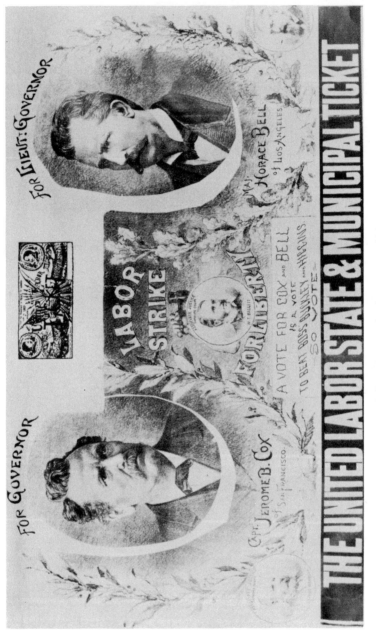

California state election poster, 1886

Bell then added the words of John Milton, describing the barristers of his day as

grounding their purposes not on the prudent and heavenly contemplation of justice and equity, which was never taught them, but on the promising and pleasing thoughts of litigious terms, fat contentions, and flowing fees.

Turning to poetry for a graceful flourish he repeated Wordsworth's squib:

> A Lawyer art thou?—draw not nigh!
> Go carry to some fitter place
> The keenness of that practiced eye,
> The hardness of that sallow face.

Finally with all its quills erect the *Porcupine* delivered its thorniest jab by quoting Ben Jonson's *Epitaph on Justice Randal*:

> God works wonders now and then;
> Here lies a lawyer and an honest man![19]

Thy Name I Love

Having served during the late war in the Northern army, Horace Bell was elected by his comrades, in 1884, as commander of the Frank Bartlett post. This was one of the two units located in Los Angeles of the Grand Army of the Republic, the national organization of Federal veterans. This office he held for three successive years. In 1886, following unbroken custom, the two groups observed Memorial Day, which fell on Sunday. In the morning the Bartlett post, accompanied by the Pasadena unit and the Sons of Veterans marched in a body to the Fort street Methodist church. Here they heard a patriotic sermon by Reverend F. P. Bresee. At the same time the Stanton post, also of Los Angeles, assembled in the Grand Opera House to hear Reverend Mr. Fay of the Unitarian society.

At two in the afternoon the combined veterans marched to Fort Hill cemetery, west of the Plaza, where General Pile of Missouri delivered an oration. After the program loving hands placed flowers upon the graves of departed comrades. Likewise the resting places of those who fought in the Mexican War were decorated, including that of Alexander Bell. In reporting the day the *Herald* recalled how this pioneer, when Frémont arrived in Los Angeles, had given three-months' pay to his men and a large sum for the general's expenses, never asking for reimbursement. In fuller appreciation of his patriotism the paper reminded its readers that he had later donated Poundcake Hill to the city as a site for the first public high school.[20]

An increasing danger to national welfare the Major thought were the hyphenated Americans—those citizens who refused to give up alien allegiances and banded together to preserve their foreign identity. He deplored the presence in California of German, Irish, and Spanish clubs. When the state elections were over he cautioned against saying that the ticket was carried by the Germans, Irish, or Mexicans. Let it rather be said that Americans of the majority defeated Americans of the minority. And he added, "As noble a sentiment as I ever heard fall from the lips of a man came from Louis Lichtenberger when he went before the political convention. He did not ask for the nomination because of his influence as a German, but because of his patriotism as an American." Bell had no patience with Irish agitators. He insisted that when emigrants from the Emerald Isle came hither they should stop their war on England. Let them send back money to the old country, if they liked, that their relatives might follow. But they must be made to understand that only Congress has the power to declare war—not the Irish.

Another facet of Bell's Americanism was his wish that all malice toward the recent rebels should be forgotten. In the spring of 1886 Jefferson Davis dedicated a Confederate monument at Montgomery, Alabama, and many Northern newspapers resented the bitterness of his address. But Bell could not blame him. Instead he honored the man who refused to "eat dirt at the feet of a government that had outraged him." The two chiefs of the rebellion, Davis and Robert E. Lee, he asserted, were the peers of any in the world and Christian gentlemen. As such they were entitled to charitable treatment. Through the fairness of General Grant, Lee had received the consideration due him. But a bigoted president had manacled Davis and thrown him into prison. Was it any wonder the poor old man was sour? To him the *Porcupine* conceded the right to say all he pleased in praise of the Lost Cause, for this is a country of free speech, it declared, and the Southerners are a brave and noble people. Generous words were these coming from a commander in the Grand Army of the Republic and one who had lost a brother in the war.

Two years later General William T. Sherman invited to a banquet celebrating Grant's birthday some of the leaders who had worn the gray. Of this act the editor approved and added: "The men who fought the Confederacy respect the men who opposed them in honorable warfare. The only people now heard cursing the 'rebels' are the 'stay-at-homes' and the politicians."

Major Bell had never heard of pacifism. He believed in war. He could not agree that its influences are entirely demoralizing. "War," he wrote, "though it does expose the evil in human nature also brings out the noble and brave. By having long periods of peace nations become effeminate and effeminacy begets corruption, which results in a few becoming very rich and powerful and the many poor and oppressed. On the whole we are of the opinion that any nation that endures a protracted term of peace is on the highway to ruin. We think the United States ought to have a war about every 25 years, thus giving each generation an opportunity to participate in at least two wars."

He predicted the coming of aircraft as a military weapon. France, he thought, held the advantage over Germany in having balloons capable of dropping bombs upon cities, fortified camps, moving armies, and war vessels. It would be only a short time he prophesied until armed airships would excite less wonder than Ericsson's little *Monitor* when it encountered the *Merrimac*. He called upon the Federal government to spend a million dollars, even $10,000,000, if need be, as premiums payable to inventors perfecting such aircraft. One of these should be kept ready at each seaport for coastal defense.[21]

[251]

California, Here We Come!

Bell gloried in the beauty of his home country. He boasted of its swelling population. Like many others he contracted the habit of speaking extravagantly of Los Angeles. Some citizens did tire, as he did, of the absence of seasons, longing to face wintry blasts and tread on snow. But after a year in northern lands a longing to return would seize the absentee, making him exclaim, "There's no place like Los Angeles!"

He recalled his own journeys to the Far West, each time riding on a horse or mule, and dragging over weary miles, each mile seeming endless. But when he reached the Golden State and beheld its beauty his heart leaped with joy and he was rewarded for all the suffering he had endured in coming. Think of present-day winter tourists, he remarked—how astonished they must feel after passing over the cold wastes of Kansas or, more desolate still, the great Colorado desert to enter a world of vernal charm by rail at the rate of 40 miles an hour!

But what was this marvelous country coming to? A few years ago it was a boundless pasture for sheep. Now it was checkered with railroads. Land worth only three dollars an acre a decade before was now in the middle '80s covered with iron-front brick business buildings, as well as cottages and mansions. Lots in Pasadena were selling for $100 a front foot. In all directions spread hundreds of orange groves and vineyards.

Since 1874 when the inhabitants numbered 7,000 he had seen the population of Los Angeles mount up in six years to 11,000. Now in '86 it was about 45,000. By 1894 he expected the City of Mary's Angels to count 100,000 people. Indeed it seemed to Bell not far in the future when her northern limits would lie at the foot of Sierra Madre and the southern touch the sea. But such a growth might be checked by an inadequate store of water. If properly developed and distributed water resources were sufficient for a city of 200,000. "But," cautioned the editor of the *Porcupine*, "we must not hug the delusion to our souls that we can lie in the shade of our orange groves and have our city in the next decade attain to the size of Minneapolis. Our moneyed men must create and encourage manufacturing."

The rapid growth of Los Angeles Bell declared had made San Francisco jealous. The southern city was older and at first outnumbered its rival. But the gold mines had given San Francisco the lead and Los Angeles a setback. Now his town was making up for lost time. He believed that the two places would some day compare with New York and Boston in that San Francisco would remain a rough seaport while her competitor would excel in culture. In fact he expected Los Angeles eventually to equal Boston in intellectual achievement.

At present her advance in numerical size had brought greater property values. The town was so situated, he thought, that the spreading of the business section would occur only toward the south. For the hills to the west and the river on the east would prevent expansion in those directions. If, as it was predicted, the population in 1890 would be 100,000 then the commercial district, although it already reached above Second street, would run still farther southward up Main. Lots in that area would then be worth a hundred dollars per front foot, as they were then at Main and Sixth.

The *Porcupine* in the spring of '86 advertised for sale 500 lots subdivided from a nursery tract two-and-a-half miles south of the post office. They had been improved with plank sidewalks and supplied with four electric light poles, each lot costing $250. In the following year Bell's paper reported that 13 acres lying at Main and Adams streets had just sold for $80,000. The land boom, the Major cynically remarked, had decreased the number of politicians. Office seekers who formerly would have gone wild over the prospect of being secretary to a woodcutter now turned up their noses at being a congressman—there was more money in real estate.

In March 1886 Pasadena held her Citrus Fair. Thursday, the eighteenth, was set aside to honor the county journalists and Bell came as a guest. Other editors were present, including Colonel H. H. Boyce of the Los Angeles *Tribune*, and Charles A.

[253]

Gardner of the *Pasadena Valley and Union*, as well as representatives of the *Times*, the *Herald*, and the *Express* of the former city, also publishers of the Anaheim *Gazette*, the Pomona *Progress*, and the Santa Ana *Standard*. All made speeches.

Bell when his turn came told the Pasadenans that their town was the most beautiful in America. It was hard to realize the changes that had taken place in only a few years. He described how the county looked when he first saw it in his early twenties.

"There were only two houses on the sixty-mile journey from Los Angeles to San Juan Capistrano. Four intervened between the Angel City and San Bernardino and as we rode from the Sierra's base to San Gabriel by way of Pasadena only two homes could be seen, that of Don Benito Wilson and the other of Don Manuel Garfias, the latter being the old San Pasqual ranch house.[22] Such was the condition of the county until the completion of the Central and Southern Pacific railroads. It was then that progress began." He predicted that the day would soon come when Pasadena would be part of a greater city reaching to Santa Monica by the sea.[23]

The county's development he attributed to an enlargement of the American mind caused by the War of the Rebellion. He gave thanks to Jefferson Davis and Robert Toombs for precipitating the conflict. But for them hostilities would have been deferred and the building of the Pacific railroad put off for half a lifetime. Consequently Los Angeles county would still be a sheep pasture and lands now worth $100 an acre would be high at "two bits." Instead of 60,000 its population might be less than 6,000.

But after the fervor of his speech had waned and the fever of the boom had run its course the Major now nearing 60 suffered a revulsion. He sighed for the good old days when his town was small. "I doubt the fact of my living in Los Angeles," he told his subscribers. "To me it has become some other place. Nine men out of every 10 are strangers to me and to have lived one's life here affords no more familiarity with present affairs than if I had come in on one of the new railroads.

"Confound the railroads! The locomotive has driven all the

sheep from the country and its whistle has caused our jack rabbits and coyotes to migrate—whither, oh, where? And we are all made strangers in our own land. Alas, ye stranger hath come in and possessed our country at a thousand dollars an acre. Alas and alack!"

The Man with a Cane

In March of '87 Bell's journalistic hedgehog stuck its sharp spines into a general who belonged to a local post of the Grand Army of the Republic. He was described as a political boss who controlled the county clerk, the sheriff, the board of supervisors, the Los Angeles *Express*, and tried to govern the *Times*. The general boasted, so the paper affirmed, that he "ran the post office and carried the Republican party in the tails of his coat." When the county supervisors were constructing a new jail the *Porcupine* charged the veteran with grafting. Soon after publishing this allegation the editor was warned by his friend, Colonel Miller, that three enemies in the post, including the general, planned to provoke a fight with him during which one would assassinate Bell. Naturally this put him on the lookout.

A few afternoons later the publisher was standing on Market street talking with Judge Anson Brunson and his old ranger friend, William Jenkins, when the accused politician came along. Then something happened which we may learn of by reading old copies of the *Herald* and the *Times* reporting a consequent trial. The former gave its account without feeling, but Harrison Gray Otis gleefully put Bell in the worst light possible.

Brunson, as chief witness, testified that he heard the plaintiff say to the defendant, "You damned brute! Don't print my name again in that dirty blackmailing sheet of yours!" Then he saw the general throw up his arm and Horace Bell's cane bend across it, and as it struck, the lower part broke off and fell upon the ground, disclosing a steel blade about two feet long. The plaintiff asserted that he raised his arm to ward off the blow. Jenkins and Edward Van Husen affirmed that when Bell stepped back after delivering the stroke the cane was held downward and that the editor made no attempt to harm the general after the bamboo scabbard fell.

Acting against the advice of his legal counsel the Major gave under oath his version. He had been warned of hostile intentions on the part of the general. As his adversary had insulted him he had struck in retaliation. Bell declared that his cane was a new gift and he did not know the end had "the trick of falling off." Furthermore his opponent had put his hand to his hip pocket as if to draw a revolver and Brunson being a man of peace had stepped between them. "I had no intention of injuring the general with a sword cane. I only desired to resent an insult."

After listening to arguments from the prosecution Judge Austin dismissed the case on the ground that the evidence being insufficient did not prove the assault was made with a deadly weapon.

In his next number Bell retold the story, but he failed to mention that his walking stick was a sword cane, such as was carried in that day by Western gentlemen. "Let it be known," he concluded, "that during the whole period of our life in Los Angeles we have never drawn a deadly weapon except on two occasions —and we have never failed to properly and on the spot resent insult."[24]

What Bell said was true. Contradicting legends still repeated in Los Angeles, men now living who knew him well confirm his statement. They assert that he carried not a gun but a cane. Sometimes it was a hickory walking stick, sometimes a small rattan. These were sufficient for self-protection and for "resenting insults." Despite the urging of friends he would not carry a gun. He was afraid to do so—it is said—because of his sudden temper.

The Good Neighbor Policy

Bell had a warm heart for Spanish-speaking people. He regretted that many *Californios* had lost their great ranchos, but it comforted him to know that their misfortune was due to compound interest and not to the American government.

When holidays came, in his middle life, it was his habit to hitch up Big Dash and Little Dash to the two-seated family carriage and set out for a pleasure drive. This vehicle was so wide and sprawling, so alive with the arms and legs of numerous active children that he nicknamed it "the tarantula." Usually it gravitated to San Gabriel, where lived a large settlement of Mexicans. Here he greeted old friends with a cordial hug and a pat on the back—the *abrazo*—even the elderly women, while Mrs. Bell sat on the back seat and looked askance.

He was proud of the compliments paid to his book by the *hijos del país*, or native sons of California. For example, Eulogio de Celis, who owned the vast rancho at San Fernando, had praised the *Reminiscences of a Ranger* because it had treated his people "most handsomely."[25] In the *Porcupine* the Major told his readers, since many were late arrivals, that "among our Spanish-American residents we have as brave and generous men, as good and virtuous women, as one can find in the best classes of American society."

He revered the name of Benito Juárez, the Mexican revolutionist under whom he had fought. This patriot he compared favorably with the Italian Garibaldi.

Bell's military service in Mexico had taught him the meaning of that country's Day of Independence. It stirred in him the same emotion, though in less degree, that he felt on the Fourth of July. When the sixteenth of September came in 1883, Bell called upon all citizens of Los Angeles to honor the memory of Mexico's beloved Father of Independence, Miguel Hidalgo. For the newcomers and other uninformed Californians he gave in his paper a full and impassioned account of Hidalgo, the parish priest of the village of Dolores, telling how in 1810 on the sixteenth of September, at dawn, he raised the cry of liberty, *el grito de Dolores*, in the courtyard of his church and began the war against Spain.

Honoring as he did the Mexicans' love of freedom Bell was amazed and angered when Porfirio Díaz, the president of Mexico, sold commercial privileges to foreign corporations. Could it be possible, he queried, that so rich and beautiful a country would forfeit its birthright to outsiders?

In the early '80s Americans were protesting against acts of violence committed by Mexicans on the Texas border. On three occasions he defended our southern neighbor. There was the case in point of Crawford, an American army officer who had been killed by Mexicans. Bell explained that the two governments on opposite sides of the Rio Grande had agreed that troops might move into the other's territory in pursuit of hostile Apaches. Sometime before, Crook, an Indian fighter in the United States army, had conceived the idea of fighting Apaches with other Apaches. But when the Indians were sent into the southern country in search of their own tribesmen, they had murdered Mexicans, stolen, and burned their property. Naturally the Mexicans retaliated by attacking Crawford's party. Bell insisted they had done right. "The sending of Apaches into Mexico as United States troops was in violation of the treaty."

In the summer of '86 newspapers complained that Mexican *vaqueros* were stealing American cattle grazing near the Rio Grande. The *Porcupine* freed its readers from resentment by quoting Colonel A. G. Bracket stationed at Fort Davis, Texas. Scouting parties, he declared, kept moving along the river, but they knew nothing of the reported thefts. Instead they saw hundreds of cattle crossing over into Mexico, but nobody drove them. They went of their own accord where they could find enough grass to live on. This was hard for them to do in Presidio county whence they came. The Texas cowboys were willing to have their cattle wander into Mexico where grazing was comparatively good, for they could drive them back when they pleased. Moreover, the colonel declared, "if any Mexican has crossed on this side and driven cattle over, he has been merely taking back his own property just as our people do from the other side." It seemed only fair to Bell that false charges should be cleared up. He would do his part in spreading the truth and creating good will.

Nicaragua never lost its lure for the Major. He loved to describe his favorite country of Central America. Beautiful and grand—so he told his readers—were the islands in Lake Nicaragua. Besides being capable of high cultivation they were healthful places to live. Bordering the lake stood primeval forests where unknown rivers awaited discovery. In the regions of Chontales and Segovia, lying between the lake and the Caribbean sea, high rolling prairies invited settlement. There wild grasses grew as high as a mule's back and rippled in the breeze up to the very hilltops. Beyond the prairie slopes, mountains towered above green valleys, ridges of timber alternated with bright rivers, and brooks dashed over rocky bottoms. Such geographical features enhanced by coal fields and placers of gold made this vast tract the most favored by nature on the continent. Then too there was no finer country than that west of the lake.

He foresaw an increasing trade with our Latin neighbors. This would make a knowledge of their language a necessity. "Much good would follow if the time wasted in teaching our boys astronomy were given to teaching them Spanish and preparing them to be clerks, bookkeepers, and telegraphers. In this semi-Spanish city the children with a little schoolroom help will become proficient in this language and we hope that our Board of Education will have our boys taught Spanish." The voice of the *Porcupine* may have had influence, for three years later a petition was offered to the Board asking for a high school class in Spanish. The editor remarked, "We say *yes*. Have it free or at any cost."

The Power of an Honest Paper

The *Porcupine* was founded to fight political corruption. Almost every official in the county, asserted Bell in 1882, took bribes: the police, the city councilmen, and even judges. The city offices were held by thieves and cutthroats, and if one were exposed the rest would retaliate. As the reformer continued his warfare he reported from time to time the progress he thought he was making.

After the fourth month of disclosures he declared that no one had questioned the truthfulness of anything he had printed. A little later he wrote that having driven the enemy underground, he expected sweeping reforms to follow. But in this work he had received no support from other papers. In the eighth month of crusading the editor proclaimed to his readers, "The police are now pretty well behaved, for they know the *Porcupine* will prick them when they deserve it."

Two years passed and the Major noted further progress. At the last election the voters had improved the personnel of the city council. Moreover the discipline of the police had bettered; that is, the chief was less open in levying blackmail—his officers were less prone to lean against lamp posts or to get drunk publicly and stagger on the sidewalks. Yet in spite of this advance Bell maintained that bribery still persisted. In 1885 after three years of publication the *Porcupine* congratulated Los Angeles on a thorough reform of the police department. No city it affirmed could boast of a more respectable body of officers. "We have no more thieves and convicts on the force and the chief is a gentleman—not a drunken Arizona cowboy."

During the late campaign Bell used his paper to oppose the candidates of his own party. In his opinion the worst Republican politicians of Los Angeles had united with "the hoodlums and carpetbaggers," and assisted by the *Times* had captured the party machinery, putting themselves up for office. Owing to the popularity of James G. Blaine, the Republican national leader, these men were elected. But Bell fought them until the fall of '86 when they were defeated for re-election. Under the caption "The Power of an Honest Paper" the *Porcupine* claimed its share of credit for their removal from office.

Los Angeles must have been doing well in 1887, for Bell had only praise for its mayor, William H. Workman. "He seems fully up to the work," wrote the Major, "and he works night and day. We predict he will make the municipal reforms his friends expect."

It was in 1888, the sixth year of his self-chosen mission, that Bell saw the most signs of improvement. Public gambling had stopped. He was pleased with the city officers. He considered the

[260]

president of the city council to be a gentleman and the city attorney possessed of high legal and moral worth. Likewise the clerk, the auditor, the street superintendent dignified the people who employed them. The civil engineer and his corps were capable. But the greatest amendment appeared among the police.

Bell's influence as a reformer was largely due to the number of people he could gain as readers. Four years after its beginning the *Porcupine* enjoyed a circulation of 6,000 copies throughout Los Angeles county. Its publisher estimated that 20,000 citizens read his paper and believed what it said. The issue which cartooned Wiley Wells as trying to sit on an angry porcupine he guessed had made 50,000 people laugh. During its palmiest days the *Porcupine* was sold at all newsstands in the city and on trains running out of Los Angeles, as well as in Santa Ana, San Diego, Colton, Pomona, and at the Palace hotel in San Francisco. Copies were mailed to subscribers in the East. In New York City they were kept on file by an advertising firm ready to make contracts with merchants. In the fifth year of his venture Bell boasted that he had made his paper highly profitable. Now he needed a permanent advertising solicitor, whom he would pay well. He hoped to raise the subscription list soon to 10,000. To reach this goal he offered to send, for three dollars, a copy of his *Reminiscences of a Ranger* (usual price two dollars) in addition to a two-dollar yearly subscription to his weekly.

Overlooking unfavorable comments, Bell reported that he continually received letters of approbation, many of them coming from the East. With natural pride he reprinted the praise of friendly editors. The San Diego *Star* coupled the *Porcupine* with the San Francisco *Star*, calling both public benefactors. The latter paper, pleased with this association, remarked, "Keep up the good work, brother Bell." The *Register* of San Jacinto (California) commended his exposure of political corruption. Back in Illinois the Chenoa *Gazette* pronounced the *Porcupine* to be "the most fearless and best edited paper on the Pacific slope."

Having achieved his measure of success Bell was satisfied. He had made his fight, he said, and "won the right of all good citizens to walk the streets of Los Angeles without paying tribute to official thieves and murderers." He did not think that the municipal government was perfect. Yet it was outwardly decent. Now he was ready to quit. Accordingly after six years of an editor's routine he turned the paper over to his son Charles to publish. From then on the father's only connection with the weekly was an occasional article written to assist his filial successor. It continued to be printed—so a few remaining copies show—as late as 1897. But on the day the Major walked out of its office the *Porcupine* lost its prickles.

In looking back over the reforms that had come to the governments of Los Angeles and its county, Bell claimed his due credit, but he was glad to share honors with others. It was in the second year of the *Porcupine's* life that Stephen M. White became district attorney. He was the man whose statue now stands on the lawn at Civic Center. Today we see him dressed in a frock coat and lifting his right hand oratorically over the traffic flowing past the intersection of Temple street with Broadway. In his old age Bell wrote generously of him: "Stephen M. White did more to aid me in my warfare against the evil ones than any other man in the county. A great man was he!"

Such success as the *Porcupine* had, he also ascribed partly to its happy conjuncture with social trends. When Bell started his paper the migration of Easterners to Los Angeles had begun. To these new citizens the editor chiefly directed his call. Most of the early settlers, he declared, were indifferent to the immoral conditions of their town. It had always been corrupt; they assumed it always would be. Twenty years after dropping his editorial pen Bell wrote: "We looked to the newcomers for emancipation and the newcomers made the change."

How will impartial history appraise the *Porcupine*? One can guess from opinions held by those who knew the man and his times. Mary Foy, the first city librarian, believes that in many instances his journalistic attacks were wholesome. The editor of the Los Angeles *Tribune* recorded in Bell's obituary that "according to the Major's friends the *Porcupine* accomplished its purpose to a considerable extent and made Los Angeles a much better place to live in." Frederick Baker, a senior attorney, points out that he painted only in black and white, his friends being perfect, his enemies wholly bad. In the words of Judge Joseph F. Chambers, "Bell often went too far in his censure, yet he did bring evil to light." And for this reason the late Joseph Mesmer, an early merchant, declared that "Los Angeles needed such a fighter as Horace Bell and such a paper as the *Porcupine*."[26]

CHAPTER IX

The Last Leaf

And if I should live to be
The last leaf upon the tree
In the spring. . . .

O. W. HOLMES

TICK-TOCK, tick-tock sounded the clock in the quiet front parlor. It seemed louder that night in the deep hush of sickness. Two weeks before, both parents had been mysteriously smitten by ptomaine poisoning. Bell having the stronger constitution quickly recovered, but his wife grew worse.[1]

She wanted to look out on her flowers in the yard and so several days ago her bed had been moved into the front parlor. Directly forward she could see through the broad bay window her white roses posing all day like lovely models, while nearby watched a pair of magnolia trees, one on each side of the walk leading down to the front gate, their great white petals now fully open. By turning her head to the right she could adore her garden on the south side of the house beyond the other window. Here were blooming her pink Duchess roses. The plumbagos offered their showy blue flowers and a large banksia shrub climbing over an arbor extended to her its dark green leaves and long sprays densely covered with clusters of yellow blossoms. Much of the day she had gazed outside and now it was dark again. The large beehive clock which she had brought from New Orleans stood on a cabinet of Chinese ebony to the right of the bay window and opposite the foot of her bed.

"Horace," sighed the invalid, "what day is tomorrow?"

"The eighth of June, my little darling."

"Then," breathed the mother, "it will be Maud's birthday. Just think! She was born 16 years ago tomorrow. I was pretty sick then, don't you remember?"

[264]

"Yes, Georgie, my darling, I can never forget that terrible time back in '83."

"Oh," she added, "I do hope her birthday dress comes tomorrow. How disappointed poor little Maud will be if it doesn't! And I want to see her enjoy it—before I go."

In the morning, after the expressman came, in stepped Maud arrayed in her new dress of pink organdie. "Look, Mamma!" she exclaimed proudly, "it came in time!"

"Oh," replied Mrs. Bell, "I am so happy! Turn around, dear, and let me see the back of the dress. It fits perfectly—and how very, very pretty!"

Solemnly the beehive clock was measuring out the last hours of Maud's birthday anniversary. Papa sat again by the bed with the nurse, both of them watching and serving—most of the children being close by. "Do you know me?" he asked softly. "Why, yes, it's Horace of course," came the answer. She felt cold. So he rose and spread an extra comforter over the bed. Did she not want something more? Yes, she would like a cup of coffee. He insisted on making it himself and after a while brought it in from the kitchen. He took her up in his arms. She drank a few swallows, then resting her head upon his big shoulder closed her eyes. The clock chimed one bell for the last half-hour of the day.

"Isn't there something else we can do, my little darling?" Horace waited a long time for an answer. Then came her words barely audible, "It is very, very pretty."

Here in his arms lay the gentle girl who had given up her people, had gone through the hazards of war, had crossed the wild plains, and spent most of her years—for him. What pictures of their life together must have raced through his mind as he tenderly clasped her! Softly she fell asleep and then in perfect peace Georgia Bell, daughter of the Herricks and Crockers, withdrew from her world of loved ones and flowers.

After the first tears everyone sat motionless lost in grief until the mahogany clock rudely broke the silence. It started to whiz, then thumped and finally gave forth a loud bang! The startled mourners looked up expecting to hear it strike 12. But it did not. Instead it had stopped and even after being rewound refused to run again.[2]

This sad event opened the last chapter of Horace Bell's life. Through sorrow his nature grew milder and his heart turned toward religion. He continued to live at the old home place, cared for by Lillian, an unmarried daughter. Maud not long after entered Mills College in Oakland as a student. Frequently his children and grandchildren came for a visit. "I anticipate great loneliness when daughter Georgia leaves," he wrote, "because the rattle and clatter, the running and tumbling, the screaming and yelling of her three children afford me solace. I like it very much. I never saw babies grow so fast and wax so strong. They are outdoors all the time. There is one fault, however, I find with them; they are always pulling the flowers and sometimes they pull the wrong ones."

In another letter he informed a son:

I have worked for two hours every morning since you went away and I have all the flower beds in perfect order, from the kitchen window to the stable—all the weeds dug up, the ground forked over. The orchard is doing pretty well. We will have plenty of figs, apricots, peaches and plums, and a few quinces. But we won't have any apples or pears. Monday I am going to stake and tie up the chrysanthemums in the long bed. Then our place will be a paradise and the most homelike on Figueroa.

We all went out to the cemetery on Decoration Day. Your Mamma's grave looks beautiful, especially so since the monument was put up. The girls continue to go there at least twice a week to cover the place with flowers.

More than a year after losing his wife the Major began to assuage his grief with social affairs. Frequently he visited San Francisco where his seventy-first year saw many gay parties. Especially did he enjoy conversing with new feminine friends. Mrs. Gillespie invited him to a stylish dinner. Some of the ladies present he thought were "simply charming." But he committed a social *faux pas*. In an unguarded moment he jokingly asked a

[266]

dinner companion if she was "an old maid." She replied she hoped not. But on discovering that she was, he found himself in "the most embarrassing position I ever got into regarding a charming old girl."

Because of their interest in him as a fellow journalist and author the Ladies Press Club of San Francisco sent two of their members to the Palace hotel to pay their respects and invite him on behalf of the group to be the guest of honor at a theater box party. One of the callers appointed to escort him was Madge Morris, a poetess and wife of the writer Harr Wagner. But since he had another social engagement for that time, the club gave him on the next day a dinner instead, followed by a reception and musical. "The best part of it was," said Bell, "in being the only gentleman present, except an Italian who played the piano for the lady singers." One of the artists was Madame Guido Spitzy, who had sung for the king of Siam.

May of this year brought him a happy surprise. Upon his arrival in the bay city the first gentlemen to call on him were General Carlos Alberto Lacayo of Nicaragua, and his companion, an ex-president of Salvador, Carlos Ezeta, the former being then the new consul of his country. The Major had known his family nearly a half-century ago when he was soldiering in Granada, where the Lacayos lived in a mansion facing the plaza. Being an officer in Walker's army and speaking Spanish fluently, Bell was a frequent guest at their home and became a favorite of Don Fernando. "I have always known you by hearing my father speak of you in a kindly manner," said Don Carlos. A gay dinner party followed, the consul being host. With a graceful speech made in Spanish Lacayo presented to his guest a one-hundred-dollar gold-headed cane. Near the top appeared the inscription *From C. A. L.* and on the grip *To Major Horace Bell.*

"Well, General," concluded the recipient in his response, "I suppose I may consider this cane as a certificate of good behavior while I was in Granada."

The next morning Maud Bell, who was present at the party, had to return to school, having stayed overnight with Daisy.

Bell accompanied his daughters to Mills College in Oakland. Together the two sisters carried a big satchel. At the end of the car line in San Francisco their father took it to the ferryboat and in so doing he brought on an old back trouble and was sick for two days. What made the handbag so heavy? Fifty pounds of candy which Lacayo had presented to Maud. "I suppose," wrote Bell telling of the incident, "Maud's classmates at Mills will be eating candy for the rest of the school year."

On the following Sunday four of these friends who were at the party went for a walk in Golden Gate Park: Lacayo, Ezeta, and Bell arm in arm with Señora Ezeta. The Major described her as "one of the most beautiful and charming ladies anybody ever met anywhere in the world."

General William Rufus Shafter having heard of Bell's colorful personality as well as his war record desired to meet him while he was in San Francisco. Accordingly he wrote the Major a note inviting him to call at his home in the Presidio[3] with General Lacayo. Shafter graciously planned for the two gentlemen to return for dinner and bring with them the Ezetas and Daisy Bell Overton now living in the bay city. The American general drove over in his carriage accompanied by his daughter Mary to get Daisy. As they rode through Golden Gate Park to the Presidio every man recognized Shafter, stopped, and took off his hat. Daisy was so elated by all this attention that she almost thought she was the hero of the battle of Santiago de Cuba.

Then came the annual banquet of the Loyal Legion, of which Admiral Watson was president. There the Major met many gentlemen whom he had known for many years, among them Admiral Beardsley. At the dinner there was a continual passing of whisky punch, the opening of wine bottles, and popping of champagne corks. "Do you believe it," wrote Bell, "I did not drink a drop! Every time they would open a bottle I would turn my glass upside down."

Soon after, he visited the Harr Wagners[4] where he was entertained by a roomful of ladies. Here he had such a good time that he stayed an hour too long and was too late to attend a banquet at the Occidental hotel. "And do you know, Jinnie," he admitted, "I enjoyed the society of those ladies better than I did that of the admirals and generals."

Next on the social calendar came a luncheon with the Ezetas in Oakland, who had a lovely home not far from Mills College. At this modish affair no gentlemen guests were present except General Lacayo and Major Bell, a circumstance highly gratifying to the latter. Among the ladies gracing the occasion there was a red-haired Spanish señorita. "And oh, wasn't she a beauty!" confessed Don Horace, "and didn't I flirt with her!"

Despite frequent trips out of Los Angeles Bell remained in the practice of law. But in 1903 he began to think of retirement. Such a goal suggested the need for an increase of his pension. A letter which tells how he obtained it is significant in his life story, being the only complete reference to wounds received in battle.

I went before the examining surgeons of the pension bureau yesterday and carried the family Bible along to show them that I was 73 years old. That was much in my favor because outside of any injury I have sustained and notwithstanding three bullet wounds which they examined and one saber cut there is nothing the matter with me. But they monkeyed around and looked at my eyes and had me close one eye and open the other, then shut both eyes, and then look cross-eyed.

Next they took a wooden mallet and prodded me on the knee-cap, then had me cross my leg, one over the other, and they pounded that brother bone with the mallet, all of which was to ascertain if I ever had my back broken or strained. Then the doctors mysteriously conversed together in one corner of the room. One said *sirocco* or some other big medical name and another said *E Pluribus.*

One of the doctors came up and pinched the skin of the small of my back. Then he punched the place with his thumb, asked me if it felt sensitive. I told him, "not a bit." Then they measured my anatomy so as to locate exactly the bullet hole that passed through my shoulder (they wanted to be sure not to get it in the wrong place). Then they measured the other shoulder from the elbow up and from my hip joint, converging the two angles at the *locus in quo* (that means the place where the point of the saber struck me under the arm) and then they measured from the point of my hip to my knee and located

[269]

the bullet hole that went through my thigh. They were likewise very particular in examining that old scar across the knuckle on my left hand.

I did not tell them anything about that bullet hole in my ankle because I had got sort of tired of their examining. So when they said to me, "Is that all?"—not wishing to untie my drawer strings or pull off my sock and shoe to show them that scar on my ankle—I pointed to that clip on my right ear. That was an eye-opener to them, for it apparently satisfied them that I had a lame back. So they very frankly told me that I had passed a good examination as an incompetent.

Now the reason I took the family Bible with me was that I wished to appear as old as possible. That is very much in favor of a person appearing before pension examiners. I knew that if I told them I was 73 they wouldn't believe it—they would put me down at 58. There being two old soldiers on the board, I knew they would question my veracity. So the Bible showed me to be 73 years old next birthday, the eleventh day of this month, and I beg everyone of you not to forget it.

His pension being enlarged he felt free a year later to retire from law. Recently he had been taking life easier and writing the historical narratives which would be published posthumously and called *On the Old West Coast*.

It was about this time that Harry Carr, a popular columnist on the staff of the Los Angeles *Times* jibed at Bell's manner of dress. For many years the Major had worn for outdoor use an Inverness cape. This was a sleeveless, cloak-like garment originated in Scotland but worn in England as a gentleman's evening coat. He always had his cape made to order by Poole, a fashionable tailor in London. Enveloping his erect form it gave him a distinctive appearance which he loved. Proudly he wore it wherever he went when the air was sufficiently cool, and as no other men in Los Angeles during those years donned such apparel he became a striking and familiar figure on the city streets. When friends told him of Carr's ridicule the Major characteristically replied, "You tell Harry Carr to tend to his own business and if I want to I'll run around town in my shirt tail."

Lillian had gone to visit Daisy in San Francisco. She returned with rosy impressions of the bay area and wanted to live there.

The Major had always liked that country and as the home place had become too expensive to keep up and a great care for the old man, they decided in 1904 to dispose of it and move to Berkeley. He agreed to transfer the big house and the lot, measuring 180 feet on Figueroa and 450 feet deep, to an investment company for $15,000. On hearing of the deal the older children were shocked at the low figure. They protested that the property was worth twice as much. They urged him to demand more, since there was only a verbal agreement. "No," he replied, "I promised Mr. Graves I would sell for that price and I can't back down. I have never broken my word."

With the proceeds from the old place Bell built a new house in Berkeley (at 1402 Le Roy avenue) which stood on a hill overlooking the Golden Gate and went there to live with Lillian. But within a year he grew restless. In a low mood he wrote to his children:

I would be happier in a log cabin among the pines on a mountain side. Why? Because I inherited this trait—love for the outdoors. My ancestors lived that way. In Scotland they were Highlanders—in America frontiersmen. I have a house here with a view of eight counties. But think of climbing steps to see it! Therefore be it

Resolved: that I am going to Rancho El Scorpion, having a two-mile frontage on a country road. It has mineral springs that one can swim and dive in. There are big oak trees, four adobe houses a hundred years old, and a prehistoric Indian town. Am going to build a bathhouse by the sulphur springs that has water white as buttermilk. Am going to have three greyhounds to be let into my bedroom at daylight for me to caress and rub noses with—also a horse (mustang preferred) and a fine saddle, bridle, and Mexican spurs, a riding suit, and sombrero.

My daily routine will be to get up at daybreak, have my cold bath and my golden hot coffee, mount my horse and gallop over to some neighbor's a few miles away, dogs following, and have my breakfast. Then I shall return home and devote six hours a day to literature and writing. Now, my dears, this is all I shall want to make me happy.

Then too the Major had other reasons for going to his ranch, which was partly owned by Charles Bell and lay near Calabasas, on the road to Ventura, about 30 miles north of Los Angeles. It would give him a chance to see his sons. At this time Albert had gone to El Scorpion to help Charles with the work. Canby having been kicked by a mule was also there recuperating. Horace Junior would be at the Van Nuys farm not too far away, and the father hoped that Walter, who traveled in Mexico for a San Francisco firm and sold Mexican laces, might drop in between journeys. "Walter is quite familiar with the Spanish language and a great rustler," Bell wrote proudly. But his stay at the ranch was not long, for less than a year later he was back in Berkeley. Then fate began to stir.

Lillian Bell had become acquainted with Ida Wintermute, whose husband taught in the medical school at the University of California. Her mother then a widow in her early seventies was coming to spend the winter in Berkeley. Wishing to have her entertained during the long visit her daughter suggested to Bell that he should be "her beau" and escort her to all the places an Easterner might wish to see.

"Will she flirt?" asked the widower roguishly now in his seventy-eighth year.

"Mamma flirt?" laughed Ida. "Why don't you try her and see, Major?"

Emily Jane Culver was a millionairess, her husband having made a fortune in the iron foundries of St. Louis. Wishing to do good with their money they had established in 1894 a private preparatory boarding school for 45 poor boys. It was located on the shore of Lake Maxinkuckee in north-central Indiana. In the second year of its history it was joined by another boys' school of 75 and became the Culver Military Academy, which is widely known today.

Mrs. Culver came to visit her daughter as planned and Bell graciously gave his time to entertaining her. One day after several months' acquaintance the two were strolling on a Berkeley hill-top enjoying the ocean view when their conversation took a personal turn. "Well," remarked the Major casually, "I couldn't afford to get married in these times. This high cost of living which we are suffering from now would make it impossible." To

Emily Jane Culver Bell,
the second wife

Bessie

Virginia   *Georgia*

The six daughters of Horace Bell, in 1899

Daisy

Lillian

Maud

Major Horace Bell in 1916

which his companion replied softly, "But I have enough for both." Then and there they agreed to marry, the erstwhile labor leader accepting the proposal of a millionairess.

For the wedding they went back to Indiana. But before that event Bell visited the scenes of his boyhood for the first time in almost 50 years. His tour took him to Indianapolis, New Albany and Corydon—also to Laconia near the burial ground of his people. In Kentucky at Louisville, Brandenburg, and Hawesville he was honored with public receptions. In October 1909 they were married at Culver, Indiana, by Reverend G. L. Mackintosh, president of Wabash College. It was an elegant affair and only relatives were present. Immediately the happy couple left for California, whereupon the local paper consoled its readers by saying: "Mrs. Culver Bell will not be lost to Indiana. She and her husband will return to her beautiful home on the lake for summer residence. They will spend their winters at Major Bell's picturesque home in Berkeley overlooking San Francisco."[5]

When they traveled Mrs. Bell carried her many jewels with her. Except those that she wore, she put them all—eardrops, brooches, rings, unset jewels, and jewels of all sizes—into a quart Mason fruit jar, which they almost filled, and slipped the glass container inside her suitcase.

Evidently it was a good match, for Bell could write several years after his marriage, "Lady Jane and I are perfect lovers. Hasn't she been good to me! I have never had an unkind word from her and I have been good to her."

Their summers at Culver were pleasant. Frequently they took a spin with friends on the lake in her gasoline yacht. Many times they would go on the twenty-mile drive around the lake or ride to town a mile away behind a liveried coachman driving a span of blooded horses. They made it a habit to visit the academy three times a week—usually on Thursdays and Sundays, for then it was that the cadets had fried chicken for dinner. Mrs. Bell wanted her boys to be well fed and have plenty of chicken, at least twice a week. So she hired men who went in wagons scouting the countryside for the best fowls.

Sometimes they watched the 300 pupils in action. After

chicken at noon the boys would have boat drill for an hour on the lake, the Bells sailing with the commander of the fleet, who directed maneuvers. Later the lads changed their clothes and cleaned up for the military dress parade. There were four companies and the Major thought they looked like regular troops at a garrison and marched as well. At six the guests would enter their carriage and ride home.

One summer the Wintermutes came and begged the elderly couple to spend the winter with them in Europe. But the Major refused by saying, "I would rather go to Tia Juana, Mexico."

During these seasons at Culver, Bell, following a lifelong practice of strenuous exercise, swam in the lake before breakfast— except when his back hurt. On a scouting trip in the Civil War his horse was shot and fell across the rider's waist, thereby causing spinal weakness. In middle life he had tried every known treatment from drinking sulphur water to letting a Los Angeles doctor singe the small of his back with a hot poker. But nothing had ever helped. Now the condition was causing more trouble.

In his eightieth year Bell wrote to his children:

This day 55 years ago I had my first baptism in blood. A gory battle was fought in Granada. I fell and was carried under fire into the church of the grand plaza. We started in with 25 hundred men. But when the campaign was over and I could fight on crutches we mustered only 35 for duty at Virgin bay. Nearly all had been killed or died of wounds or fever.

God was good to me, thanks be to Him. Get down on your knees, my dears, and thank the Loving God for having spared you a father.

All of you know how the chief of police stole into my office and turned loose on me with a big revolver. God saved me from that and six other attempts on my life; three of them being in Los Angeles, one in San Francisco, one in Arkansas, and another in Mississippi. I was in the first battle of the Civil War, was present at the final surrender.[6] Was exposed to many dangers. God has guided and shielded me till now I am almost 81. How good he has been to me! Every morning and evening, often at midnight, I kneel in prayers of thanksgiving.

I pray for all my children and grandchildren. I pray for friends.

[274]

I pray for my enemies living and dead. And may He be merciful to me a sinner. For more than two years I have been prayerful and as good as I knew how to be. Have prayed for purity of mind, for a clean heart, and a clear conscience. I feel that He has answered my prayers.

Yes, my dear children, I beg you to pray as you were taught by your Christian mother, and pray for your loving father.

Three years later Bell expressed his creed in a letter to his son Charles:

I am at the mercy seat trying to make amends for—no, I will not say a misspent life—but for all my sinful acts committed during my long, eventful life.

I believe in a just and forgiving God. And I believe in His Son Jesus Christ and the Holy Ghost—world without end, amen!

In the summer of 1911 Virginia visited her father and his wife at their home in Culver. Early one evening on going to his room to retire he failed to close his door. When the daughter chanced to pass through the hall she saw Bell in his red dressing gown, kneeling by the bed in prayer. She thought she saw tears on his cheeks. In the morning at the breakfast table he informed her: "I want all you children to know that I have become a Christian. I have seen the light! Your mother's prayers have been answered. And I can truly say that I love everybody. Yes," he added, "I even love Harrison Gray Otis." This he repeated over and over again to all the family until his death: that he had become a Christian and felt no enmity toward anyone living or dead—not even to Otis.

His words were followed by action. For on November 17, 1913 he publicly confessed his Christian faith, was baptized and received into the Immanuel Presbyterian church in Los Angeles, the church his first wife had joined many years before. At last her prayers for him were completely answered.

Like a bud the soul of Bell had unfolded. His character was not retrogressive, or static, but upward-moving. As a young man on the frontier he was ruled by an urge for violence—the will to

[275]

fight for the thrill of action. In later maturity his combativeness found vent in patriotic service. The war over, his aggressive instinct answered the call of civic reform and what to him were worthy ideals. Now in his last period his spiritual nature flowered forth and more light came. Mellowed and sweetened he had learned life's lessons. And as he looked back upon many hazardous experiences he felt that it was not chance or fortune which had favored him with survival, but Providence.

It was in 1916 when the Bells were living at no. 227 on the Tunnel road in Berkeley that he went alone to visit his daughter Georgia in San Francisco. He left his home by the electric train on the Key System, crossed over the bay on the ferryboat and landed at the Terminal building in the city. From there he walked to a streetcar. No sooner had he sat down than the car was filled with passengers, many having to stand.

At once he saw a lady holding on to a hand strap for want of a place to sit. Promptly the Major rose and with the bow of a *caballero* gave her his seat. Now in his eighty-fifth year his back had become worse—so much so that he could not stand for more than a few minutes without feeling faint and nauseated. Yet he stood up in the car all the way out to the 1400 block on Geary street.

When he reached his daughter's home she remarked, "Oh, Papa, you look so very tired! Let me make you a cup of tea."

"No," he answered, "just let me sit down and rest a while."

Then after persistent quizzing she discovered the cause of his weakness. "Why, Papa," she warned, "you are too old to give up your seat. You must never do that again."

Rising to his full height and slowly nodding his head to stress his words he replied, "Madam," (a term of address he used to impress his wife and daughters) "when I am too old to give my seat to a lady, it will be time for me to die."

A year later he began to go for long periods to a hospital at Livermore, a few miles south of Berkeley. It was his back again— and now there were complications. Gratitude to his wife filled his mind. "Lady Jane is very good to me," he wrote to his children; "she pays for my care and curing. But for her love in sending me to this sanitarium you would be without a father and she a widow." Every morning as long as he was able he insisted on getting up at four, having a cup of coffee, and massaging himself with a brush. But as months wore on he slowly grew weaker. His condition was described by his daughter in a letter written at Livermore to the family:

I came into his room unannounced and he knew me and turned his cheek for me to kiss and said, "Well, if it isn't my little ol' Daisy."

I stayed with him until after 10 and he was perfectly conscious all the time and his faculties never clearer. Yesterday sick as he was—in fact dying—he insisted on getting up, dressing, and having his breakfast, but later he had to go to bed.

This morning I am sitting beside him. His mind is clear and he looks wonderful, but he is very feeble. He insisted on having his glasses (in fact he keeps them beside him on his bed) and then asked for the newspaper. To my utter astonishment he turned the paper until he got to the large headlines and then said,

"I want to see what the Italians are doing on the Piave."

It is wonderful how everyone here loves him. Dr. Robinson told me last night that he considers Papa one of the sweetest-natured men he has ever known. Even the girls in the office love him. The type writer spoke of him this morning with tears in her eyes and said, "He is a grand old gentleman."

On the next day Daisy wrote again:

Do you know Papa just insisted on the nurse brushing his hair and mustache and then rubbing him with his massage brush. He said he had not had his exercise this morning. I wish you could see him now as he lies in bed. He looks wonderful—seems very peaceful and is in no pain. He asked me to pray for him.

Then came the twenty-ninth day of June in 1918. Dear ones heard the feeble voice utter, "I—I love—everybody." With these words on his lips Horace Bell set forth on his greatest adventure into an unknown country.[7]

His passing marked the end of an epoch, the settling of America, for the last continental territories had recently entered the

Union. When his life ended, nearly all the pioneers had vanished, and the last frontier. He had himself seen California wax great. Before his eyes Los Angeles changed from a primitive pueblo to a modern metropolis and he gave of himself for her betterment. He witnessed the coming of the Iron Horse, the piping of melted snows from the High Sierras to water a thirsty land, and the migration of a half-million homeseekers to his loved town.[8]

Sometimes when the light of day has gone, when the noise of traffic has subsided in the older business district of Los Angeles, and the multitudes of pedestrians have diminished, it is easy to imagine a gallant old gentleman, with a white mustache, walking by on the streets.

> Look, gentle reader,
> Here he comes now!
> Tall and erect he emerges
> From under the trees of the ancient Plaza
> And proudly advances up Main;
> His white tie and white vest
> Showing under a cape-like coat
> Give him a stylish appearance.
>
> When he reaches the City Hall
> On the site of the old courthouse
> He stops and stares at the great white tower
> Rising 28 stories high
> And he seems to say: "Great Jehoshaphat!
> So many changes since 1918!
> And what has become of the Temple Block?"[9]
>
> After pausing a moment to reminisce
> He turns two blocks west
> Then moves southward on Broadway
> Swinging his cane as he goes
> And tapping, recurrently tapping
> Tapping the walk
>   With his cane.

[278]

Notes and Sources

CHAPTER I—"O PIONEERS!"

[1]Facts concerning Horace Bell's genealogy came from Bell's letters to his children and his family Bible.

[2]Reference to the migrations of the Scottish Highlanders to America appears in James Boswell's *The Journal of a Tour to the Hebrides*, October 2, 1773.

[3]For the story of the Parson Homes colony see *The Scotch-Irish in America* by Henry J. Ford (Princeton University Press, 1915), pp. 181-285, 377. Also *Scotch-Irish Pioneers in Ulster and America* by Charles K. Bolton (Boston: Bacon and Brown, 1910), pp. 58; 79-85; 130-177; 270. For Mather's remarks see *The Diary of Cotton Mather* in the Massachusetts Historical Society Collections, Seventh Series (1912), VIII, 548-549. The words of Sewall may be found in the *Diary of Samuel Sewall*, Collections of Massachusetts Historical Society (1882), Fifth Series, Sewall Papers, III, 191, 215.

[4]The novel in which Zadok Wright appears as a character is entitled *The Latimers: A Tale of the Western Insurrection of 1794*, by Henry C. McCook (Philadelphia: G. W. Jacobs & Co., 1897).

[5]The story of Daniel Sullivan comes from G. L. Cranmer's *History of Wheeling City and Ohio County, West Virginia* (1902), pp. 129-134—a rare book in the Indiana State Library.

[6]*How Dear to This Heart*. Its sources are largely Bell's personal letters and William H. Roose's *Indiana's Birthplace: a History of Harrison County, Indiana*.

[7]*To Hangtown or Bust*. Sources: Bell's *Reminiscences of a Ranger* (edition of 1881), p. 255 or (edition of 1927), p. 260; Bell's manuscript *Saddle and Sword* in the Huntington Library, Chap. 51, pp. 2, 8, 9; and Hubert H. Bancroft's *History of California* (San Francisco, 1887), VI, 144-145.

Two of Bancroft's writers spent many days in Bell's office in Los Angeles in the year 1887, recording his memories of pioneer history. Consequently Bancroft's description of the emigrants' transcontinental passage to California, cited above, may have come from the lips of Bell himself. The Major complained that the historian never gave him any credit for his contribution, a claim which one can verify by looking into the volume.

[8]*Among the Diggings*. This section has been drawn mostly from Bell's "Tales of the Trinity," published in the *Golden Era*. Briefer sources are his letter to Bancroft in the Bancroft Library and "Some Tales of the Early Days," in the Los Angeles *Herald*, Sept. 10, 1900, which reports Bell's speech in San Bernardino recalling his life in Sacramento and the first celebration of California's admission to the Union.

[9]On the site of Alexander Bell's store and house, at the southeast corner of Aliso and Los Angeles streets, there stands today a modern commercial building, which is occupied by the George R. Hadley Company, producers of bookkeeping devices

and business systems, no. 330 North Los Angeles street. On the north wall of the Hadley building, facing Aliso street, appears a plaque with this inscription:

On this site stood
The Military Headquarters of
Gen. John C. Fremont
War Governor of California
1847
Marked by
Eschscholtzia Chapter
Daughters of the American Revolution
Los Angeles, California
1915

[10]Pancho Johnson, who carried the message from Commodore Sloat, was undoubtedly a Spanish-American and probably a relative of Mrs. Alexander Bell.

[11]In the Los Angeles Daily *News* of July 25, 1871 appears this obituary: "Yesterday at a few minutes before 10 o'clock A.M., Alexander Bell died at his residence in this city. Born in Washington county, Pennsylvania, January 9, 1801, he was in his seventy-first year. He had been a resident of this county for 31 years. The funeral will take place at his residence, corner of Los Angeles and Aliso streets, at eight o'clock this morning. The French Benevolent Society of which he was an active member will attend the funeral in a body."

Alexander Bell was first buried in old Calvary (Catholic) cemetery, which was on the west side of Buena Vista street (now North Broadway) and north of College. Sometime after 1903 his body and that of his wife were removed to the new Calvary cemetery at 4201 Whittier Boulevard.

He left nothing to his nephew Horace, but willed half of his property to his widow and half to her grandnephew, who was their adopted son, James H. Bell. The young heir was the son of Henry Mellus, who came to Los Angeles in 1835 with Richard Henry Dana, Jr. on the brig *Pilgrim*, as related in Dana's *Two Years Before the Mast* (Boston: Houghton Mifflin Co., 1911), pp. 93, 478.

In 1847 Henry Mellus had married Anita, daughter of James (Santiago) Johnson of Los Angeles, and niece of Mrs. Alexander Bell. In 1860 he died while he was mayor of the town. Their son James was then adopted by the Bells. This information comes from Henry D. Barrows, who was executor of Bell's will. Thus through the Melluses and Bells are two important books of early Americana joined by human relations, Dana's *Two Years Before the Mast* and Bell's *Reminiscences of a Ranger*.

[12]The Death Records of St. Vibiana's cathedral in Los Angeles show that the funeral of Mrs. Maria de las Nievas de Bell was held in the cathedral on October 27, 1889. Her age at time of death was 96 years (Courtesy of Rev. Michael J. Ryan). As a widow Mrs. de Bell lived until her death with her niece Mrs. Sam Hamilton on the west side of Spring street between Eighth and Ninth streets.

[13]For source materials on Alexander Bell consult Bibliography at end of book.

[14]Benjamin Davis Wilson for whom Mount Wilson north of Pasadena was named died in 1878. Through the marriage of his daughter Ruth he became the grandfather of a distinguished American soldier of World War II, General George S. Patton, Jr. (Los Angeles *Times*, March 19, 1943).

[15]*Suelto, carajo!* means "Let [them] loose, damn it!"

[16]The story of Alexander Bell's birthday gift to Horace and the promise of a ranch if the young man would marry comes from Mrs. Virginia H. B. Phillips,

who heard it told in the family when she was a little girl. For the only reason that Uncle Aleck had picked Maria Dolores as a wife for Horace, Mrs. Georgia Bell was always a bit jealous and would never call on her.

Maria Dolores Dominguez was born in 1838 and died September 7, 1924, aged 86. She married James A. Watson. At the time Horace Bell was friendly with her she was 14 years old. She had five sisters: Anita, who first married William Dryden, then later Judge Charles Geyer; Victoria, who married George Carson; Susanna, who wedded Dr. Gregorio del Amo; Maria del Reyes, who became Mrs. John F. Francis; Guadalupe died unmarried. (These facts were supplied by Mrs. J. R. Lacayo of Los Angeles, granddaughter of Maria Dolores.)

Harris Newmark in his *Sixty Years in Southern California* (Boston: Houghton Mifflin Co., 1930) gives the history of the Dominguez family and their Rancho de San Pedro, which contained about 48,000 acres. Don Manuel, the father, died in 1882. (pp. 173-174)

[17]The incident of the beating Horace received from Wheeler may be found in the Los Angeles *Star*, January 14, 1854, in the Huntington Library.

[18]A copy of the first advertisement for the wagon train going over the San Fernando Pass from San Francisco appears in the Historical Society of Southern California *Quarterly*, March 1947, p. 47.

[19]*Adobe Days*. Unless otherwise indicated, facts concerning Horace's activities during this period are taken here and there from *Reminiscences of a Ranger*.

Chapter II—"SOLDIER OF FORTUNE"

[1]The true name of the poet whose quotation heads this chapter was Cincinnatus Hiner Miller. He took the pen name of Joaquin from Murietta, who figures in the first chapter, out of sympathy for the bandit, since Miller regarded him as having been treated wrongfully.

[2]For the full story of James King and the San Francisco *Bulletin* see Gertrude Atherton's *Golden Gate Country* (New York: Duell, Sloan and Pearce, 1945), pp. 143-152. King appended "of Wm." to his name to distinguish himself from another James King, William having been the name of his father.

[3]The phrase "Manifest Destiny" as used by Walker was a common expression in the 1840s and '50s intended to mean the supposed inevitability of a continental expansion of the United States. Originally it referred to the annexation of Texas.

[4]*Carajos* is used here as a general term for profanity.

[5]Dr. John Brinkerhoff of Los Angeles appears in *Reminiscences of a Ranger*, Chapter XXV. His name is also shown in the *Census of the City and County of Los Angeles for the Year 1850*, by M. H. and M. R. Newmark (Los Angeles: Times-Mirror Press, 1929), p. 63. He was a native of New Jersey and lived in the Bella Union hotel. At the time of the census-taking he was 28, so that at the end of the Walker campaign his age was 35.

[6]After his surrender to Commander Davis, Walker was returned to the United States. Eluding Federal authorities he sailed from Mobile, Alabama, on a second expedition to Nicaragua, but was arrested at San Juan del Norte and sent home with his men. In August 1860 Walker evaded British and American naval forces and started again for Nicaragua. Landing in Honduras he was picked up by the British and turned over to the Hondurans, who put him to death on September 12. (*Dictionary of American Biography*)

[7]In 1860 Walker published at Mobile, Alabama, a history called *The War in Nicaragua*, its object being to induce volunteers to enlist in a new expedition to that country. In this book he makes no mention of Bell except to say that Bell deserted him near the end of the war (p. 411). In the *Porcupine* of February 3, 1883, Bell wrote that the book treated him "cruelly and unjustly," that he was present at the last fight in Rivas, and that shortly after the capitulation was agreed upon he and Walker had quarreled. He added that Walker's book ignored or vilified every important person who had disagreed with him. The author "portrayed every man who had forsaken his standard as either a traitor, coward, or deserter to provide an excuse for his failures."

[8]This chapter is a *rifacimento* of Bell's typescript "Manifest Destiny," owned by the Los Angeles Public Library. It was first published in the *Golden Era* under the title, "Confessions of a Filibuster." Bell reprinted it in his *Porcupine* in 1882-83.

Chapter III—"CHAMPION OF FREEDOM"

[1]The news of the Bell jail delivery was told in the Los Angeles *Southern Vineyard* on December 10, 1858 (Huntington Library). The editor recalled Horace as being a former resident of Los Angeles and a relative of Alexander Bell, "one of our most esteemed fellow citizens." He expressed neither sympathy nor disapproval.

[2]The poem "A Chime of Bells," by Forceythe Wilson may be found in the New Albany Daily *Tribune* of August 10, 1858.

[3]Charles Alexander Bell, brother of Horace and John, was born in Boone township, Harrison county, Indiana, on the first day of January 1836. In July 1861 he was mustered into the service of the United States as second lieutenant; later he was made adjutant of the Twentieth Indiana Regulars and continued as such until the battle of Gettysburg. For his gallantry during this fight he was promoted to a captaincy. His regiment was first under fire in April 1862 when it served as sharpshooters in the engagement between the *Monitor* and the *Merrimac* at Hampton Roads, Virginia. The Twentieth took part in most of the battles of McClellan's peninsular campaign and in most of the battles in which the Army of the Potomac engaged.

In the fall of 1863 with his regiment he accompanied Major General E. R. S. Canby, when the latter was sent to New York with a military force to quell the draft riots.

When General Grant's army crossed the Rapidan in 1864 on its march to Richmond, Charles Bell's regiment numbered 1,040 men with a full complement of officers. When the army settled down before Petersburg, the regiment had only 63 men. They were commanded by Captain Bell. At the opening of this campaign he was the youngest captain in his regiment. All his superior officers had been killed or wounded during the bloody march.

Charles participated in all his regiment's engagements and survived without receiving a scratch. But on July 8, 1864 while he was superintending the construction of some earthworks in front of Petersburg, Virginia, and was supposedly in no great danger, the fragment of an exploding shell struck and killed him. On the day of his death he was commissioned colonel of his regiment. His remains were sent to Indiana and buried in the Bell plot in Rehoboth cemetery within two miles of the place where he was born. (From Horace Bell's private papers)

Nothing more is known of John Bell than that after returning to California he settled in Chico (Butte county), dying there many years ago—date unrecorded.

Mrs. Elizabeth Bell, mother of Horace, died March 7, 1862. David W. Bell, her husband, died February 13, 1872.

[4]Sources of Chapter III. *Life of Walter Quinton Gresham* by Matilda Gresham, I, 78-91. Both the author and her husband knew the Bell family intimately. In 1858 Mr. Gresham was practicing law in Corydon, Indiana. He was engaged by Horace to defend his father and brother in their trial at Brandenburg. Gresham was the one who led a party to the governor of Indiana, asking that he demand of the state of Kentucky the return of David and Charles Bell. Later Horace confided in the lawyer his plan for breaking the jail. Said Gresham to Horace, "The audacity of your plan will almost warrant its success." After Horace had been kidnaped and jailed, Gresham endeavored to obtain his release. In the preface of Mrs. Gresham's book appears the statement: "Horace Bell was afraid of no man."

Consult also Charles H. Money's "The Fugitive Slave Law in Indiana," *Indiana Magazine of History*, XVII (September 1921), 287-297, which gives a full story of the Bell case. For contemporary newspaper accounts see in the Indiana State Library the New Albany (Ind.) Daily *Tribune*, August 9, 1858; and the New Albany Daily *Ledger*, October 25-30, 1858.

CHAPTER IV—"WANDERLUST"

[1]Benito Juárez was president of Mexico from 1858 to 1863 and again from 1867-1872.

[2]For confirmation of statements made concerning Cortés and Marina see: Hubert H. Bancroft's *History of Central America* (San Francisco, 1887) VI, 539-551; William H. Prescott's *History of the Conquest of Mexico* (Philadelphia: Lippincott Co., 1891), Book II, Chapter 5; and the original source, Bernal Díaz' *The True History of the Conquest of Mexico*, translated from the original Spanish by Maurice Keatinge (New York: McBride & Co., 1938), pp. 77-89, 150.

[3]The legend of Doña Marina's promise to return to Chinameca and the age-old watching for her appearance I find no mention of in histories. Probably Bell got the myth directly from the Indians, as well as from Romero, and was the only writer to record it.

[4]This story of Bell's experiences in southeastern Mexico is taken from the Major's own account as it appears in his newspaper, the *Porcupine*, under the caption "Chinameca" in the issues of August 11 and 18, 1883.

CHAPTER V—"CONFINED TO QUARTERS"

[1]Down to this point Chapter V derives from Andrew J. Grayson's *History of the Sixth Indiana Regiment in the Three Months' Campaign in Western Virginia* and the *Dictionary of American Biography*.

A certificate in the biographer's possession issued by the adjutant general of Indiana proves that Horace Bell was enrolled as quartermaster sergeant of the Sixth Regiment of Indiana Volunteers and mustered into the military service of the United States at Indianapolis on April 27, 1861 for the term of three months. This record also shows that he was mustered out at Indianapolis on August 2, 1861.

CHAPTER VI—"SADDLE AND SPURS"

[1]The conversation between Bell and General Wallace is taken from the general's memory as he recorded it in Lew Wallace's *An Autobiography*, I, 455-456.

Many years after the battle General Lew Wallace visited Los Angeles on a speaking tour. On November 9, 1894 at the Unitarian church, corner of Third and Hill streets, he delivered an address called "The Third Division of the Tennessee Army at Shiloh." On the next evening he gave a lecture on his popular novel, *Ben Hur*, after which the Loyal Legion honored him with a banquet. (The *Herald*, November 10, 1894)

[2]Bell's saying, "Fortune favors fools as well as the brave," was a blending of two Latin proverbs: *Fortuna favet fatuis* and *Fortes fortuna adjuvat*. The first, meaning "Fortune favors fools," is an ancient anonymous adage. Its English form may be found in John Gay's *Fables*, no. 12, line 120. The second, "Fortune favors the brave," appears in Virgil's *Aeneid* X, 284; in Terence's *Phormio*, Act I, sc. 4, l. 26; in Cicero's *De Finibus* III, 4; in Ovid's *Metamorphoses* X, 586; and also in Chaucer: *Legend of Good Women*, 1773; *Troilus* IV, 600; *Thopas*, 830; and *The Reeve's Tale*, 4210. Perhaps Horace acquired these proverbs from his reading at school, or they may have been common expressions of his day.

[3]The story of Georgia's courtship and marriage comes from her daughter, Mrs. Phillips. The *Encyclopaedia Britannica* (1946) under the caption "Edward VII" tells briefly of the Prince of Wales' visit to Canada and the United States as "Lord Renfrew."

[4]Raphael Semmes (1809-1877)—pronounced *semz*—commander of the steamer *Sumter*, began his career by destroying Northern commerce in the West Indies. Later with the swift steamer *Alabama*, built in England, he captured and burned many more vessels. In June 1864 his ship was blockaded at Cherbourg, France, by the Union ship *Kearsage*. The *Alabama* fired the first shot, but after an hour of fighting she began to sink and raised the white flag. Semmes was rescued by the British and fled to England. This was the most important sea battle of the Civil War. (*Encyclopaedia Britannica*)

[5]The story told in this chapter is for the most part a revision of Bell's typescript "Of Civil War Times." Except for the incident concerning Rochelle, it has never before appeared publicly in any form—so far as the biographer knows. Another source is Bell's letter of August 19, 1899, privately owned, written to J. M. Quinn of El Monte, California, a member of the Historical Society of Southern California.

Chapter VII—"MOSAIC GLIMPSES"

[1]The description of Los Angeles in the late 1860s comes from Mrs. Georgia Bell as remembered by her daughter Virginia. Some details were gathered in interviews with Mr. Edward Fitzgerald and Mrs. Rachel Edelman Barnett, both early residents of Los Angeles.

Mr. Fitzgerald explained why the name of Fort street was changed to Broadway. The German citizens being unable to pronounce a "t, h" called Fourth street "Fourt," thus causing confusion. Since it was not desirable to change the name of Fourth street and break the sequence of numbered streets, the city council gave Fort street its present name. He also recalled that about this time the name of Charity street was changed, the reason being that parents living there were embarrassed to hear it said that their children "lived on charity." So Charity street became Grand avenue.

[2]From here on, excepting those parts otherwise designated, the information in this chapter comes from Virginia H. B. Phillips.

[284]

[3]The incident of Wiley McNear may be found in *Saddle and Sword*, Chap. 45, pp. 6-8, a manuscript in the Huntington Library.

[4]The old home lot of the Bells is now crowded with buildings. The general offices of the Bekins Van and Storage Company cover the site of the residence. At the southwest corner of Pico and Figueroa stands a branch of the Citizens National Bank. Adjoining it on the west is a Masonic temple. Mrs. Bell's old house number, 1337, appears over the door of a liquor bar on the west side of Figueroa. The three old palms still standing by the lane leading to the Bekins offices were planted there by the Major himself.

[5]Georgia street was named by the Major in 1875. About 1887 the city council lengthened the name to Georgia Bell to avoid a duplication. Sometime later the street was renamed Nevada; Virginia became De Long street and Charles street Sixteenth, as they are now called. In 1897 Bell made a formal protest to the council against dropping his wife's name. They responded by reaccepting the name, Georgia street, as it originally was and as it still is today. See the *Porcupine* of February 6, 1897 in County Museum. The Los Angeles Trade and Technical Junior College, 644 Seventeenth street, now occupies the site of the original Georgia Street School.

[6]The Temple Block or building, where Bell had his law office on the second floor for many years, was built in 1858 by John Temple and located at the junction of Main, Spring, and Temple streets. Three stories high it stood in the commercial center on the north apex of a triangular block, the site of the present City Hall, and faced all three streets. The first building back of its south walls and separated from it by a short street was the courthouse. The term block was used for all big buildings and was not limited to divisions of land.

[7]The incident relating to Judge Gray was recalled by Mrs. Willoughby Cole of Los Angeles, the judge's granddaughter.

[8]George W. and Helen P. Beattie are co-authors of *Heritage of the Valley* (Pasadena: San Pasqual Press, 1939), a history of San Bernardino valley and vicinity.

[9]The story of the Serrano rancho is taken from Rose L. Ellerbe's "History of Temescal Valley" in *Annual Publications of the Historical Society of Southern California*, XI (1920), 12-20. The incident of the red pepper, however, comes from Mrs. Phillips. The legal facts concerning the Serrano rancho have been verified by referring to a copy of the Petition of Josefa Montalva *et al.* to the Board of Commissioners for ascertaining and settling land claims in the state of California. (courtesy of George W. Beattie)

[10]Little Judy Fitzgerald was the late Mrs. Willoughby Cole (Geraldine), who told to the biographer the following anecdote concerning Mrs. Bell.

[11]The following letter written by Mrs. Georgia Bell on May 21, 1895 in Los Angeles gives a further glimpse of her personality:
"My sweet little Daisy Bell, . . . and now my dear Daisy about your happiness. The information of your engagement caused a great sadness to settle about my heart. Of course being that you are both so young, your love may grow with your years, but I should have preferred that you should wait until you were about 22 years old before you married. But I am so glad that this young man in whom you have centered your affections is so moral and gentle and I hope that he is a Christian.

"Walter is still going to Woodbury's [a commercial school] and at noon he goes to Papa's office and they go to lunch together and then after school he goes up and comes home with Papa.

"I don't suppose you know that the electric road between Pasadena and Santa Monica will run between Pasadena and here and the tracks are laid down Georgia Bell street to Washington and they are working hard to get it in running order by the first of August. The cars are beautiful. Won't that be handy for us?

"We have been housecleaning for the last two weeks and are all tired out. I have a beautiful light carpet in my room and a handsome moquette carpet on the hall.

"And now, my dear Daisy, I must say good-by and I pray the Lord's blessing on my absent children.

Your loving Mamma"

[12]Following are the birth years of the Bell children: Charles Alexander, 1863; Elizabeth Victoria (Mrs. Frank E. Walsh), 1865; Horace Junior, 1870; Virginia Herrick (Mrs. James A. Phillips), 1871; Georgia (Mrs. Stanley Richmond), 1873; Albert Herrick, 1874; Daisy (Mrs. Charles P. Overton), 1876; Lillian (Mrs. John T. Gray), 1877; Walter Frederick, 1879; Edward Robert Canby, 1881; Maud Ethel (Mrs. Edgar A. Jones), 1883.

[13]Bell had a habit of embarrassing his daughters when he was introduced to their young gentlemen friends. During the early 1890s it was not uncommon for men settling in Los Angeles to assume a new name, and many unmarried newcomers would attend church services in order to meet eligible young ladies of good families. When the Major was introduced to a strange young man who was calling at his house, he would invariably say, "How do you do, Mr. — —," and then smoothly add, "And what was your name before you came here?"

[14]For more about Truman see Franklin Walker, *A Literary History of Southern California*, pp. 109-110.

[15]The account of the first city centennial is indebted to: Bascom A. Stephens' "A Succinct History of the City of Los Angeles"; Los Angeles *Herald*, September 6, 1881; and Laurance L. Hill's *La Reina*, p. 63—here appears a photograph of the procession.

[16]The *Times* on December 25, 1881 gave a long and favorable review of *Reminiscences of a Ranger*. The writer remarked: "As the story is founded on fact and deals principally with Southern California and Los Angeles, it will be accepted as a representative book and will eventually constitute a part of the history of the country."

[17]While Helen Hunt Jackson was living in Los Angeles gathering material for her novel *Ramona*, the Major took her in his buggy to many places for local color and to interview people for historic facts. She demanded so much of his time that Mrs. Bell became jealous of her. When her book came out he was greatly disappointed. "Oh!" he said to his family, "she has spoiled it historically! That's the way with these writers"—meaning that she had been faithless to actuality and guilty of romanticizing. Regarding her aberrations see Harry Carr's *Los Angeles* (New York: Appleton-Century Co., 1935), pp. 337-339.

[18]In 1904 Bell brought to the bookstore of Norman C. Holmes at 257 South Main street about 200 copies of his *Reminiscences of a Ranger* and sold them to Holmes for less than 50¢ each. The book merchant put them on display in front of his store marked with the price of a half-dollar. When the Major returned he said to Holmes in a vexed mood, "I've got a notion to whack you with my cane.

I don't want my books depreciated by selling them so cheap. They ought to sell for not less than a dollar and a half. They are true history and I want them circulated."

Bell had made the mistake of trying to sell them himself.

According to Holmes the demand for *Reminiscences of a Ranger* did not come until 1910. By this time Los Angeles had grown to be a large city and many new citizens and tourists began hunting for histories of Los Angeles and vicinity. The price was then $2.50. A little later Californians began collecting Californiana and the *Ranger* was considered as one of the first books to get. At the time of this writing the cost of a first edition is not less than $25.00.

Chapter VIII—"THE FRETFUL PORCUPINE"

[1]The material in this chapter has been gathered from all the copies of Horace Bell's newspaper, the *Porcupine*, which are known to be in existence. See Bibliography.

[2]After his first few numbers the editor seems to have forgotten his primary purpose of reducing taxes. He never mentioned it again and his interests turned toward civic improvements. Perhaps he realized that both objectives were incompatible.

[3]The story of King's attack is told in the *Porcupine* of June 30, 1883, in the *Express* of June 25, and the *Times*, June 25 and July 1. The cartoon accompanies the account in the *Porcupine*.

[4]The Georgia Street Police Station, Division no. 15, on the west side of Georgia street near Pico has a receiving station, where medical care is given in emergencies.

[5]For a detailed representation of Los Angeles as it looked in 1881, approximately the time of this chapter, see the picture of a scale model of the city made to celebrate the fiftieth anniversary of the founding of the Los Angeles *Times*. In the model all buildings and residences of the central area were recreated in miniature form. In the picture a key identifies streets and structures. This picture and illustrated historical accounts of the city may be found in the Anniversary Numbers of the *Times*, which are invaluable for local history. See Bibliography.

[6]The Los Angeles State Normal School opened in 1882 and was located at Fifth street and Grand avenue, the present site of the Public Library. In 1914 it was moved to North Vermont avenue. In 1919 it became the Southern Branch of the University of California and in 1927, the University of California at Los Angeles. In 1929 it was settled in West Los Angeles, ultimately taking the name, University of California, Los Angeles.

[7]San Fernando street ran by the Southern Pacific depot on North Main street and was crossed by the railway lines to San Pedro, Wilmington, and Santa Monica. The lines going to San Fernando and Ventura crossed the Arroyo Seco road, which ran into San Fernando street.

[8]In 1853 a surveyor named Washington acting for the U. S. general land office established a point on the top of San Bernardino mountain, marking it with a monument. His astronomical observations proved it to be 34 degrees and 7 minutes of latitude north of the equator. Through this point he then ran a line due east and west, which is the Base Line referred to by Bell. All townships in southern California are numbered in relation to it. The Base Line road runs east and west of the city of San Bernardino and coincides with the Base Line.

[9]The promotion of La Ballona as a harbor project, now called Playa del Rey, is described in Glenn S. Dumke's *The Boom of the Eighties in Southern California*, p. 64.

[10]The memorial service for General U. S. Grant was held in the city on August 8, 1885. Major Horace Bell was Grand Marshal, Hon. G. Wiley Wells, orator, and General Horace H. Sargent, poet. (From Bascom A. Stephens' *A Succinct History of Los Angeles*)

[11]Harrison Gray Otis' comment on Bell as a politician appeared in the *Times* of August 8, 1886.

[12]Henry George in the fall of 1886 ran for the office of mayor of New York City and was defeated. He was also defeated as a candidate for the office of secretary of state on the United Labor Party ticket in 1887.

[13]Concerning the convention of the United Labor Party which met in San Francisco, September 24-28, 1886 read Winfield J. Davis' *History of Political Conventions in California, 1849-1892* (Sacramento, 1893), p. 526; also the San Francisco *Alta California*, issues of September 25, 26, 30, 1886 in California State Library. The state election was held on November 2, 1886. The official returns for the office of lieutenant governor were as follows: R. W. Waterman 94,969; M. F. Tarpey 92,476; A. D. Boren 5,836; Horace Bell 1,658. (From Davis, p. 532)

[14]To verify the statements made concerning the Baldwin-Perkins trial see William A. Spaulding's *History and Reminiscences of Los Angeles City and County, California*, I, 263 and Carl B. Glasscock's *Lucky Baldwin*, pp. 225-235.

[15]Concerning the Baldwin-Bell suits refer to actions numbered 4740, 4741, 4742, 4743, 4762 recorded in office of the Clerk of the Superior Court, Hall of Records, Los Angeles. These actions were dismissed on May 10, 1889. For newspaper accounts of the trials see the Evening *Express*, January 15, 16, and 25, 1886.

[16]The account of Bell's trial for contempt of court is drawn from the Los Angeles *Express*, issues of April 13-20, 1886, and also from the San Francisco *Call* of April 20, 1886. A copy of the application to the Supreme Court for the writ of habeas corpus in the case of Wells versus Bell may be seen in the Southwest Museum, Los Angeles.

[17]The story of the pamphlet and the subsequent lawsuits has been taken from the Los Angeles *Herald*, issues of February 25-March 18, 1887, and the *Express* of March 16-May 5; December 19 and 20, 1887; and January 6, 1888. These are filed in the office of the *Herald & Express*.
The official record of the Supreme Court's decision appears in *California Reports*, Vol. 74 (1887-1888) case no. 20346, January 3, 1888, pp. 482 ff., to be found in lawyers' offices.

[18]Sources: The *Porcupine*, November 11 and 13, 1886; the *Express*, November 11, 1886; the domestic scene comes from the memory of Bell's daughter Virginia.

[19]The quotation from Wesley may be verified by referring to *The Works of the Rev. John Wesley* (London, 1872), Vol. IX, "The Doctrine of Original Sin," p. 220. But Wesley was quoting verbatim from Jonathan Swift's *Gulliver's Travels*, Part 4, Chapter 5.
The words of Milton may be found in his essay *Of Education*.
The Wordsworth lines are from his poem, "A Poet's Epitaph."
The "Epitaph on Justice Randal" appears in *Ben Jonson*, edited by C. H. Herford, P., and E. Simpson (Clarendon Press, 1947), VIII, 444. Compare with Benj.

Franklin's variation in *Poor Richard's Almanac* (1733): "God works wonders now and then/Behold! a lawyer, an honest man."

These quotations suggest that Bell was a wide reader.

[20]The first public high school stood on Poundcake Hill for many years until it was replaced by the Hall of Records at the Civic Center. The hill was so named because of the poundcake parties held in homes located there. A picture of the hill and school appears in the Los Angeles *Herald & Express*, June 16, 1948.

[21]In 1884, three years before Bell made in the *Porcupine* his prophecy concerning armed aircraft, Captain Charles Renard of the French war department produced the first man-carrying airship that ever returned against the wind to its starting point. It is this fact to which Bell alludes in his remarks.

[22]Don Manuel Garfias, who became treasurer of Los Angeles county in 1852, married Luisa, daughter of Francisco Avila. The last Mexican governor gave him Rancho San Pasqual, 13,600 acres, as a wedding gift. This rancho, which lay northeast of Los Angeles and across the Arroyo Seco, was destined to be the site of Pasadena and neighboring cities of the northwestern San Gabriel valley (From the Los Angeles *Times*, December 4, 1931). In the early '70s it was owned jointly by B. D. Wilson and Dr. John Griffin. (See Dumke's *The Boom of the Eighties in Southern California*, p. 85.)

[23]If Bell had wanted to, he could have told the Pasadenans in his speech of the part he played in the founding of their town. Major Erie Locke had been sent out from Indiana to find the best spot in southern California to establish a colony of Indianians. He went to Major Bell, since the latter was also a native of Indiana, to get information. Bell and his wife drove him over in their buggy to the present site of Pasadena on the old San Pasqual ranch. So pleased he was with the Bells' suggestion that Locke chose the site as a desirable place to live and later returned with a group of people who founded Pasadena, which originally was called "the Indiana colony."

[24]Sources: Los Angeles *Times*, March 8 and 31, 1887; Los Angeles *Herald*, March 31, 1887; the *Porcupine*, March 12, 1887.

[25]After wresting it from the padres the Mexican government sold the rancho of San Fernando Mission a year later, that is in 1846, to Don Eulogio de Celis—121,000 acres for about 11¢ an acre. This money was used to equip and maintain the Mexican army against American invasion. De Celis at once stocked his ranch with cattle and before the war was over sold the animals to both sides. (Los Angeles *Times*, December 4, 1931)

[26]Mary Foy knew Horace Bell during the years of the *Porcupine* and graduated from the Los Angeles High School in the same class with Charles Bell. When he was a court clerk Joseph F. Chambers knew Bell as a practicing attorney.

Chapter IX—"THE LAST LEAF"

[1]Sources—mostly Bell's letters written during his last years to his children, which were collected and preserved by his daughter, Daisy Bell Overton. The story of Mrs. Bell's death was told to the author by Virginia H. B. Phillips.

[2]A biographical sketch of Georgia Bell appears as her obituary in the *Annual Publications of the Historical Society of Southern California* (1897-1899), IV, 279-280. She was born in Springfield, Massachusetts, April 23, 1845. Her parents

were Albert and Virginia Crocker Herrick. Another obituary appeared in the Los Angeles *Times*, June 9, 1899.

A likeness of Georgia Bell may be seen in a mosaic of colored tile on an interior wall of the Thomas A. Edison Junior High School, 6500 Hooper avenue, Los Angeles. This was made during the depression as a WPA Federal Art Project—size about eight feet by 10 feet. Mrs. Bell is central in a group of California pioneers—seven men besides herself, including miners and horsemen—all typical figures of the old West. Cattle and mountains add to the Western setting. This likeness of Mrs. Bell was copied from her picture in her husband's book, *On the Old West Coast*, p. 80.

[3]The Presidio is a military reservation located in the northwest portion of San Francisco and bordered by the Golden Gate. It contains 1,564 acres. Officers have quarters there where guests can be entertained, or they may be entertained in the officers' club.

[4]Harr Wagner (1857-1936) was from 1881 to 1890 owner and editor of the *Golden Era*. In 1916 he organized the Harr Wagner Publishing Company to publish Western books by Western authors. He wrote three books of Western history himself. These facts explain the Wagners' interest in Bell.

[5]The facts concerning the Major's second wedding and his visit to Indiana are taken from the Corydon (Indiana) *Republican*, October 28, 1909.

[6]When Bell wrote that he was in the first battle of the Civil War he alluded correctly to the Skirmish at Philippi on June 3, 1861, which historians regard as the first military action in the conflict. In saying that he was present at the final surrender he was evidently thinking of the last fighting in Louisiana, which continued after Lee's surrender at Appomattox.

[7]Bell's obituaries appeared in the Berkeley Daily *Gazette*, July 1, 1918; the Oakland *Tribune*, July 1, 1918; the San Francisco *Chronicle*, July 1, 1918; the Los Angeles *Tribune*, July 3, 1918; and the Los Angeles *Times*, July 2, 1918. His remains were buried beside those of his first wife in Rosedale cemetery, not far from their old home place. At his request there were carved on a grave marker these words from the citation given him when he was discharged from the Federal army:

"HIS GALLANTRY, RESOLUTION, INTELLIGENCE
AND PROMPTNESS HAVE BEEN MARKED AND
COMMENDED. HE HAS RENDERED THE
U. S. GOVERNMENT GREAT SERVICE."
FROM RECORDS OF THE WAR DEPARTMENT
AT WASHINGTON.

But recently the stone was removed, time having dimmed the letters.

[8]On November 15, 1913 a celebration was held to mark the completion of the new aqueduct bringing water from the Owens river to the San Fernando valley. For picture and account see Laurance L. Hill's *La Reina*, pp. 124-130.

[9]An old picture of the Temple Block and the courthouse clock tower showing behind it appears in the Los Angeles *Herald & Express* of June 16, 1948. The last picture of the historic Temple Block, taken shortly before it was torn down to make room for the new City Hall, may be found in Hill's *La Reina*, p. 191. Here one sees the steel frame of the new City Hall rising high above the old building and abutting its south and west walls. The City Hall was dedicated on April 26, 1928.

Bibliography

BELL'S UNPUBLISHED WRITINGS

Bell Collection of Manuscripts. Henry E. Huntington Library. San Marino, California.

Bell Collection of Manuscripts. Los Angeles Public Library. Los Angeles, California. (These are duplicates of four items in Huntington Collection.)

Personal Letters to His Children, 1895-1918. Privately owned.

Biographical and Historical Notes. Privately owned.

"Of Civil War Times." Typescript privately owned. Pp. 179.

Letter to Hubert Howe Bancroft, 1887. Bancroft Library. Berkeley, California.

BELL'S PUBLISHED WORKS

"Confessions of a Filibuster," The *Golden Era*. San Francisco, California, May 7-Oct. 1, 1876. Bancroft Library.

"El Basquo Grande," The *Graphic*. Los Angeles: Graphic Pub. Co. Vol. XXX (April 10, 17, 24, 1909). Los Angeles Public Library. (A short story)

On the Old West Coast. Lanier Bartlett (ed.). New York: Wm. Morrow & Co., 1930.

The *Porcupine*. Los Angeles, 1882-1883. Huntington Library. Eighty-one issues, 1884-1897. Los Angeles County Museum. Los Angeles, Calif.

Reminiscences of a Ranger or Early Times in Southern California. Los Angeles: Yarnell, Caystile & Mathes, 1881; reprinted, Santa Barbara, Calif.: Wallace Hebberd, 1927, and Los Angeles: Primavera Press, 1933.

"Tales of the Trinity," the *Golden Era*. San Francisco, Oct. 11, 1879. Bancroft Library.
Nov. 15, Dec. 13, 1879; Jan. 10, Feb. 21, 1880. California State Library. Sacramento, Calif.

"Ysabel of Atlantis," *Touring Topics*. Lanier Bartlett (ed.). Beverly Hills: Automobile Club of Southern Calif. Nov. 1930, pp. 20-29. (a short story)

CONCERNING HORACE BELL

Anonymous. *Life of Horace Bell.* no pub., no date. Huntington Library.

Glasscock, Carl B. *Lucky Baldwin.* Indianapolis: Bobbs-Merrill Co., 1933.

Grayson, Andrew J. *History of the Sixth Indiana Regiment in the Three Months' Campaign in Western Virginia.* Madison, Ind.: Courier Printshop, no date. Indiana State Library. Indianapolis, Ind.

Gresham, Matilda. *Life of Walter Quinton Gresham, 1832-1895.* Chicago: Rand McNally & Co., 1919. Vol. I.

Money, Charles H. "The Fugitive Slave Law in Indiana," *Indiana Magazine of History*, XVII (September 1921), 287-297.

Roose, Wm. H. *Indiana's Birthplace: a History of Harrison County, Indiana.* New Albany, Ind., 1911. Indiana State Library.

Shuck, Oscar T. *History of the Bench and Bar of California.* Los Angeles: Commercial Printing House, 1901. Pp. 782-783.

United States War Department. *The War of the Rebellion: . . . Official Records of the Union and Confederate Armies.* Washington, D. C., 1880-1901. Ser. I, Vols. XLI & XLVIII. See index.

Walker, Franklin. *A Literary History of Southern California.* University of California Press, 1950. Pp. 51-59.

Walker, William. *The War in Nicaragua.* Mobile, 1860. Library of Congress. Washington, D. C.

Wallace, Lew. *An Autobiography.* New York: Harper & Bros., 1906. Vol. I.

CALIFORNIA NEWSPAPERS

(For complete dates see notes)

San Francisco *Alta California*, 1886
San Francisco *Call*, 1886
San Francisco *Chronicle*, 1918
Los Angeles *Express*, 1883, 1886-1888, 1904
Berkeley Daily *Gazette*, 1918
Los Angeles *Herald*, 1881, 1885-1887, 1894, 1900
Los Angeles *Herald & Express*, 1948
Los Angeles Daily *News*, 1870, 1871
Los Angeles *Southern Vineyard*, 1858
Los Angeles *Star*, 1854

Los Angeles *Times*, 1881-1883, 1886-1887, 1899, 1918, 1931
Los Angeles *Tribune*, 1918
Oakland *Tribune*, 1918

INDIANA NEWSPAPERS

(For complete dates see notes)

New Albany Daily *Ledger*, 1858
Corydon *Republican*, 1909
New Albany Daily *Tribune*, 1858

CONCERNING ALEXANDER BELL

Anonymous. *An Illustrated History of Los Angeles County*. Chicago: Lewis Pub. Co., 1889. California State Library.

Barrows, Henry D. "Captain Alexander Bell and the Bell Block," Historical Society of Southern California *Quarterly*, III (1895), 11-18.

Bowman, Mary M. "Stories of Old California," Los Angeles *Express*, Nov. 25, 1904. Los Angeles Public Library.

Los Angeles *County Records*, 1849. A, 1088-1090; II, 875. Huntington Library.

Newmark, Marco R. "Pioneer Merchants of Los Angeles," Historical Society of Southern California *Quarterly*. September 1942, p. 79. (Picture of Bell's Row)

Los Angeles Daily *News*, July 25, 1871.

The *Porcupine*, June 5, 1886. Los Angeles County Museum.

Wilson, J. Albert. *History of Los Angeles County*. Oakland, Calif.: Thompson & West Co., 1880. Los Angeles County Library.

MORE ABOUT LOS ANGELES

Dumke, Glenn S. *The Boom of the Eighties in Southern California*. San Marino: Huntington Library, 1944.

Los Angeles *Herald & Express*, June 16, 1948. (Pictures of the Temple Block, Poundcake Hill, and other early landmarks)

Hill, Laurance L. *La Reina: Los Angeles in Three Centuries*. Los Angeles: Security Trust & Savings Bank, 1929.

Publicity Department. *El Pueblo: Los Angeles Before the Railroads*. Los Angeles: Security Trust & Savings Bank, 1928.

Spaulding, William A. *History and Reminiscences of Los Angeles City and County*. Los Angeles: Finnell Co., 1931. 3 vols.

Stephens, Bascom A. "A Succinct History of the City of Los Angeles," Los Angeles Evening *Express*, Oct. 20-Nov. 1, 1885. Los Angeles Public Library.

Los Angeles *Times*. Anniversary numbers, Nov. 8, 15, 22, 29, and Dec. 4, 1931. (For picture of Scale Model see issue of Nov. 29, photogravure section, pp. 4, 5.) Los Angeles *Times* Library. Los Angeles Public Library. A. K. Smiley Public Library, Redlands, California.

Index

Prescott, plantation, 133, 135-6, 143,
  145-6, 152-4
Presidio, the, San Francisco, 268
Presidio county, Tex., 258
Press, Santa Barbara, 201
Price, Pugh, 22-4
Prince of Wales, Albert Edward, 111
Progress, Pomona, 244, 254
Puntarenas, Costa Rica, 73
Purdy, Tenn., 107, 109

Ramirez, Juanito, 23-4
Ramona (novel), 198
Ranchito, Calif., 31
Rancho del Chino, 39
Rancho Providencia, 31
Rancho El Scorpion, 271-2
Rancho San Pedro, 37
Randal, Justice, 249
Rangers, Los Angeles, 39, 195
Ranney, Justice, 243
Red Bluff, Calif., 23
Red river, La., 119-21, 124-6, 134, 144,
  153-4, 156, 159, 164
Redding's Springs, Calif., 24
Redlands, Calif., 226
Redondo Beach, Calif., 227-8
Register, San Jacinto, 261
Reindeer (boat), 121
Reminiscences of a Ranger, xvi, 197-9,
  257, 261
Republican party, 202, 234-6, 244-6, 255,
  260
Requena, Doña Gertrudes, 32
Requena, Don Manuel, 32
Requena street, 39, 210
Retribution (boat), 112
Revolutionary War, 6, 9
Rhea, Mlle., 184
Rich mountain, W. Va., 104
Richmond, Va., 155, 157, 159
Ridden, Bill, 118
Riley, General, 32
Rio Grande, 131, 168, 258
Rip Van Winkle, 184
Rivas, Nicaragua, 53-4, 56-65, 67, 73-4
Rivas, Patricio, 44-5, 71
Riverside, Calif., 39, 226
Riverside county, Calif., 180
Robb, Charles, 223
Robinson, Cornelius D., 111

Rochelle, Pancoast, 121-2, 153
Rock creek, Calif., 24
Rockefeller, John D., 235
Rocky mountains, 18-20
Romero, Padre, 87-91, 93-7
Rose (a dog), 25-8
Rowland, Billy, 40
Royal, William B., 22, 25-7
Russell, Mr. (jailer), 232

Sacramento, Calif., 18, 21
Sacramento river, Calif., 24
Sacramento valley, Calif., 22
Saddle and Sword, 172
Salinas, Tex., 168
Salmon river, Calif., 22, 25
Salvador, Salvadorans, 68, 267
Sam (colored man), 23
San Antonio, Tex., 167, 169
San Bernardino, Calif., 39, 169, 226, 254
San Bernardino county, 179, 226
San Carlos, Nicaragua, 58
San Clemente island, 171
San Diego, Calif., 31, 36, 38-9, 171, 261
San Fernando, Calif., 38, 41-2, 173, 220,
  257
San Fernando Mission, 41
San Fernando pass, 41
San Fernando street, 221
San Francisco, Calif., 26, 28, 42, 44, 60,
  97, 160-2, 196, 237, 253, 261, 266-8, 270,
  272-4, 276
San Gabriel, Calif., 169, 254, 257
San Gabriel Mission, 39, 220
San Gabriel river, Calif., 31
San Jacinto, Calif., 261
San Jacinto, Nicaragua, 47
San Joaquin Ranch, 38
San Jorge, Nicaragua, 56, 59-63, 65
San Juan Capistrano, Calif., 40, 254
San Juan del Norte, Nicaragua, 44
San Juan del Sur, Nicaragua, 61, 63, 66,
  69, 70, 74
San Juan Guichicova, Mex., 90-1
San Juan river, Nicaragua, 44, 58, 73
San Luis Obispo, Calif., 40
San Luis Rey Mission, 180
San Pasqual, Calif., 31
San Pasqual Rancho, 38, 254
San Pedro, Calif., 28-33, 189
San Pedro street, 34, 40, 220